Michaela Melián
Red Threads

Spector Books

Index

Foreword

This book was produced for the occasion of Michaela Melián's first Berlin survey exhibition **Red Threads** at the KINDL – Centre for Contemporary Art in Berlin. Michaela Melián adds a very special accent to current contemporary art, one that fits extremely well with the KINDL's program. It is not only her feminist and thus political approach to social issues, but also her method of linking visual art and music and using diverse media techniques that is impressive in its consistency.

With the method of artistic research and with a feminist gaze, Melián approaches the social phenomena she observes in an intense way. Each of her works reveals a richness of form and a joy in experimentation, without neglecting personal and psychological aspects. In large installations and compositions and in her use of time-based media, Melián formulates an explicitly political claim. At the same time, the artist develops her very own aesthetic signature, thus allowing sensuality and social-analytical conciseness to converge. At the center of the exhibition is the work complex **Tania**, newly developed for the KINDL, which comprises a mural and a sound installation on the myth surrounding the guerrilla Tamara Bunke (1937 – 1967) alias Tania between Berlin, Havana and Bolivia. Tamara / Tania's multifaceted existence as a private person and a media object encounters a reception of her biography that is interwoven with diverse social discourses.

In her research, Michaela Melián examines Bunke from various angles and illuminates different stages of her life. The results of her research culminate in 250 drawings that Melián assembles into a mural, recalling both the Latin American "murales" and the murals in public spaces in the Eastern part of Berlin. Oscillating between mosaic and rasterized or pixelated image, the **Tania** mural consists of impressions of 1 x 1 centimetre rubber stamps that trace the contours of the drawings and were stamped onto the wall in a collective act by the artist and KINDL staff. In addition to the original mural, a 16-channel sound installation has been created for the exhibition, which is played on converted pressure chamber loudspeakers with cables that spin a web throughout the space. The artist has used songs from Socialist resistance movements, as well as fragments of indigenous South American music. This alludes to the fact that Tamara Bunke collected indigenous music as part of her cover identity as a music anthropologist in Bolivia. The sound installation creates a musical loop that accompanies the entire exhibition and expands the viewer's range and scope of associations. The exhibition also features a selection of works Melián has created over the past 30 years. Older and more recent works have been assembled into a contemporary composition in such a way as to create a mesh of leitmotifs (or read threads). The new work complex **Tania** is complemented by early drawings (1990, 1992), a flag (1994 / 2022) with a fictitious portrait of Tamara Bunke, and the large-scale sculpture *Mossberg Model Bullpup* (1993), which visitors can sit on. Other central works such as the installation *Heimweh* (2012) on a poem by Else Lasker-Schüler, the tapestry *Girl-Kultur* (2019), which refers to the image of the New Woman and the architectural "kitchen discourse" in modernism, the audio sculptures *Mannheim-Chairs* (2015 / 2016), and the video installation *Speicher* (2008) condense in the exhibition into a multimedia body of work that engages all the senses. This interweaving invites the viewer to put the works in context with each other and again and again draws the audience back to Melián's questions about social memory as well as language and identity. Melián's drawings, objects, her multimedia installations, and audio works refer to a complex web of historical facts and their traces in our present day. The artist contrasts the stories of places and people with phenomena of everyday culture and specially composed sound collages, thereby devising a form of commemorative culture that brings to mind historical narratives that have been omitted, suppressed, or concealed. Tracks and trajectories become visible as if they were Ariadne's threads guiding visitors to the exhibition on their own paths through the dense weave of ideas, questions, stories, images, and sounds.

In this book, art theorist Hanne Loreck provides an in-depth overview of Michaela Melián's working methods. A conversation which took place at the KINDL on 11 May 2022 between the artist and the curator Joanna Warsza, reproduced here in excerpts, deals with the backgrounds and approaches of Melián's work. The artist Nadja Abt provides us with a guided tour through the exhibition, Katja Kynast and Magdalena Mai contribute texts on the individual exhibits.
We hope that the book will find an attentive readership and that it will reach all those with an interest in art who did not have the opportunity to experience the exhibition *Red Threads* at the KINDL – Centre for Contemporary Art in Berlin.

Kathrin Becker, Ingrid Wagner

          Read Threads

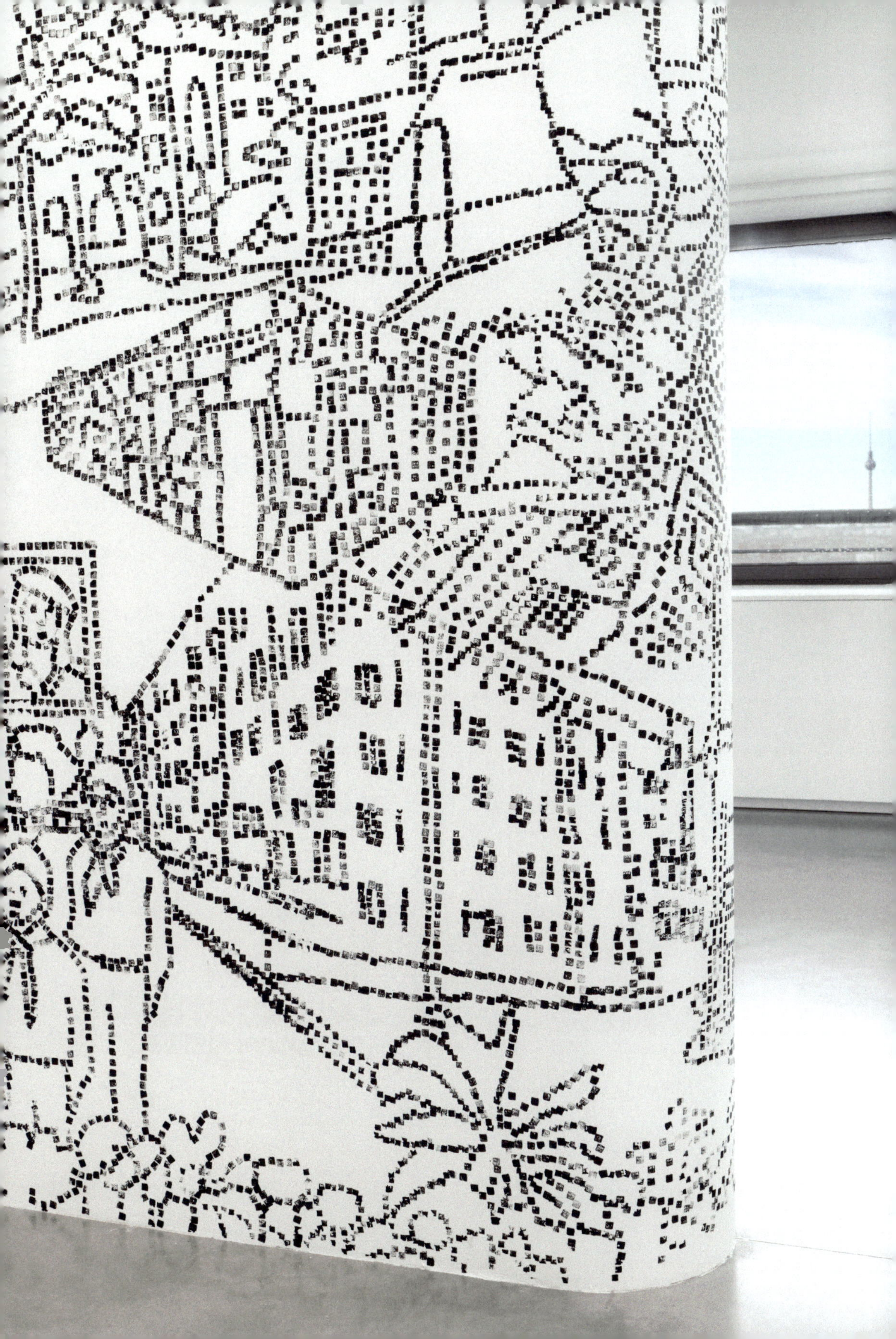

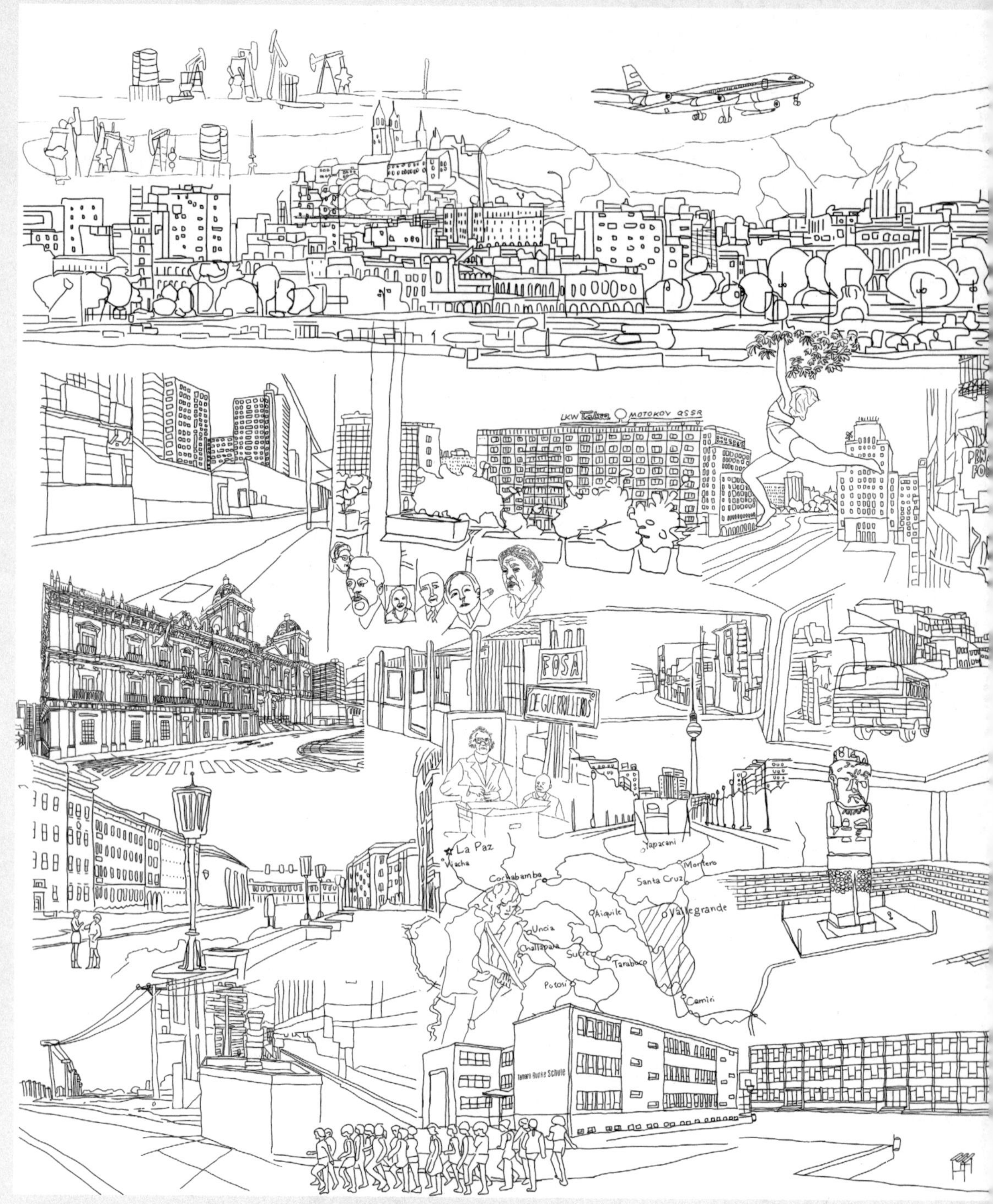

LKW MOTOKOV QSSR
FOSA DE GUERRILLEROS
La Paz
Viacha
Cochabamba
Yapacani
Montero
Santa Cruz
Aiquile
Vallegrande
Uncia
Challapata
Sucre
Tarabuco
Potosi
Camiri
Tamara Bunke Schule

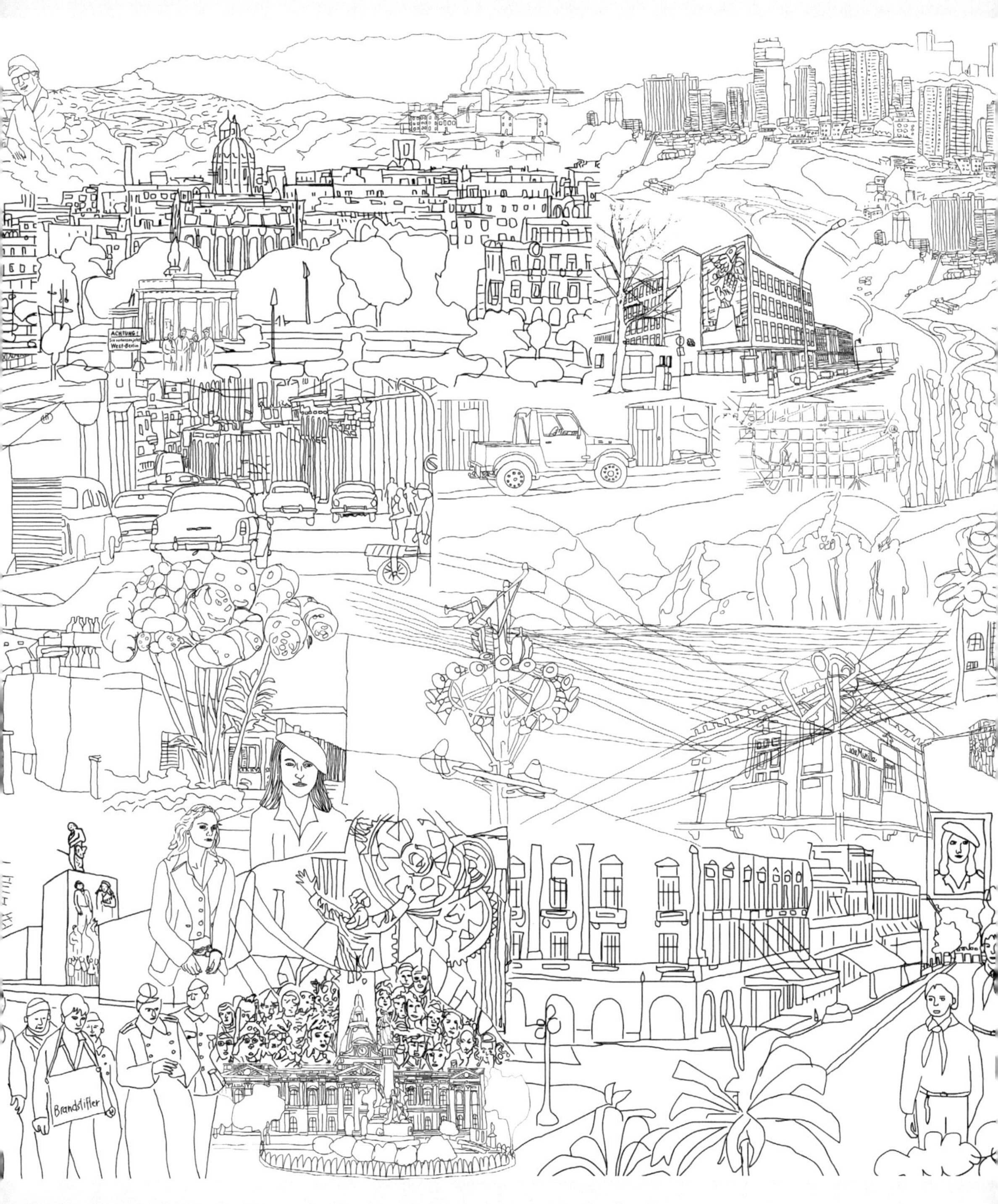
ACHTUNG !
Sie verlassen jetzt
West-Berlin
Brandstifter

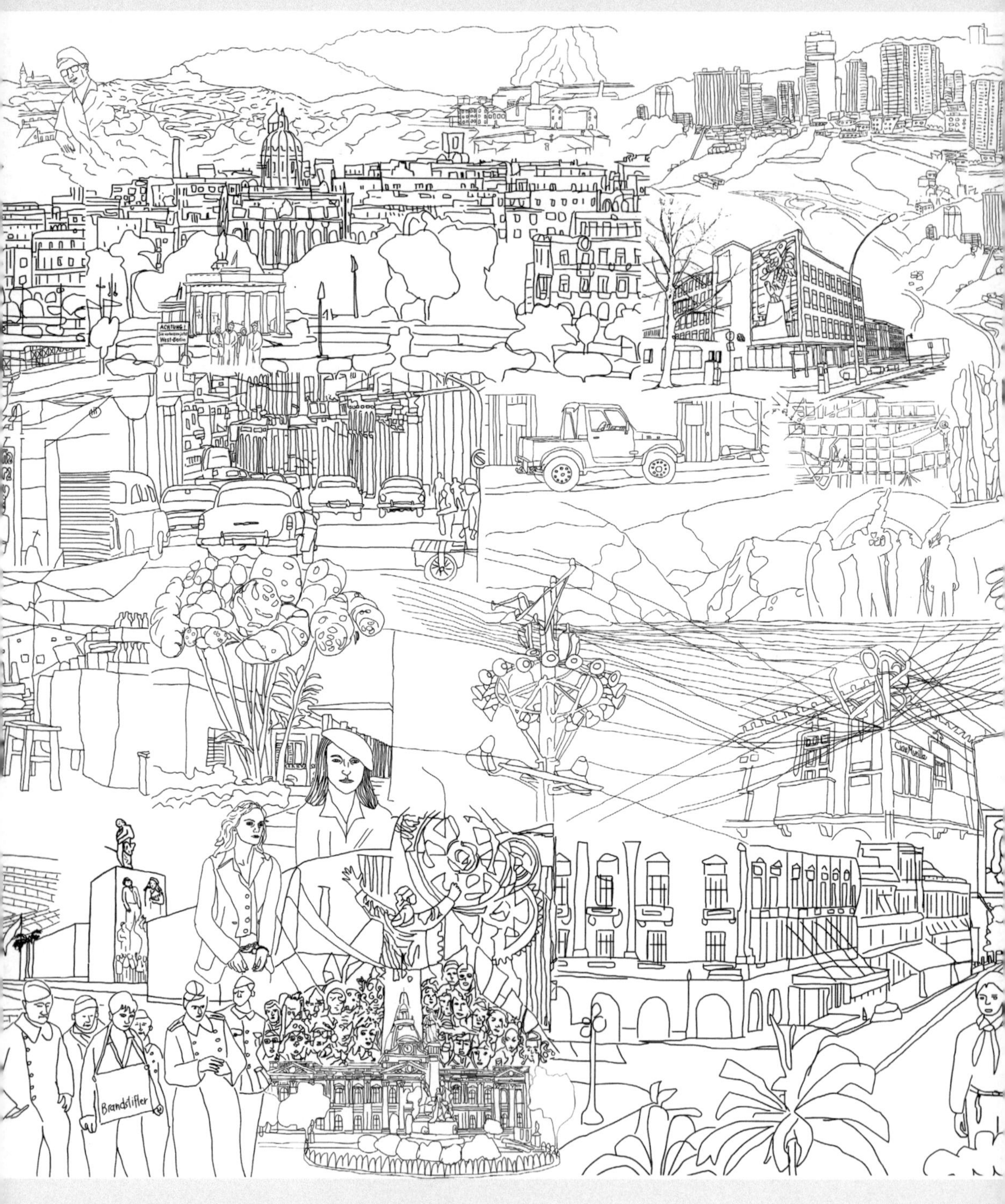

ACHTUNG !
Sie verlassen jetzt
West-Berlin
Brandstifter

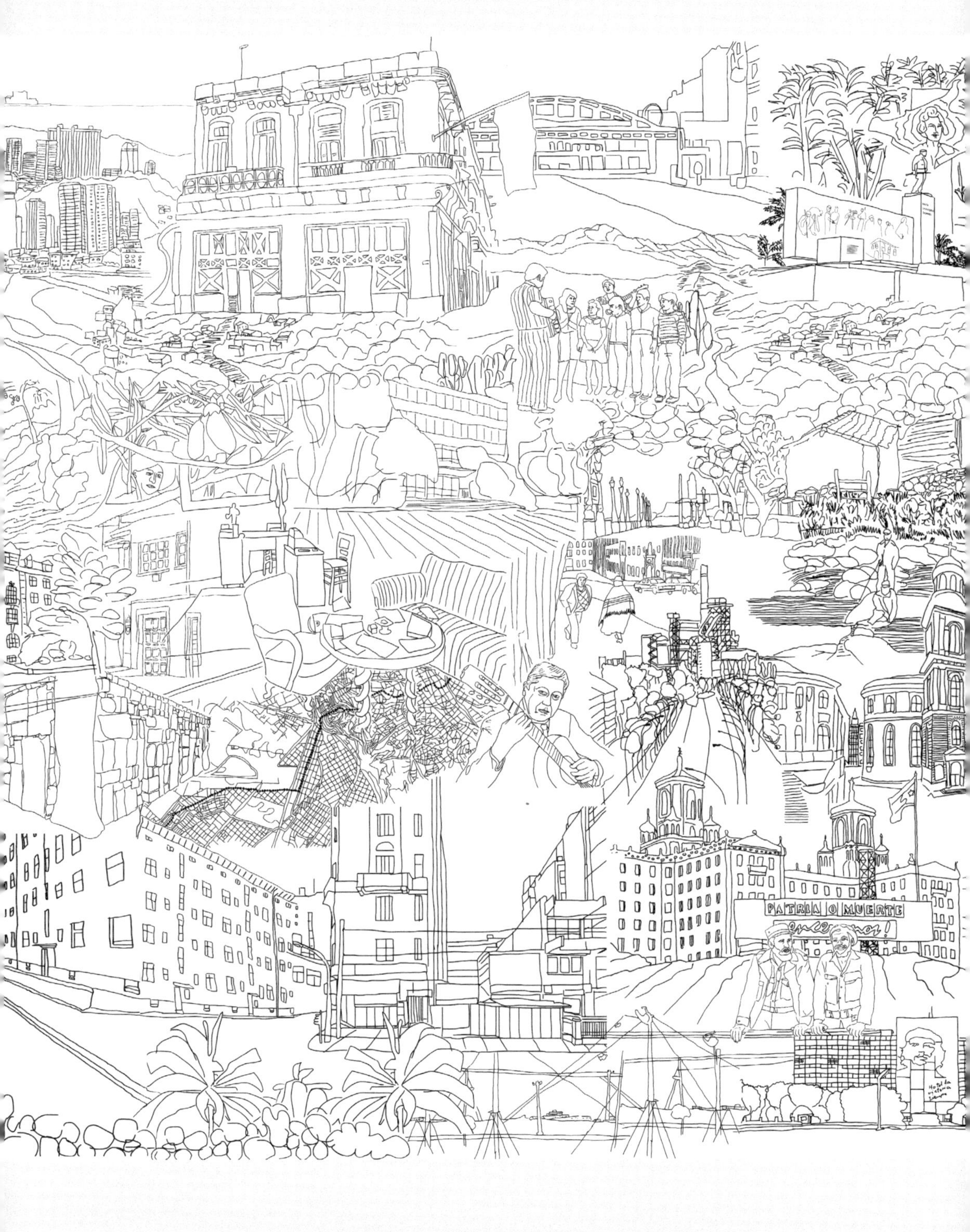

PATRIA O MUERTE
venceremos!

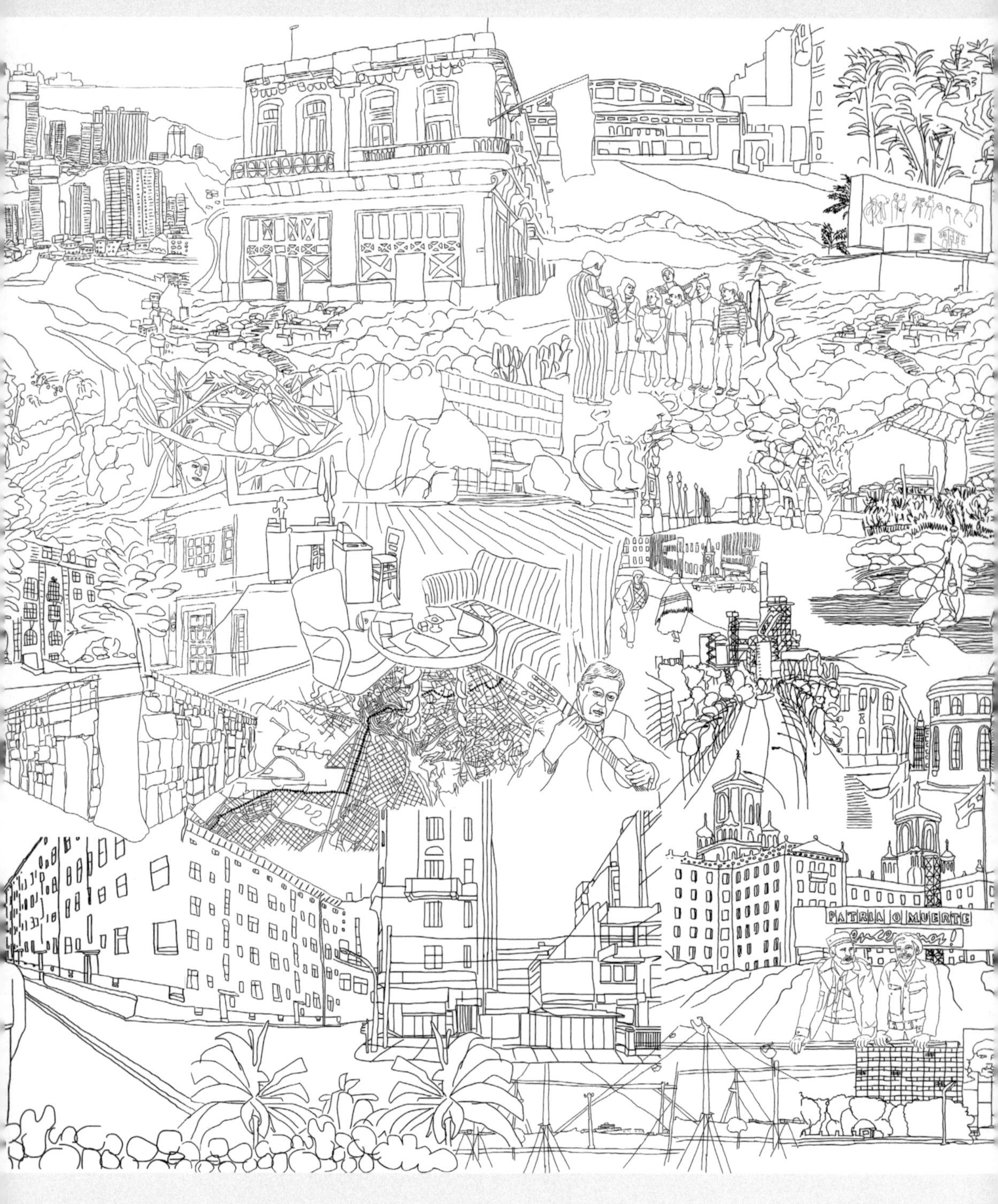
PATRIA O MUERTE
venceremos!

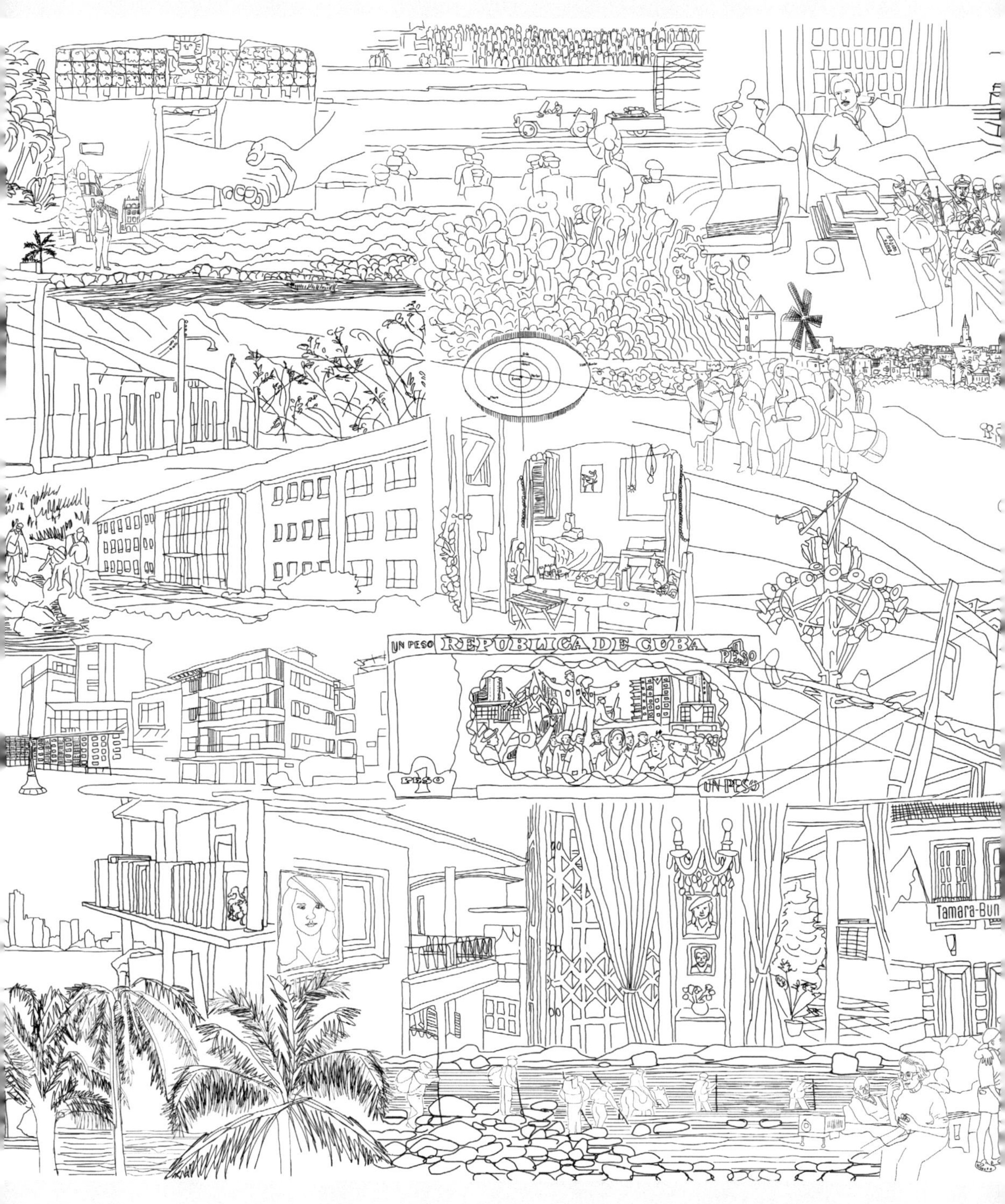
UN PESO
REPUBLICA DE CUBA
PESO
UN PESO
PESO
Tamara-Bun

UN PESO
REPÚBLICA DE CUBA
PESO
UN PESO
Tamara-Bunke-Oberschule

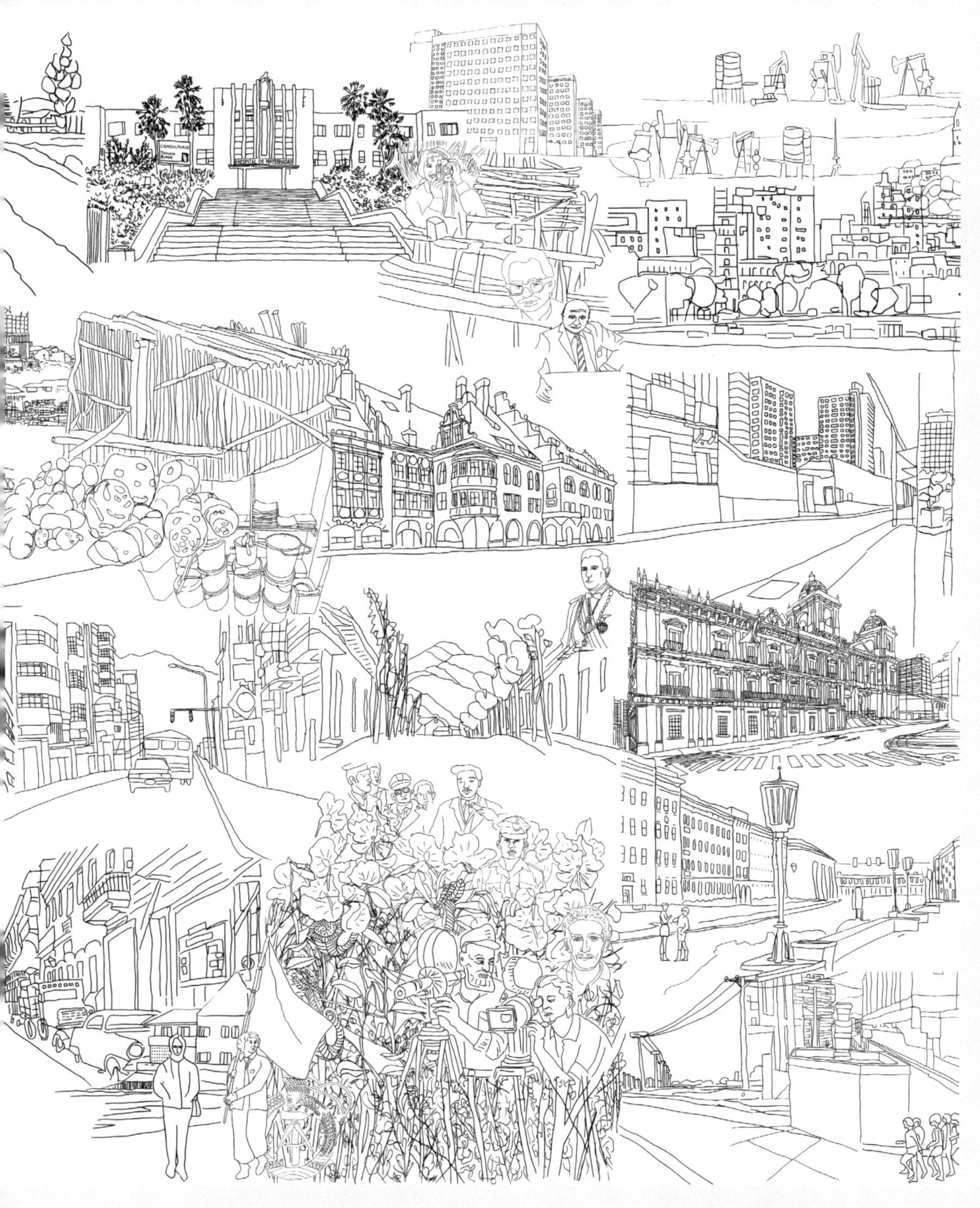

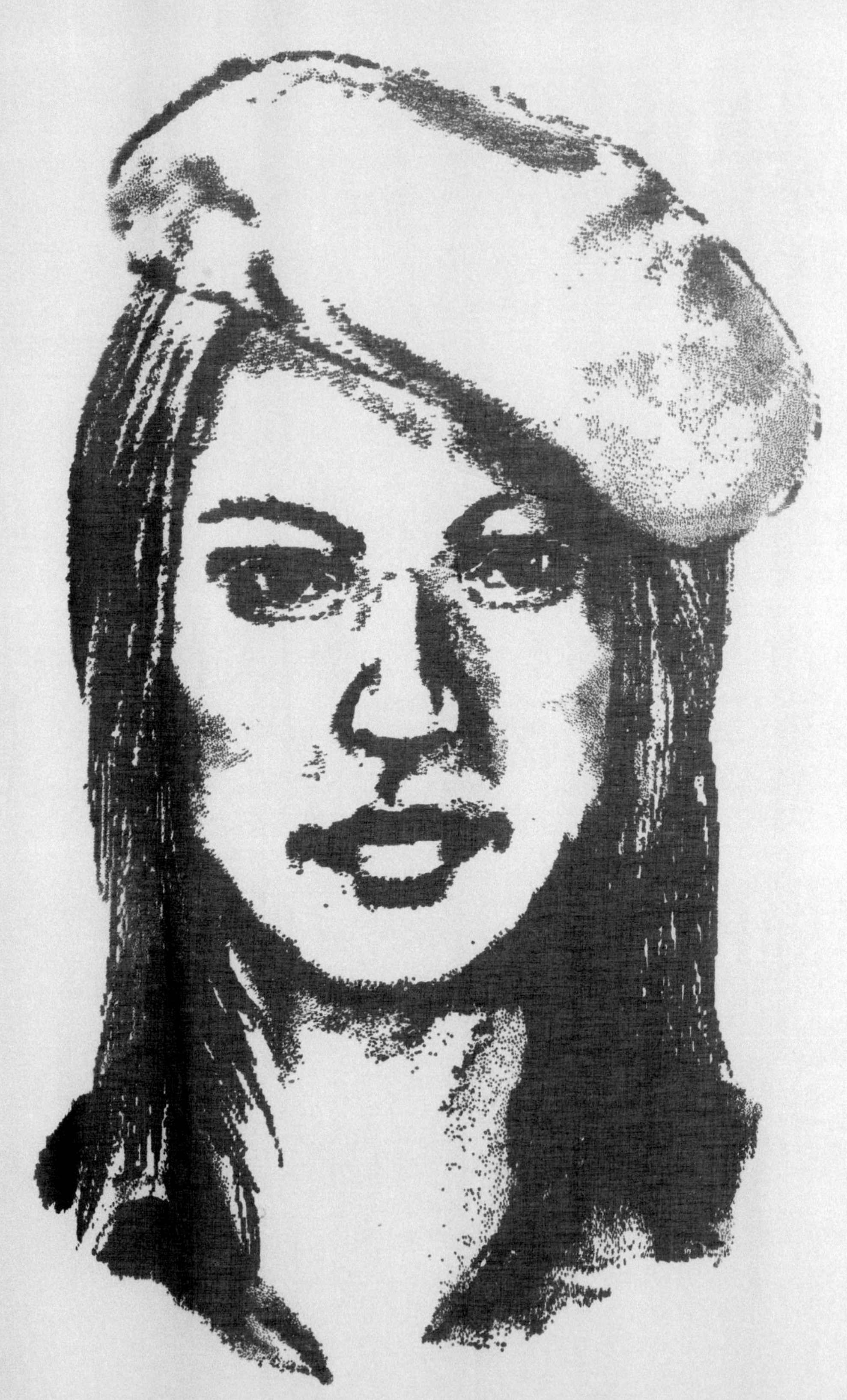

Text Index of
Exhibited Works

Katja Kynast, Magdalena Mai

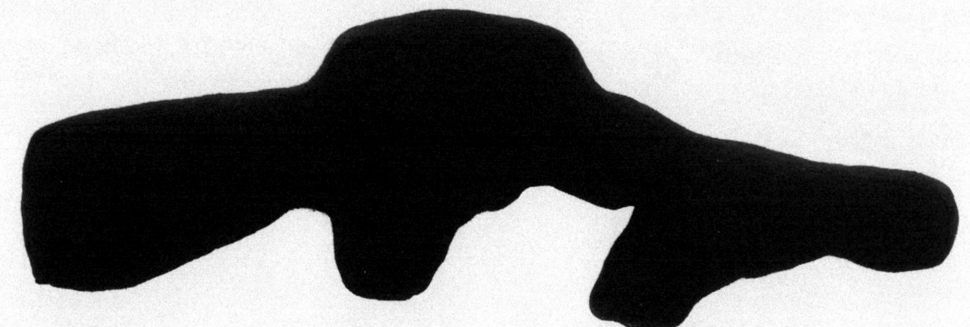

Mossberg Model Bullpup, 1992

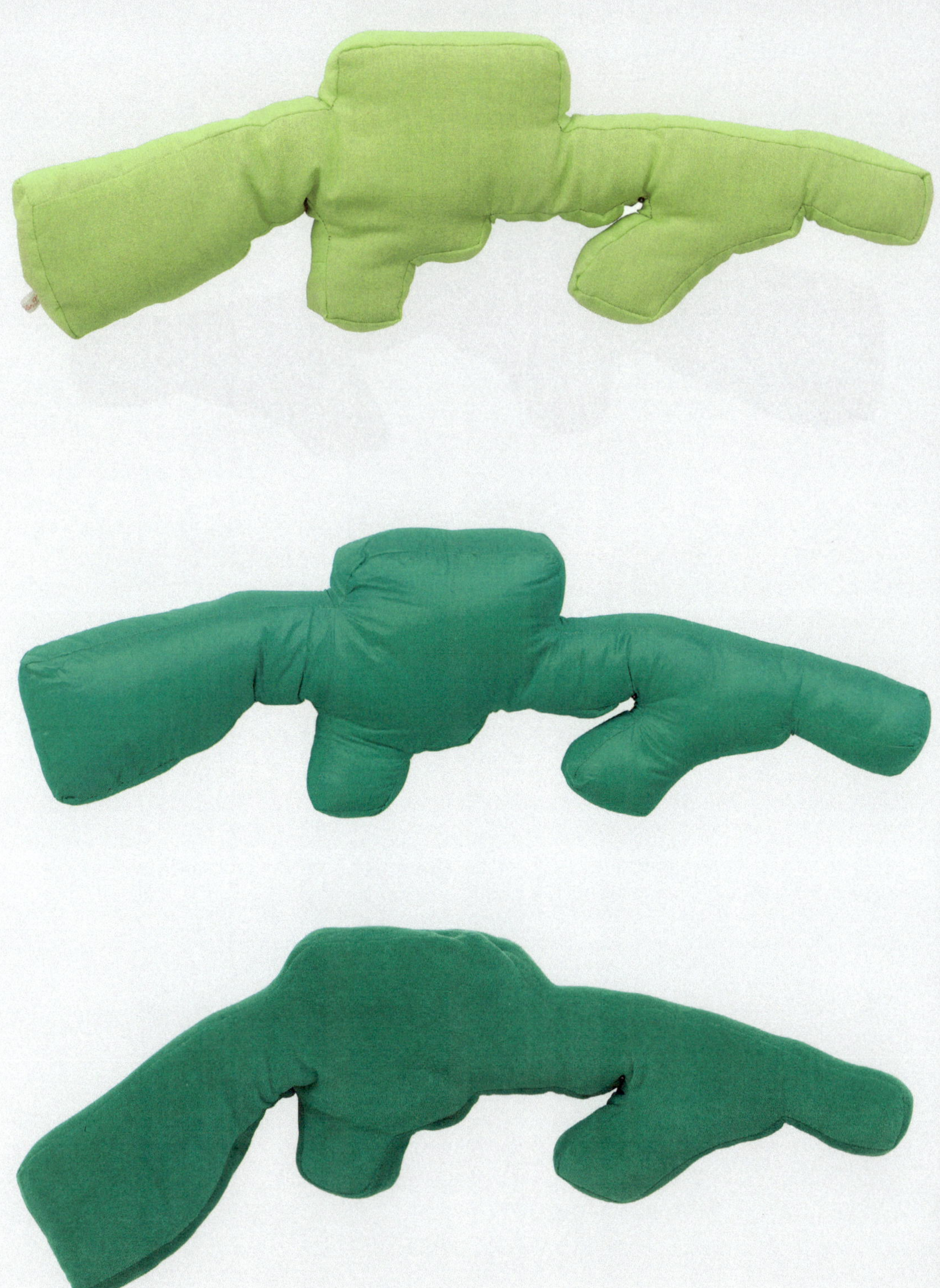

20   *Mossberg Model Bullpup,* 1992

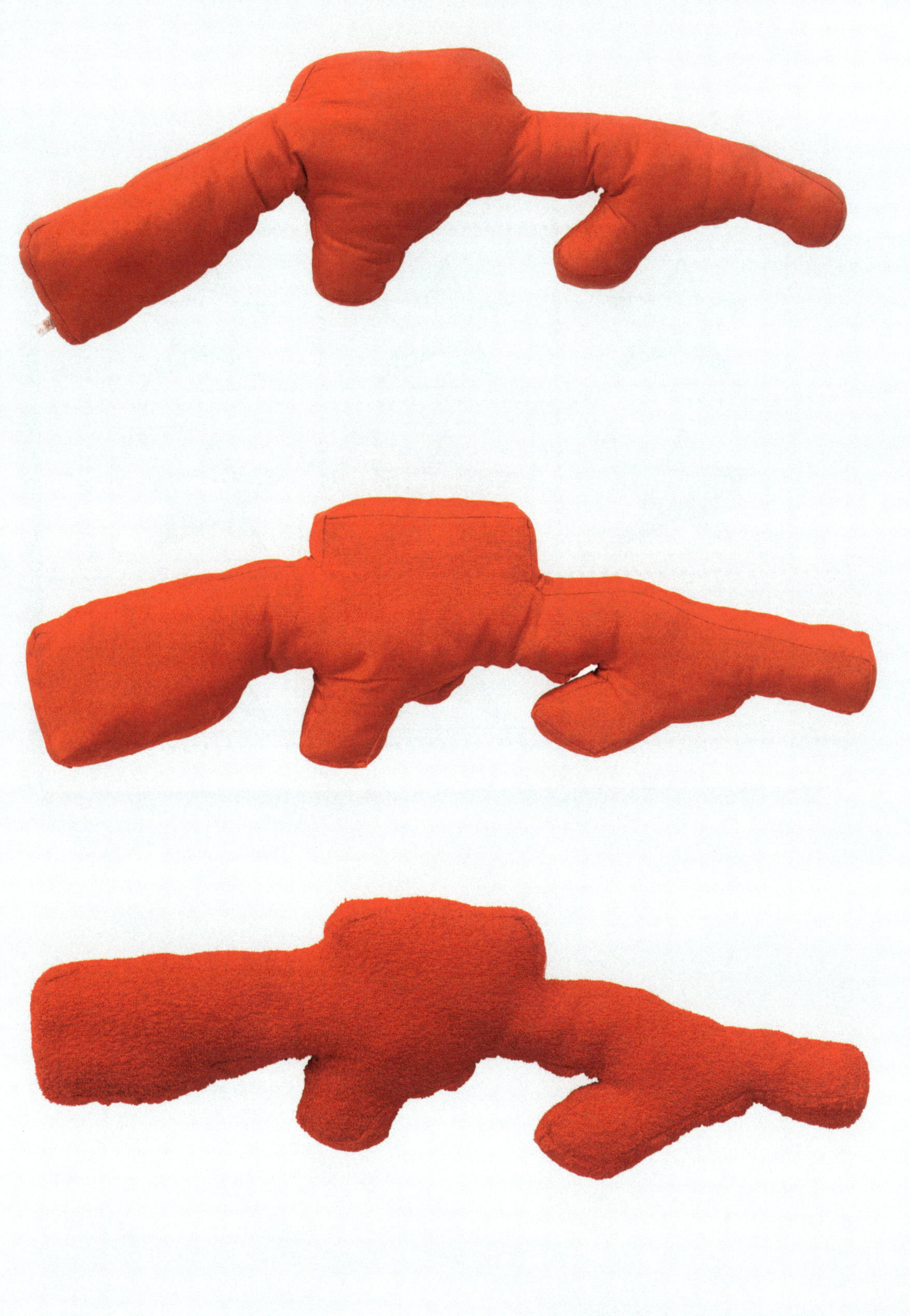

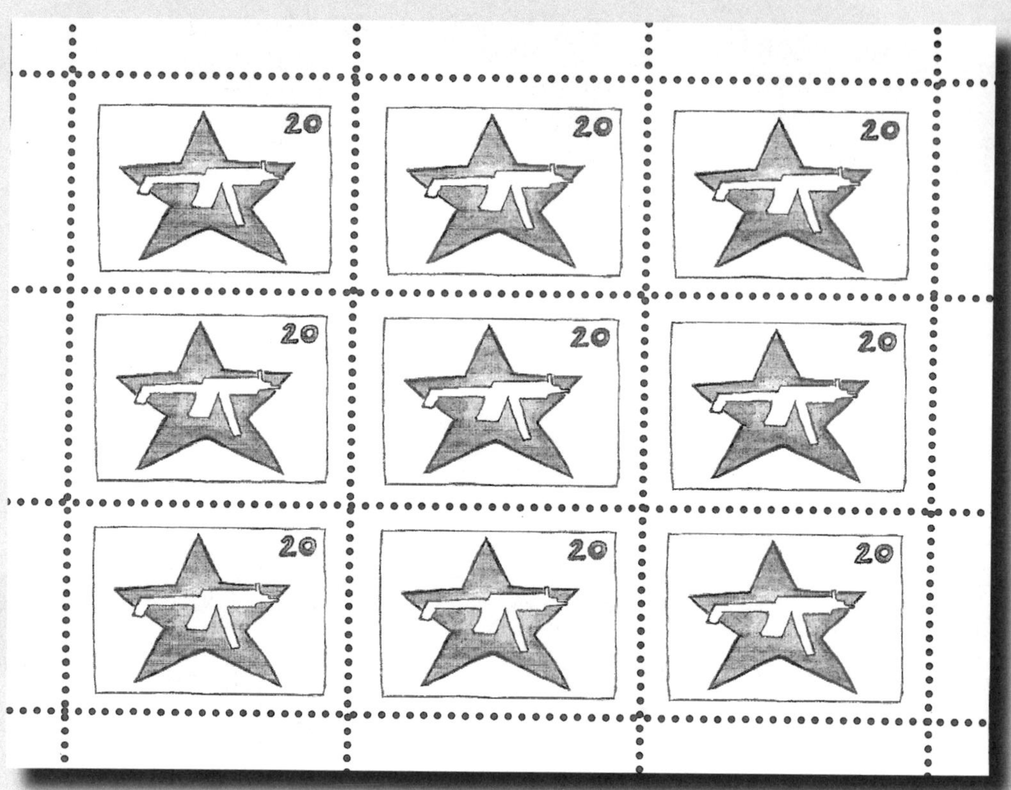

   Briefmarkenset 20, 1989–1992

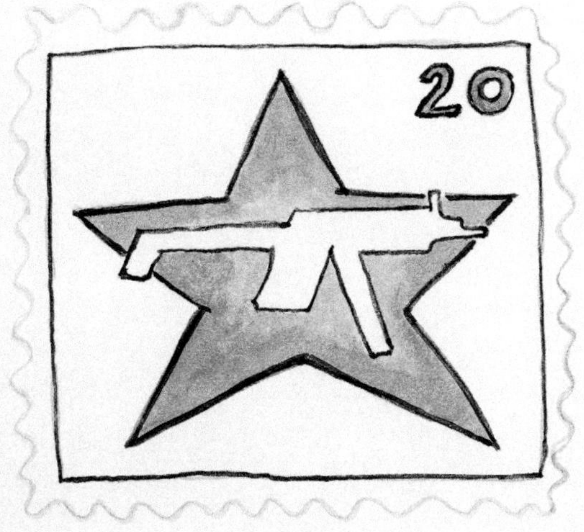

Briefmarke, 1988

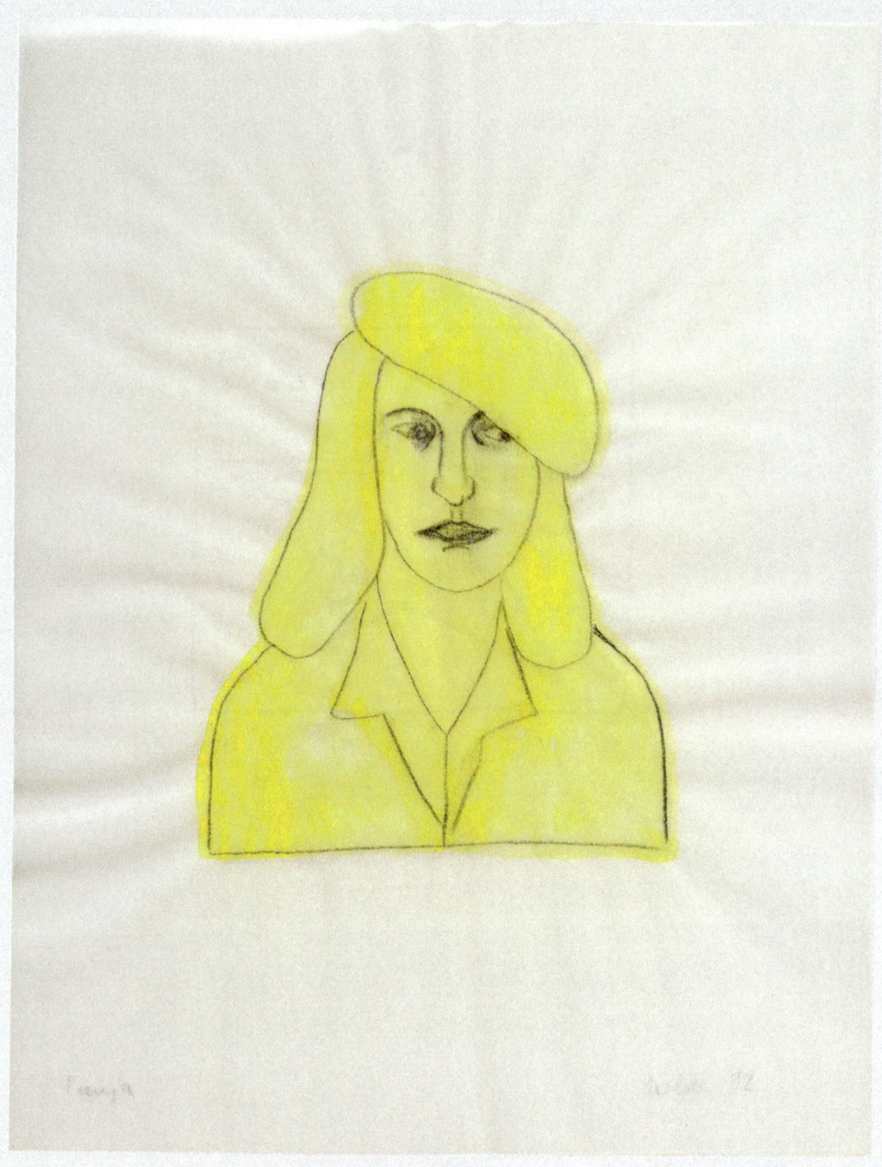

24   *Tania,* 1992

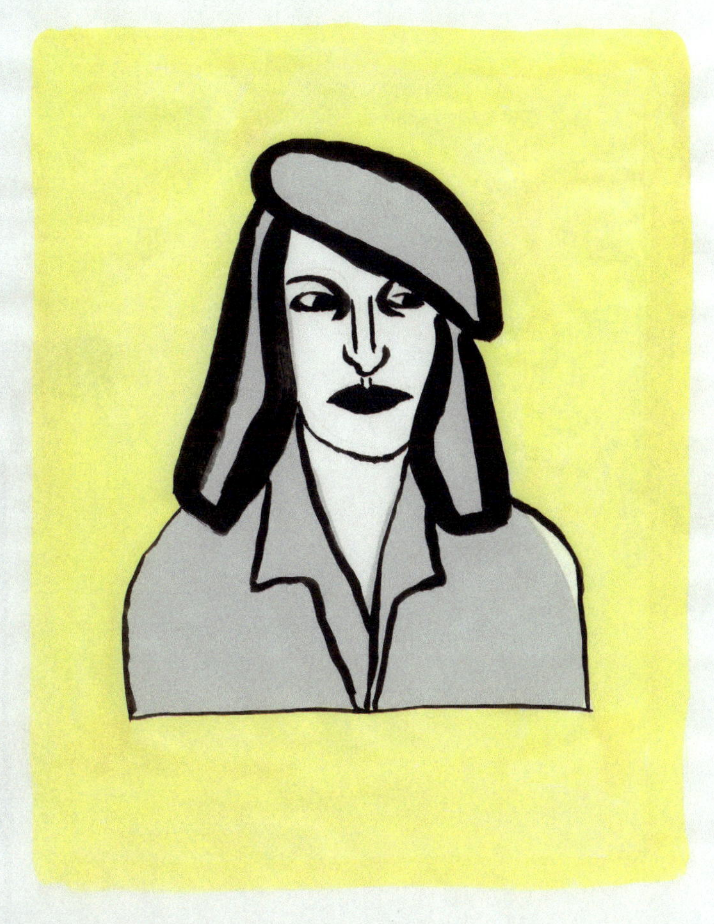

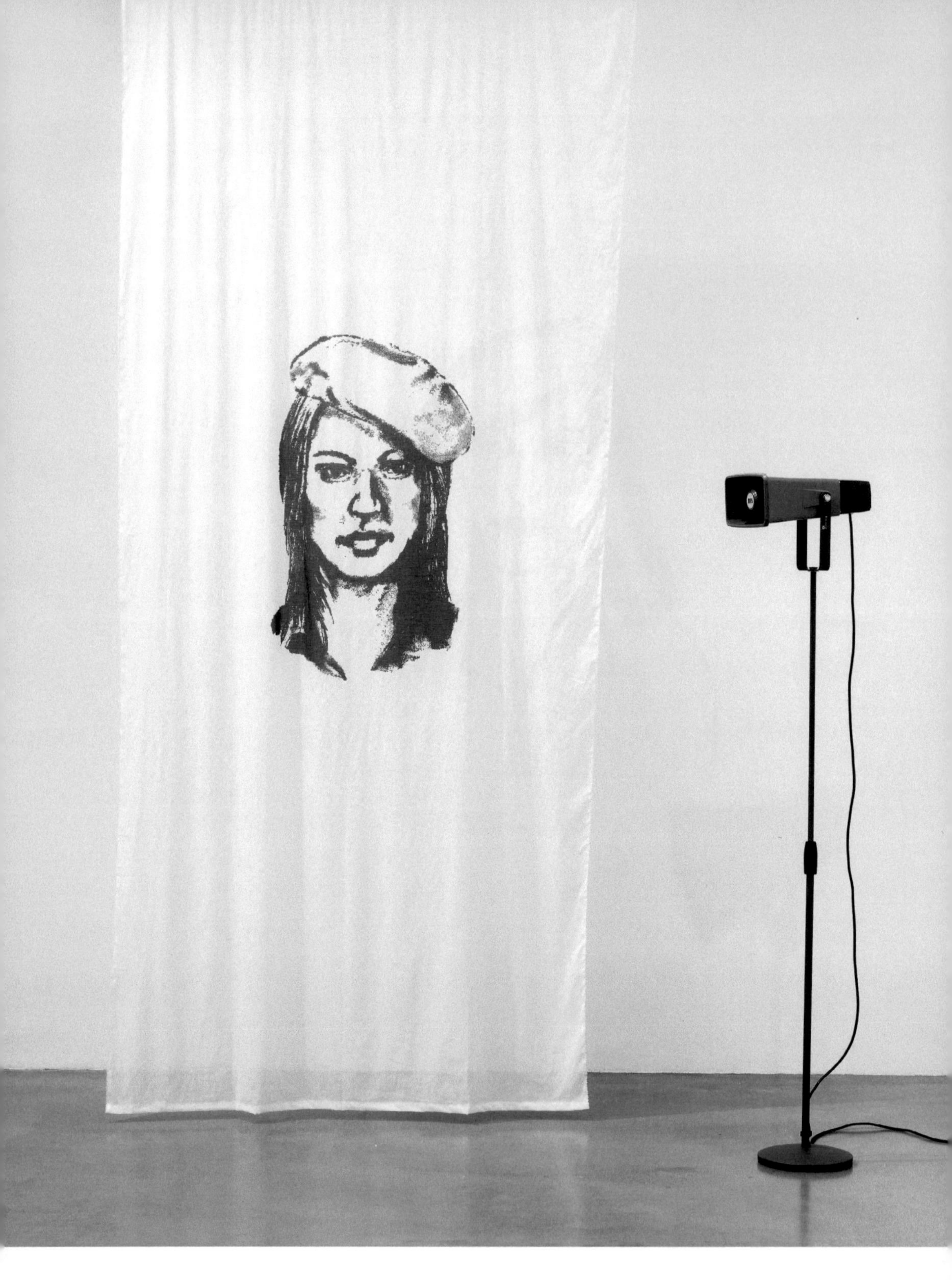

Tania, 1994 / 2022 (Flag)

Tania, 2022 (Sound installation)

Tania
1992
Pencil, ink,
oil on transparent paper
2 Drawings,
each 32,5 cm x 24 cm

Tania
1994 / 2022
Flag
Printed muslin,
drawing
420 cm x 140 cm

Tania
2022
Mural
Rubber stamp, ink,
330 cm x 1400 cm
16-channel-sound installation,
45 min.,
Pressure chamber loudspeaker,
audio tracks
Music:
Michaela Melián
Production:
Michaela Melián,
Felix Raeithel,
Jürgen Galli

Tania is the nom de guerre of
Haydée Tamara Bunke Bíder.
Bunke was born in Buenos Aires in
1937 into a communist German-
Jewish family in exile. After the war,
she moved to East Germany with
her parents, joined the Free German
Youth, and later studied at the
Humboldt University in Berlin. In the
1960s she left East Germany for
Cuba and then joined the guerrilla
group led by Che Guevara in
Bolivia, where she was ambushed
and shot in 1967.

For the **Tania** series, Michaela
Melián researched reports, events,
and places from Tamara Bunke's /
Tania's life. The great themes of the
20th century intersect in her life
story: Nazism, war, socialist modernism, emancipation, and liberation. However, her biography can
only be pieced together from unreliable narrations, forged documents,
cover identities, projections, and
suggestive documentation, and
constantly eludes understanding.

Melián does not censor the representations of Tania, and instead
collects as much material as
possible in order to channel it into
an artistic and intellectual process
that makes it possible to also address the political and media conditions of these representations.
The models for the 250 drawings
that Melián made as the basis for
the new mural **Tania** are excerpts
from documentaries, views of
La Paz (where Tamara Bunke lived
as an agent of the Cuban secret
service amid the political elite
of Bolivia), images of indigenous
sculptures that she researched
in her cover identity as ethnologist
Laura Gutiérrez Bauer, current
Google Street View images of the
places where she lived, including
socialist modernist Berlin, postcards
from Western European capitals
that Bunke travelled to during her
training as a spy or agent, photographs of oil derricks in Cuba, the
Bolivian Andes, and Bunke's funeral
in the Central Committee of the
Socialist Unity Party of Germany
with Anna Seghers as a speaker.
Melián digitally assembled the
drawings into a dense network,
which, in pixelated form, was
stamped onto the wall in repetitive,
collective manual labour with little
rubber stamps and paint. In this
way, both thematically and formally,
Melián creates a work that shifts
between image and design, archival
document and vision of the future,
information and noise.

Central processes and themes from Melián's work as well as from this exhibition are distilled in the *Tania* series. This includes potentially endless research, which enables a broad and incomplete view of history and biographies. It also includes the sequential processes of duplication and translation into other media, from film to drawing to Photoshop or from photo to description to drawing. In this way, and independently of the "artist's stroke of genius", Melián can address the conditions under which identities and spaces are created and represented. Traditional artistic forms of representation of identity and space include portraits and cityscapes or vedute, many of which can be found in the mural *Tania*. How is identity formed? How do we want to live? What is the space that is granted, that is fought for? These are the central questions of this work and other works in the exhibition, such as the tapestry *Girl-Kultur*.

The site-specific nature of the work is intended as an examination of the history and social reality of the city of Berlin and its artistic genres. In its form, the mural not only echoes South American murals, but also socialist mosaics, the best-known of which include *Aus dem Leben der Völker der Sowjetunion* (*From the Life of the Peoples of the Soviet Union*) on Karl-Marx-Allee, where Bunke's parents lived.

The work developed out of the mural created in 2004 for the Werkleitz Biennale in Halle on the same thematic complex. In this updated version, the views form a dense thicket that is impenetrable in places. The mural does not offer a sovereign, possessive, urban view of the threads that run through the world. Instead, identities, places, and stories repeatedly dissolve into unknown figures, forms, and indistinct flickering.

The second part of the installation *Tania* and a central part of the series in this exhibition is the newly developed sound installation *Tania*, which deals with Tamara Bunke's musical canon. For this work, Melián assembled snippets of sound from protest songs that she recorded herself ranging from 10 to 20 seconds in length: *The Internationale*, *Peat Bog Soldiers*, *Bella Ciao*, and the *Anthem of the 26th of July*, also known as the *Cuban Revolutionary March*. There are also pieces from musical cultures that Tania researched in her cover identity as an anthropologist. The Inca flutes refer to the recordings found in the backpack that Tania was carrying when she was shot. The recordings are played throughout the exhibition space on a dozen pressure chamber loudspeakers like those often found in public transport.

A vinyl record in an edition of 100 (12-inch EP, signed and numbered) will be available during the exhibition.

The artist's engagement with Tania, and with the genre of the portrait, conventions of the creation of identity and identifiability, and their limits began in 1992 for the work complex *Tania – Subject, Predicate, Object*. Melián had reconstructions of Tamara Bunke's likeness made on a computer system used by the state criminal police in Munich. A photo of Tania served as a model, which Melián verbally described to an officer. What are typical characteristics of a person? What features make them identifiable? Only "male" facial features based on racist stereotypes were available in the police database. The resulting image, which is featured in the mural, the drawings, and on the muslin flag at the entrance, is also reminiscent of the iconic likeness of Che Guevara and thus alludes to the missing (female) counterpart.

        Katja Kynast, Magdalena Mai

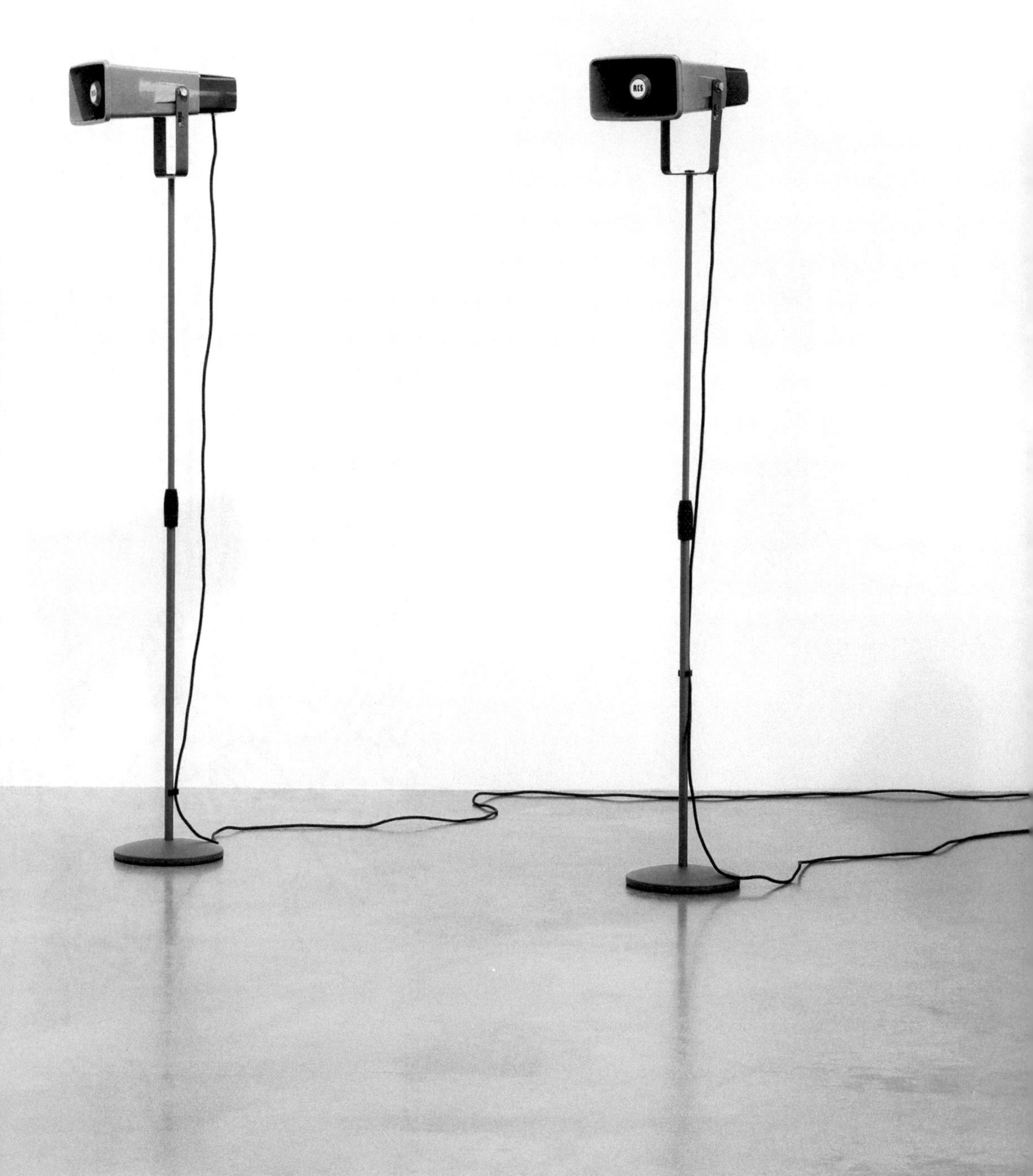

Tania, 2022 (Sound installation)

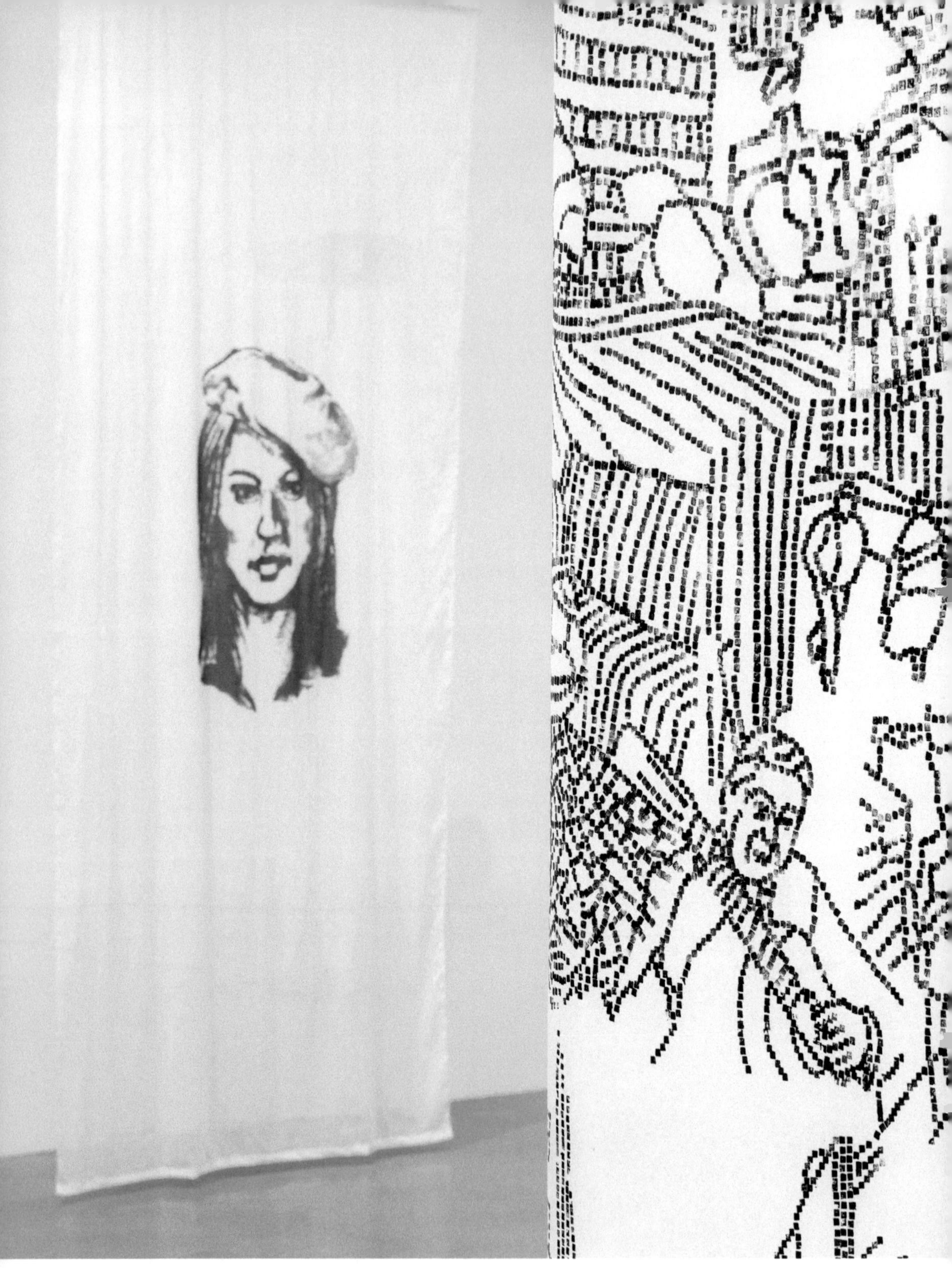

30   *Tania,* 1994 / 2022 (Flag)

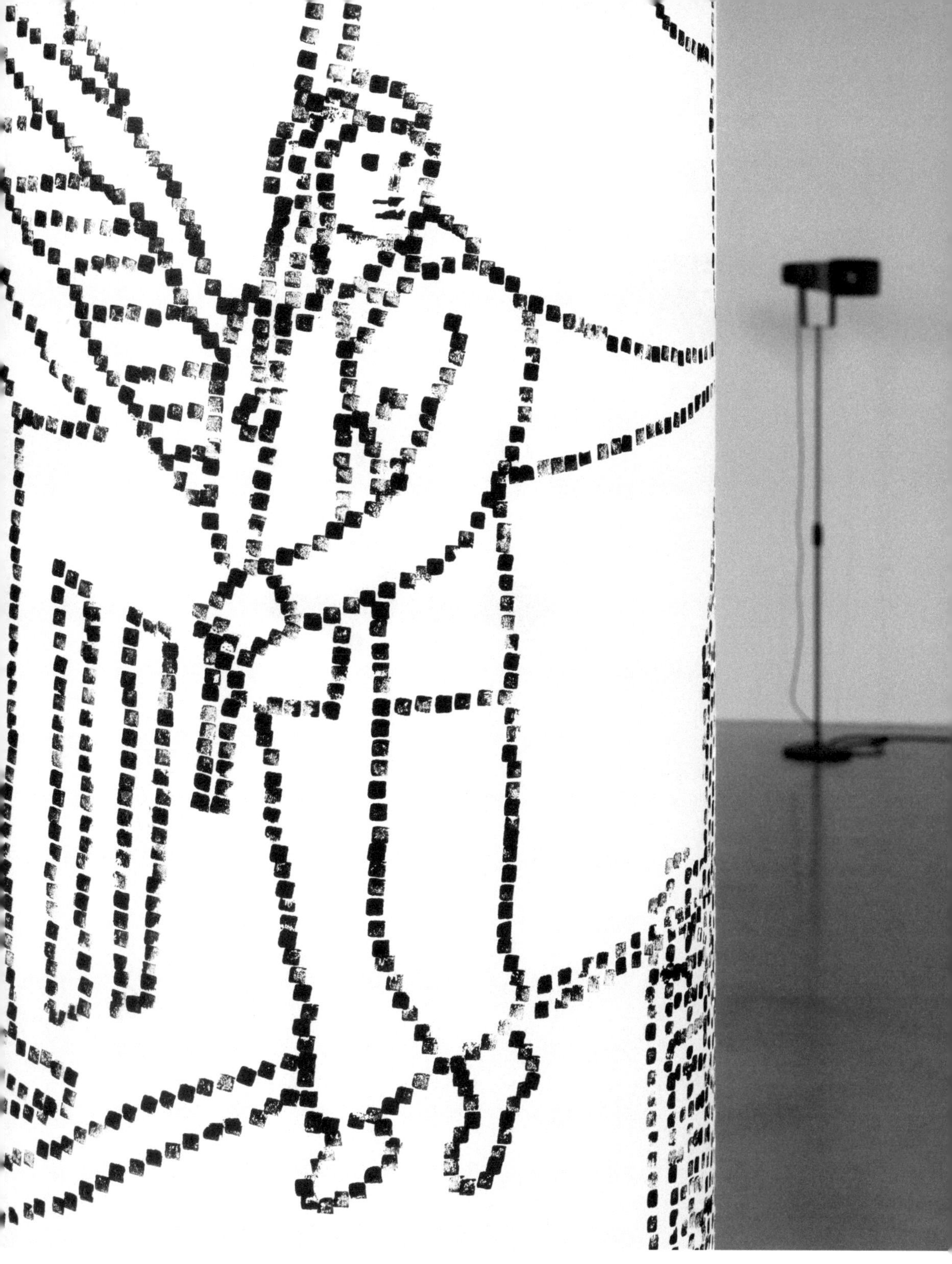

Tania, 2022 (Mural)

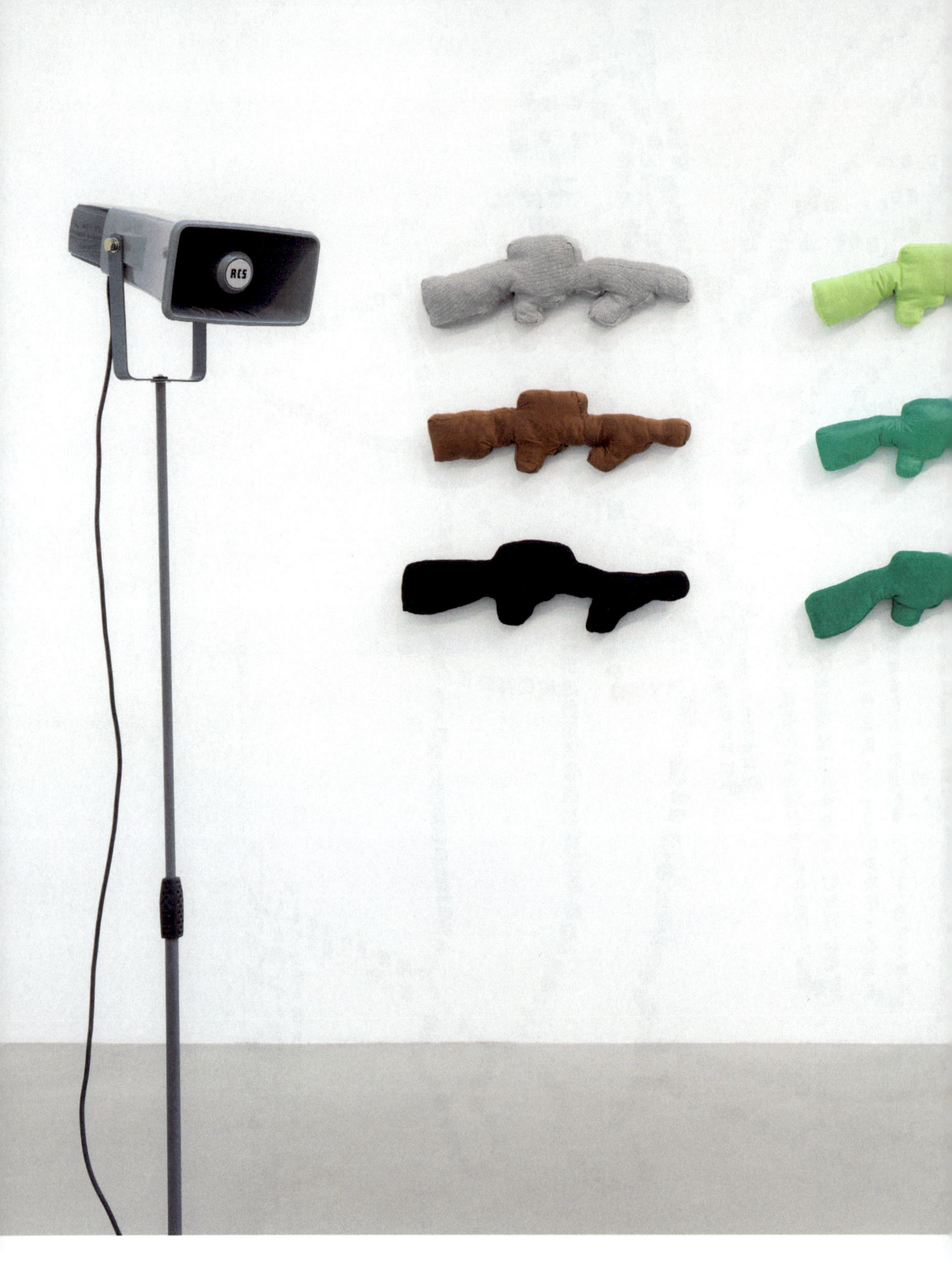

   Tania, 2022 (Sound installation)   *Mossberg Model Bullpup,* 1992

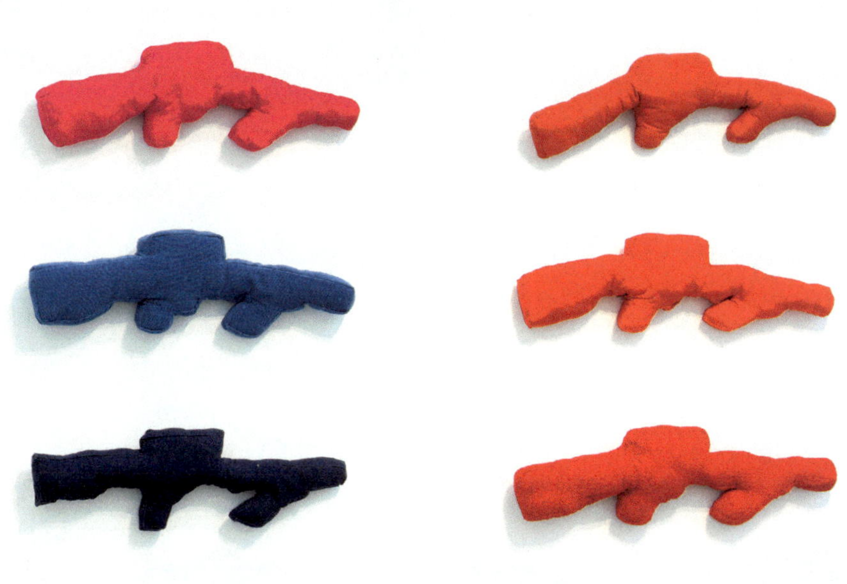

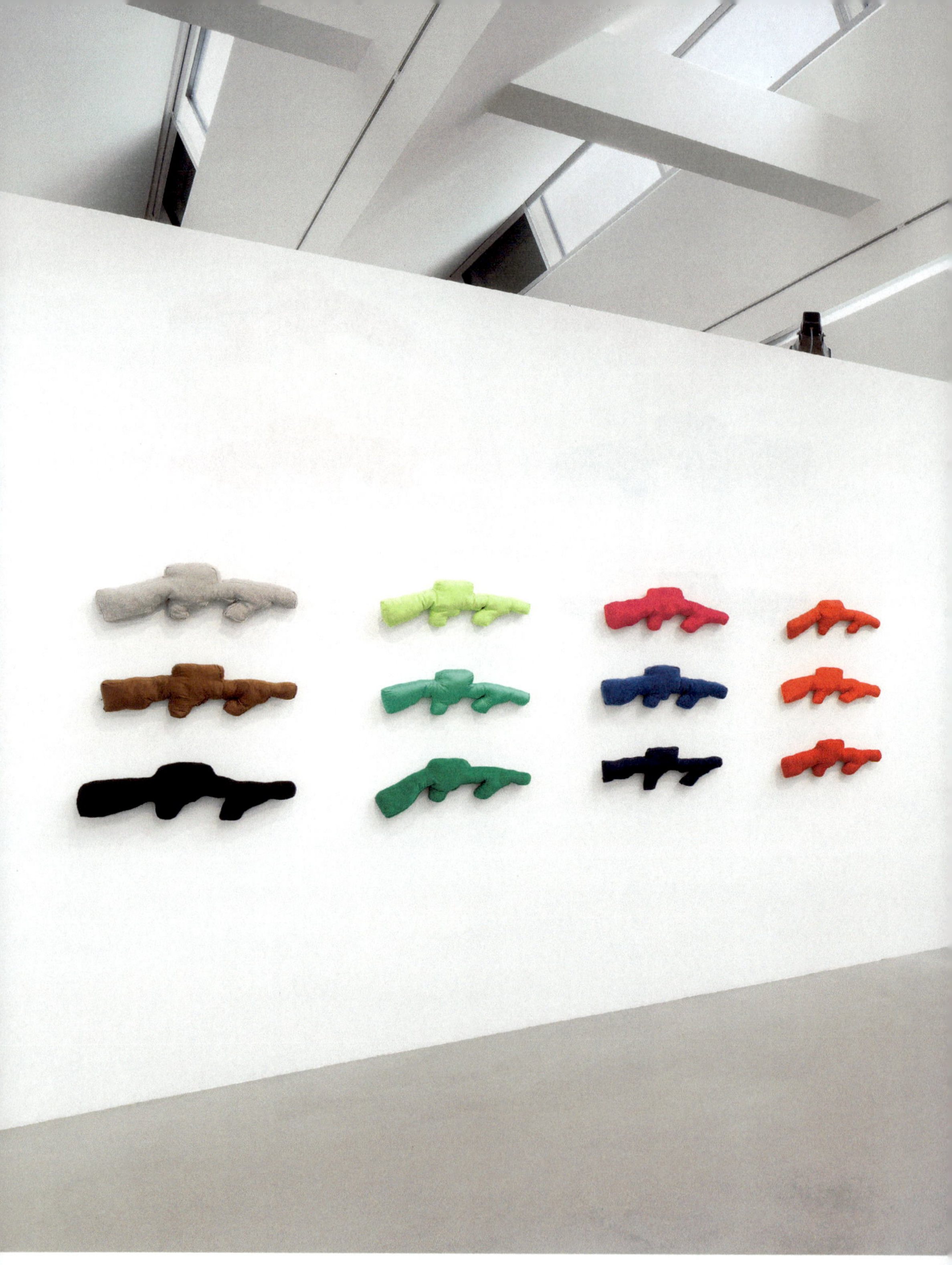

34   *Mossberg Model Bullpup,* 1992

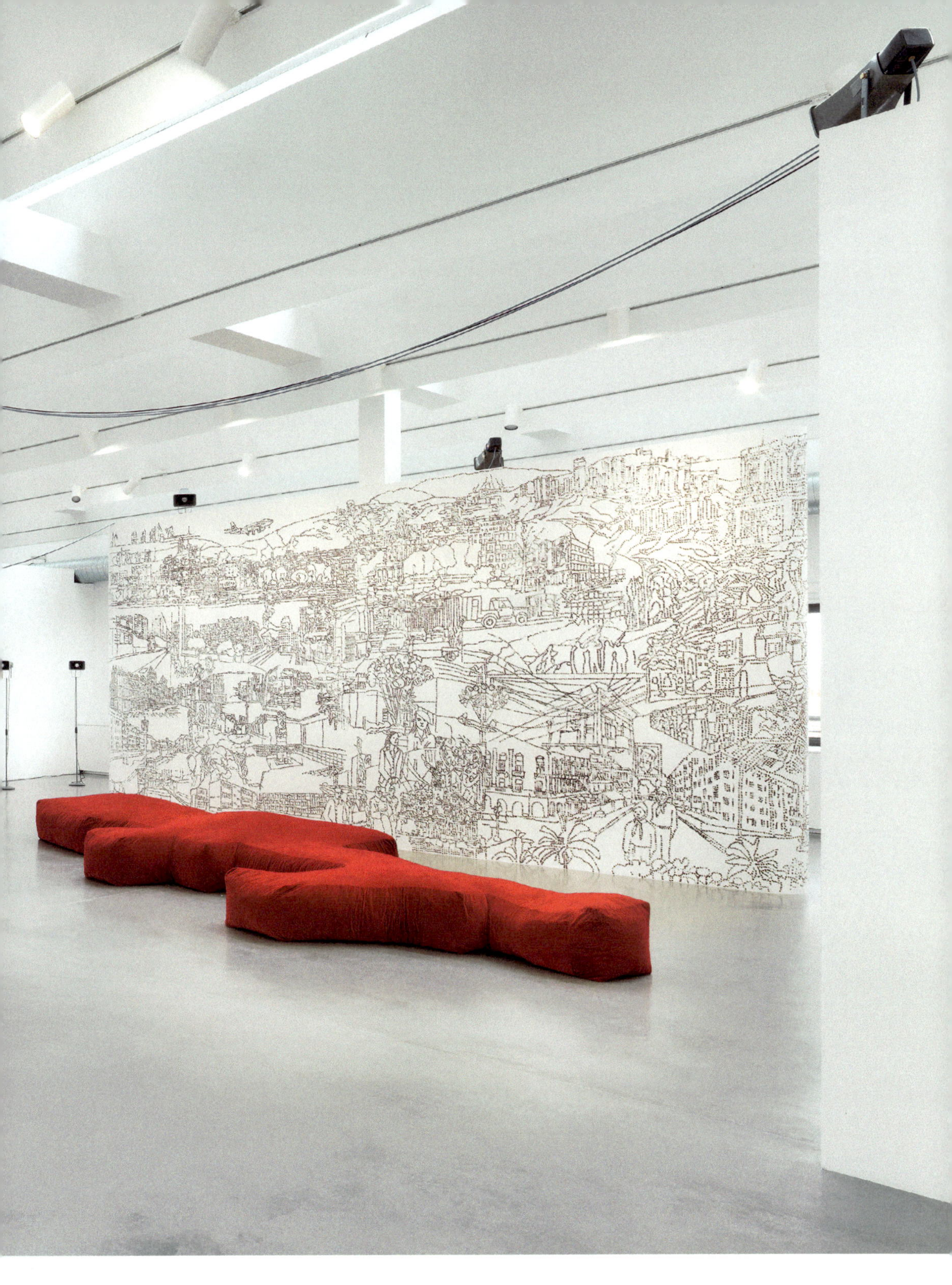

Mossberg Model Bullpup, 1993   ***Tania,*** 2022 (Sound installation, Mural)

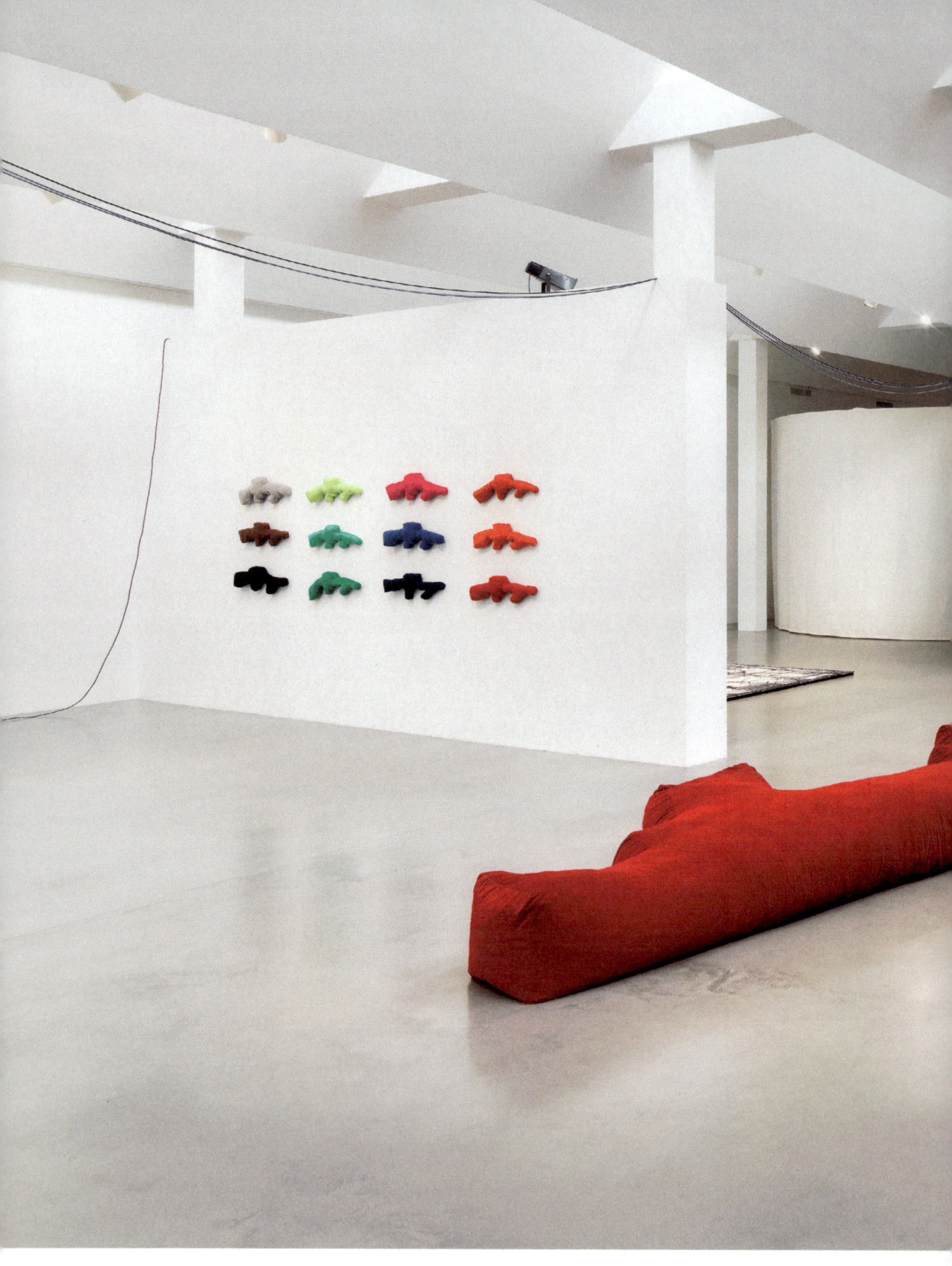

 Mossberg Model Bullpup, 1992   *Mossberg Model Bullpup,* 1993

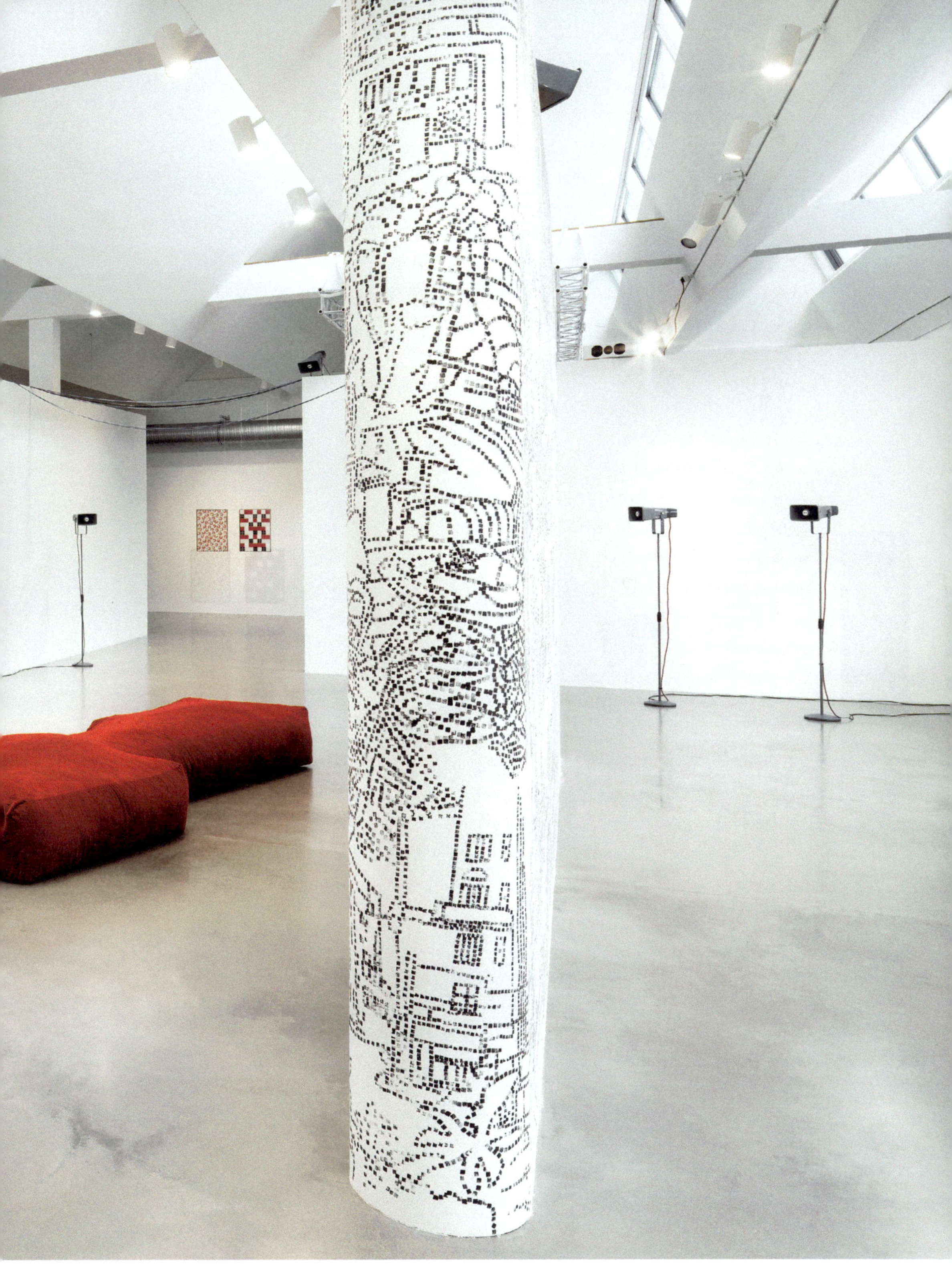

Tania, 2022 (Sound installation, Mural)

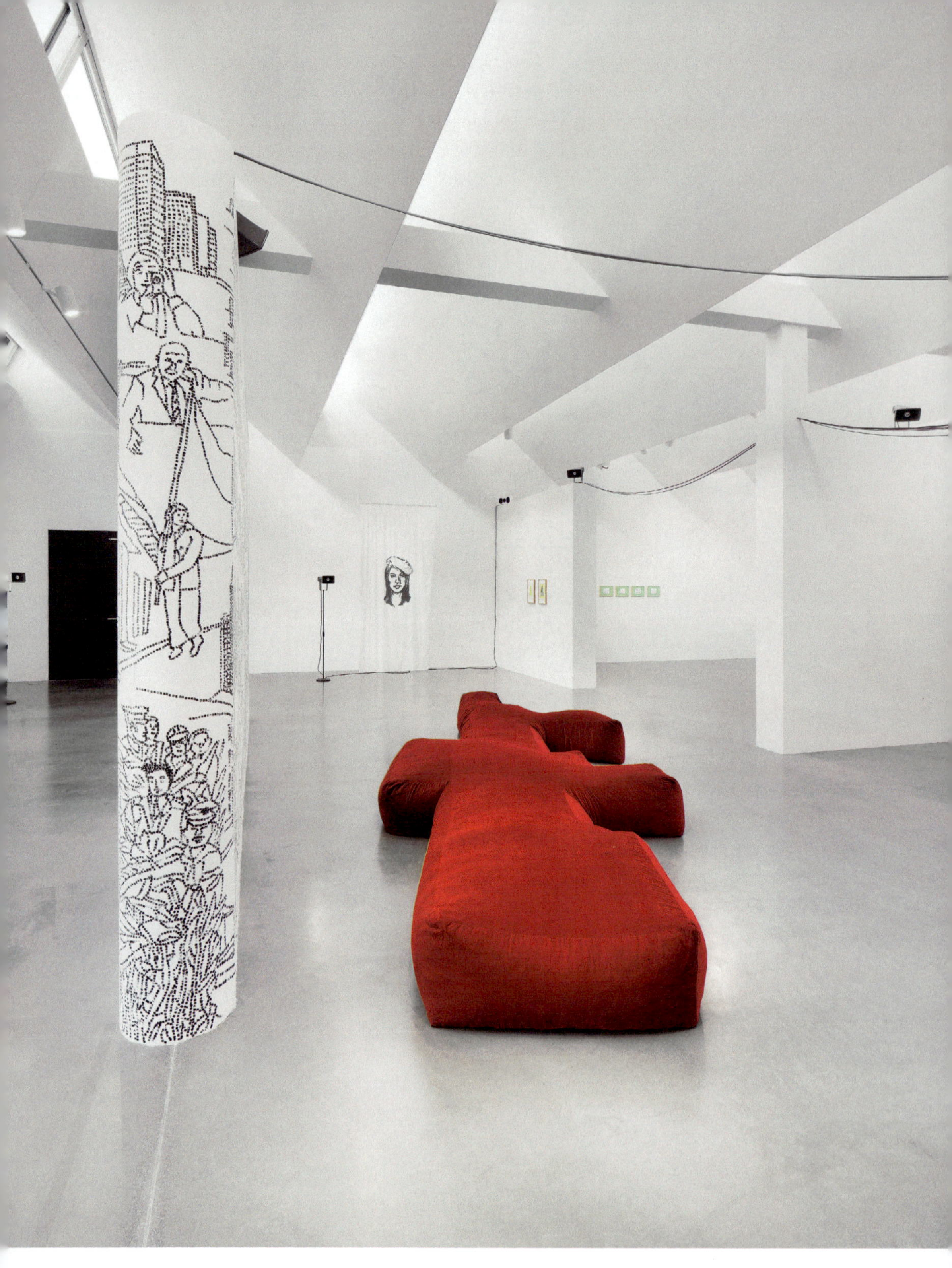

  Tania, 2022   *Mossberg Model Bullpup*, 1993

Briefmarke
1988
Drawing
Tempera on paper,
29,8 cm x 18,7 cm

Briefmarkenset 10, 20, 33, 45
1989 – 1992
Ink print on gummed paper
4 sheets,
each 11,5 cm x 13,5 cm

Mossberg Model Bullpup
1992
Sculpture
Various materials, filling
12 pieces,
each 21 cm x 63 cm x 5 cm

Mossberg Model Bullpup
1993
Sculpture
Velvet, filling,
45 cm x 650 cm x 220 cm

Michaela Melián began making
use of weapons in her artworks
against the background of the Gulf
Wars and the Yugoslav Wars.
In her research she came across
the Mossberg Bullpup, an unusually
shaped shotgun with a short barrel
and plastic grip. The firearm was
marketed as a "self-defence weapon," but was also used by the Los
Angeles Police Department (LAPD),
among others. Since the late 1980s,
the gun has appeared in various
forms in Melián's work: in drawings,
as multiples made of velvet, silk,
terry cloth, cotton, and wool in different colours, and as a soft velvet
sculpture on which visitors can sit.
In these works, Melián breaks
with the cliché of a fascination with
weapons, or turns it around with
soft shapes, the feel of different
materials, a paintbox, and an invit-
ing red sofa in the exhibition space.

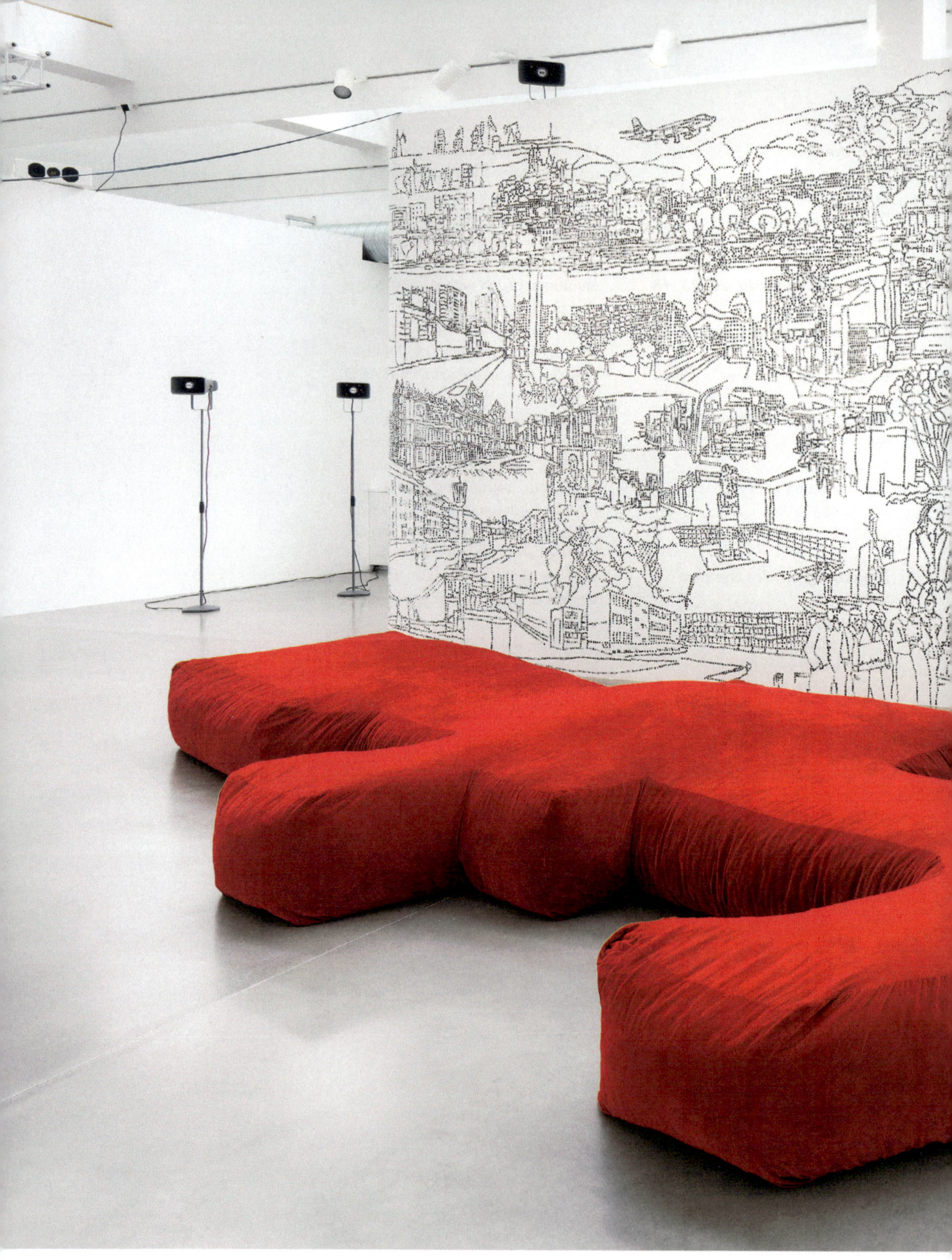

40 *Tania,* 2022 (Mural, Sound installation)

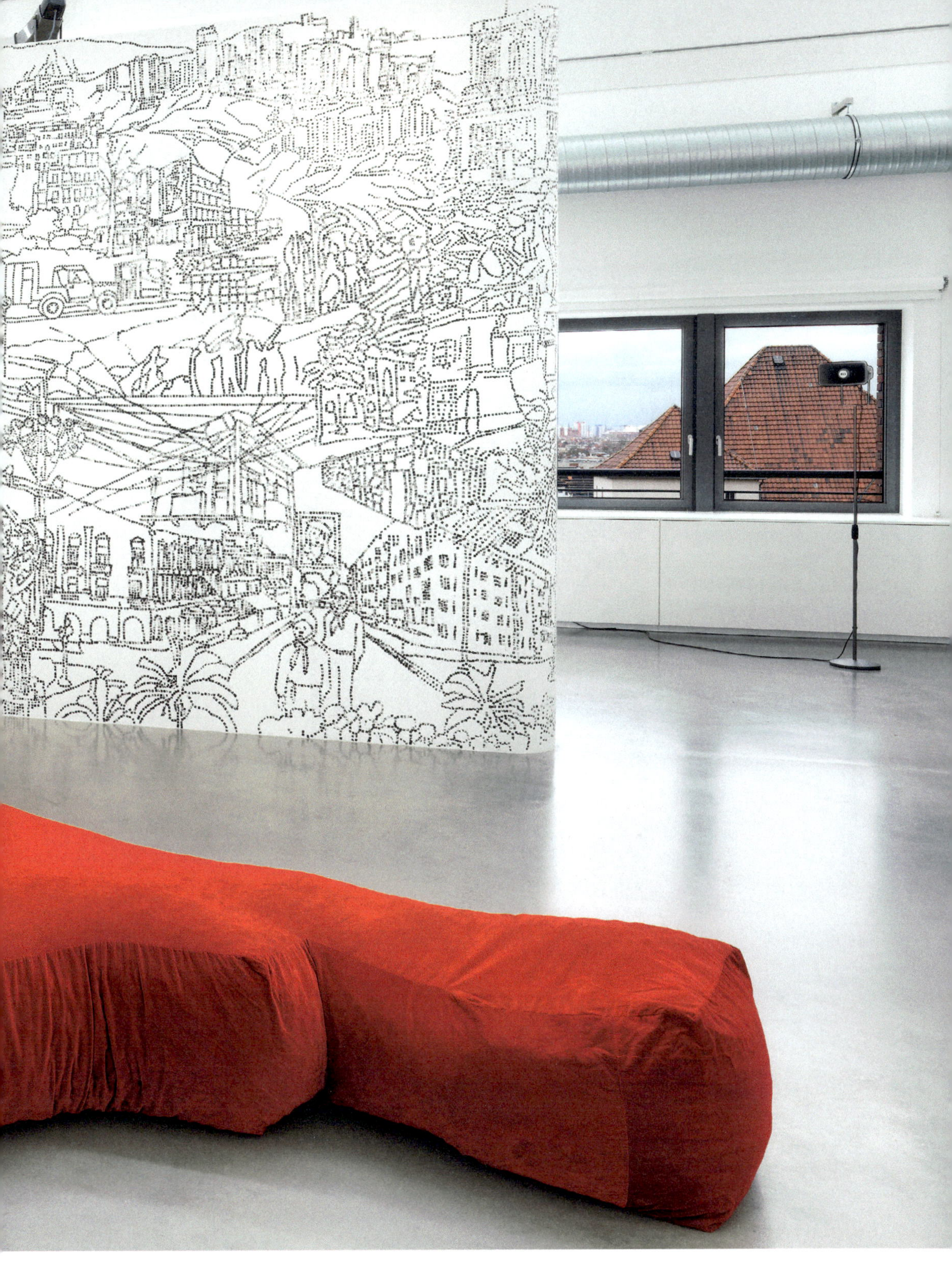

Mossberg Model Bullpup, 1993

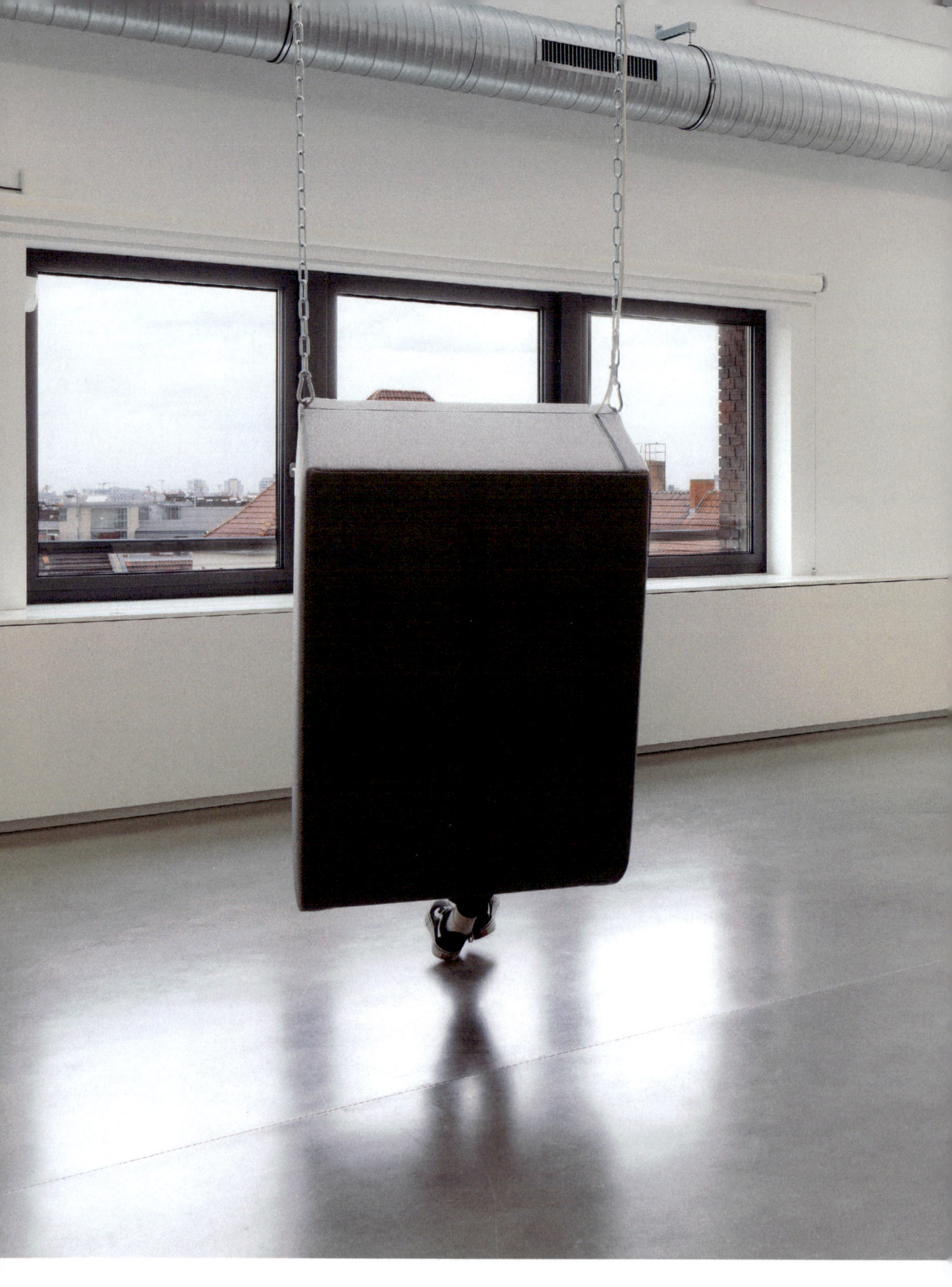

   Mannheim Chair, 2015 / 2016

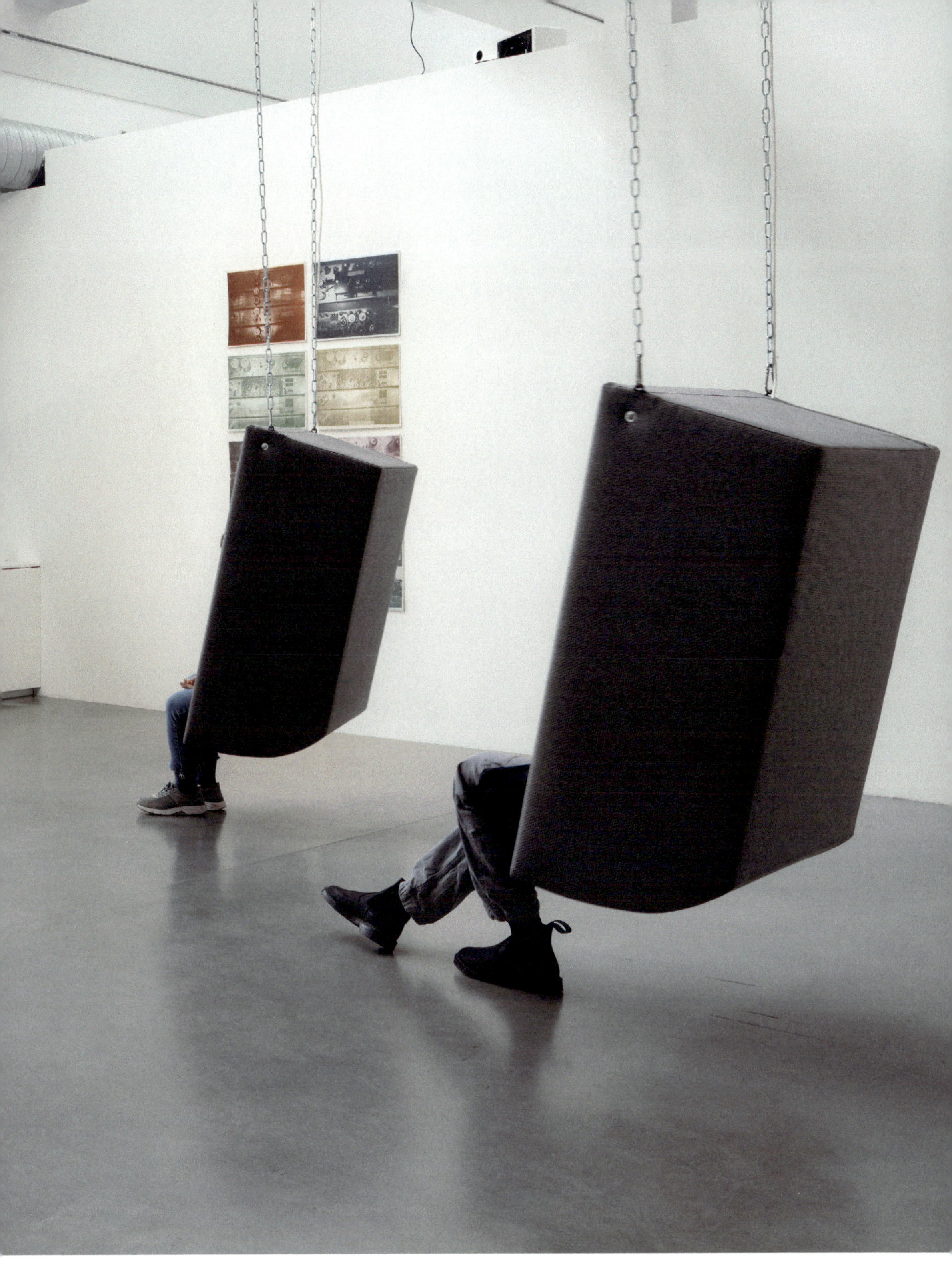

Studio, 2011

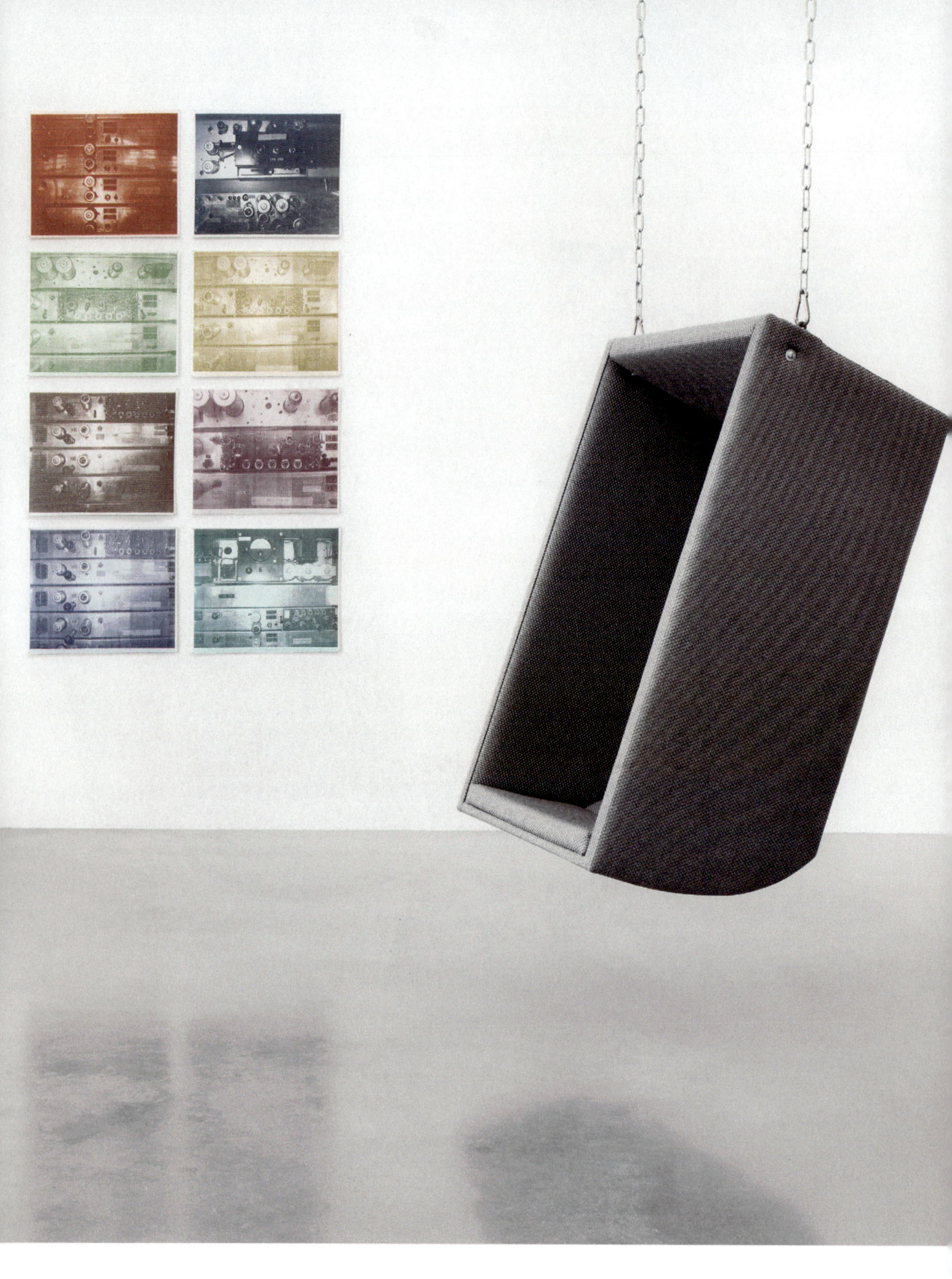

  Studio, 2011

Mannheim Chair, 2015 / 2016

Mannheim Chair
2015 / 2016
Sound sculpture
Wood, fabric, steel, sound system,
soundtrack variable
3 pieces,
each 120 cm x 75 cm x 50 cm

In the sound sculpture ***Mannheim Chair*** hanging from the cross-beam, which was originally developed for a sound installation in the old library at the Kunsthalle Mannheim, the chair becomes a multimedia exhibition display. Michaela Melián adds a sonic functionality to the chair with an integrated sound system: Visitors who sit in the chair can immerse themselves in the musical atmospheres of the pieces while gently rocking and enjoying a view of the skyline with the TV tower through the window in the exhibition space. Thus, the traces in the exhibition connect with the real place of Berlin, with its history and the receiver, who now appears as part of the coordinate system. The object that causes the body to rock is also a protected resonant space in which sound—including pieces from the projects ***Speicher*** (2008) and ***Music from a Frontier Town*** (2018)—can be experienced.

Studio
2011
Sewn drawing, print
Inkjet and thread
on paper
8 sheets,
each 42 cm x 52 cm

Frequency Hopping
2013
Sewn drawing, print
Inkjet and thread on paper
12 sheets,
each 50 cm x 65 cm

The series ***Studio*** and ***Frequency Hopping*** refer to the historic Siemens Studio for Electronic Music, which was one of the leading sound laboratories in Germany after the 2nd World War. It opened in Munich in 1956 and was headed by the composer Josef Anton Riedl. Due to its unique equipment— one-of-a-kind devices that were developed out of military technology—it is considered an important site for the development of electronic music as an early form of digital culture. In 1966 the studio was handed over to the film department headed by Alexander Kluge and Edgar Reitz at the Hochschule für Gestaltung in Ulm, and it was used as a set for Kluge's science fiction movies due to its futuristic-looking devices. When the HFG Ulm was closed in 1968, the equipment was put in storage. Since 1993, the recording studio has been part of the permanent exhibition at the Deutsches Museum in Munich.

In the works on paper in these two series, the artist depicts the historical, electroacoustic devices from the recording studio. The detail shots of mixing consoles, synthesisers, and recording equipment look like digital landscapes.
By sewing threads onto the photographs and piercing the paper with a sewing machine, Melián creates a kind of punch card in mechanical écriture automatique, which adds a shimmering, flickering vibration to the studio landscapes.

The ambivalence of the instruments developed out of military technology is particularly evident in the title ***Frequency Hopping***. The title refers to a groundbreaking invention from 1941 by the actress and scientist Hedy Lamarr, which made it possible to obscure radio signals from torpedoes by rapidly changing frequencies so that the source could not be located and the signal could not be interfered with.
The threads cover the picture of the studio landscape like a veil and interweave topography, music tracks, memory, and different temporal layers.

Speicher
2008
Video installation
with soundtrack,
53 min.
Voices:
Peter Brombacher,
Christos Davidopoulos,
Chris Dercon,
Hans Kremer,
Stefan Merki,
Laura Maire
Music:
Michaela Melián,
Carl Oesterhelt
Sound technicians:
Susanne Herzig,
Wilfried Hauer
Camera:
Michaela Melián
and Surface Frankfurt
Editing:
Margarete Hentze,
Michael Hiebel
Director:
Michaela Melián
Production:
Michaela Melián,
Ulmer Museum,
Lentos Kunstmuseum Linz,
Cubitt Gallery, London,
Bayerischer Rundfunk, Munich,
German Federal Cultural
Foundation

"Up and away, over and past.
Put distance between, leave the
crap behind."
"Walking tour through the Harz
mountains with a map of London."

Speicher pays homage to the lost
multimedia artwork VariaVision: *Unendliche Fahrt* (1965) by Alexander
Kluge (texts), Josef Anton Riedl
(music), and Edgar Reitz (film). The
installation on the theme of travel
offered a new form of simultaneous
perception of film, music, and
language via several synchronous
channels.

Based on the iconic work by Kluge,
Riedl, and Reitz, Michaela Melián
portrays travel and movement in
a collage of images, text, and music.
The non-linear, narrative elements
are based on sources and reports
from different times and contexts.
The camera moves slowly through
the winter night of a drawing made
with a sewing machine. "Farewell,
distance, cities, from city to city,
arrival, landscape, never-ending
journey, punctuality, sleep, com-
muter traffic, safety, freight transport, vacation, seasons, rails, speed,
weather." The subject of travel is
explored in the work as a search, as
a longing for the foreign between
romantic hiking scenes, emigration,
and flight.

For the soundtrack of the video installation ***Speicher***, Michaela
Melián brought the Siemens Studio
for Electronic Music at the
Deutsches Museum in Munich back
to life and turned the sounds and
noises produced with the historical
instruments into a musical composition. The studio itself is present
in the specific sound of the one-of-
a-kind electroacoustic instruments,
as well as in the length of the film,
which measures the distance
between Munich and Ulm—the distance that the studio has travelled
over the years (see text on ***Studio***
and ***Frequency Hopping***).

       Katja Kynast, Magdalena Mai

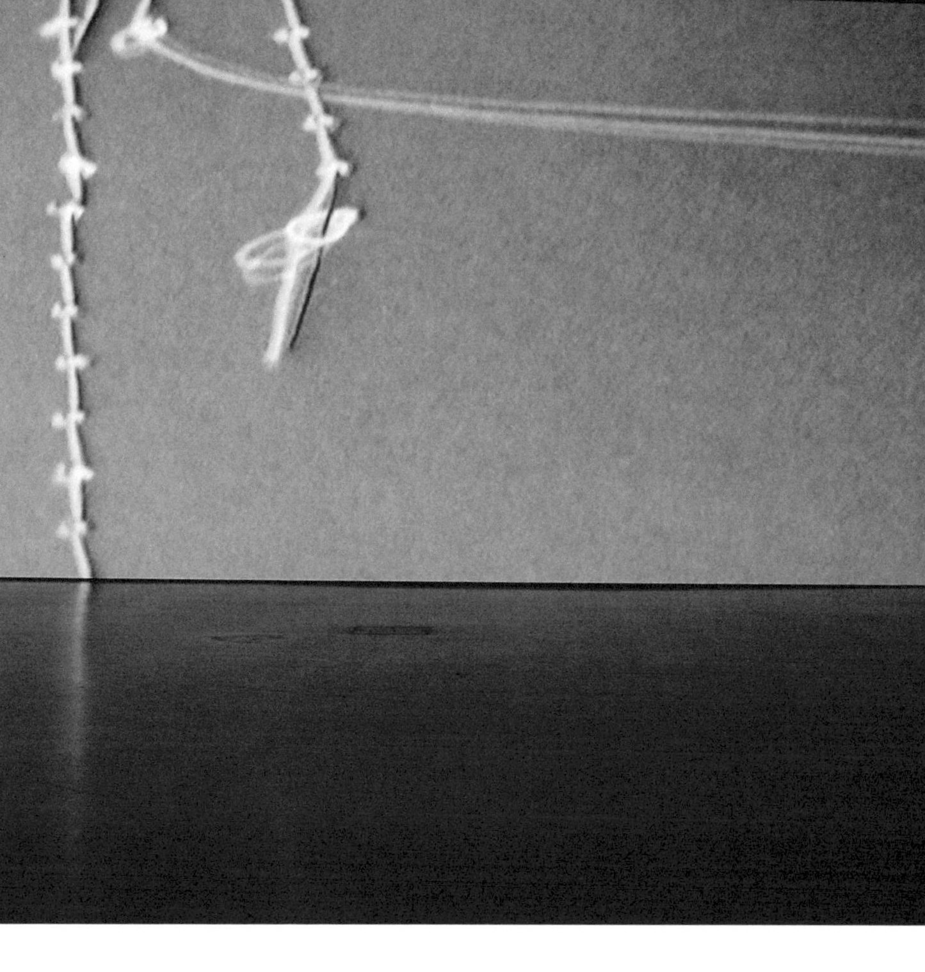

Speicher, 2008

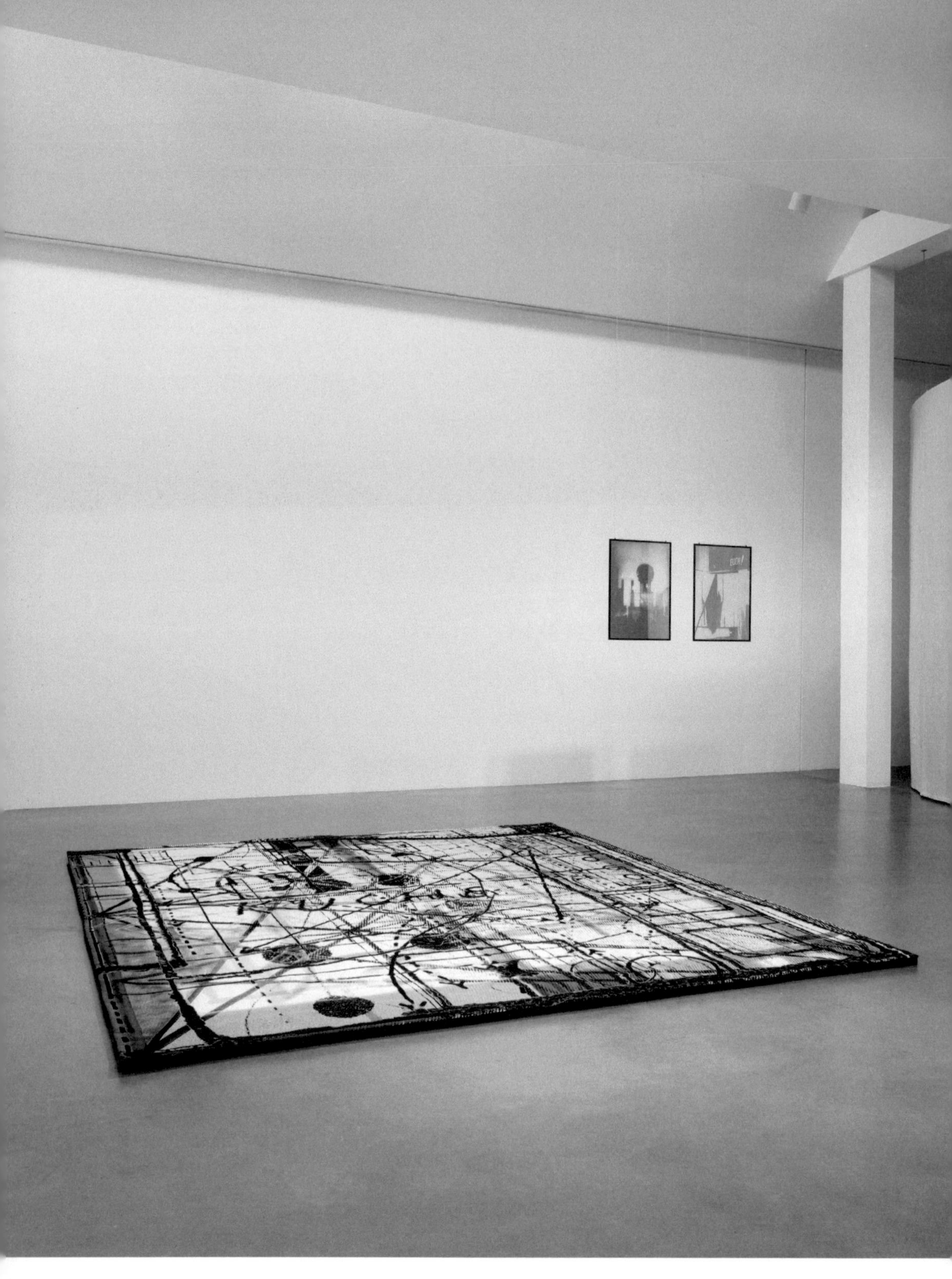

   Girl-Kultur, 2019   *In a Mist,* 2014 / 2015

Girl-Kultur
2019
Tapestry
Wool, cotton,
300 cm x 290 cm
Loan from the Staatsgalerie Stuttgart, transfer of the Ministry of Science, Research and the Arts Baden-Württemberg, 2019

Michaela Melián's works include numerous references to female biographies and their ambivalent perception. Stereotypical roles and gender hierarchies are also themes in the carpet from the installation ***Girl-Kultur***. Here Melián questions the image of the New Woman in the context of gender-associated spaces and efforts for liberation in the modern era.

In the spirit of the Neues Bauen movement in architecture, the "functional design" of the kitchen was meant to save time, energy, and materials, with everything within reach in just a few steps. It aimed to rationalise space and movement and to optimise housekeeping. Did this result in an improved standard of living or the measurement of female economic output? Was the modern kitchen a relief or a prison?

The densely tangled lines that cover the tapestry visualise the ideal (meaning short) paths of a housewife in a demonstration kitchen. Melián assembled drawings and photographs of kitchen designs from the 1920s and combined them with movement diagrams by Erna Meyer and Margarete Schütte-Lihotzky, among others. While the carpet unmistakably echoes the discipline of weaving, which was reserved for women at the Bauhaus, the title refers to the book Girlkultur by the German psychologist Fritz Giese (1925), which compares the rhythm and attitude to life of modern women in America and Europe.

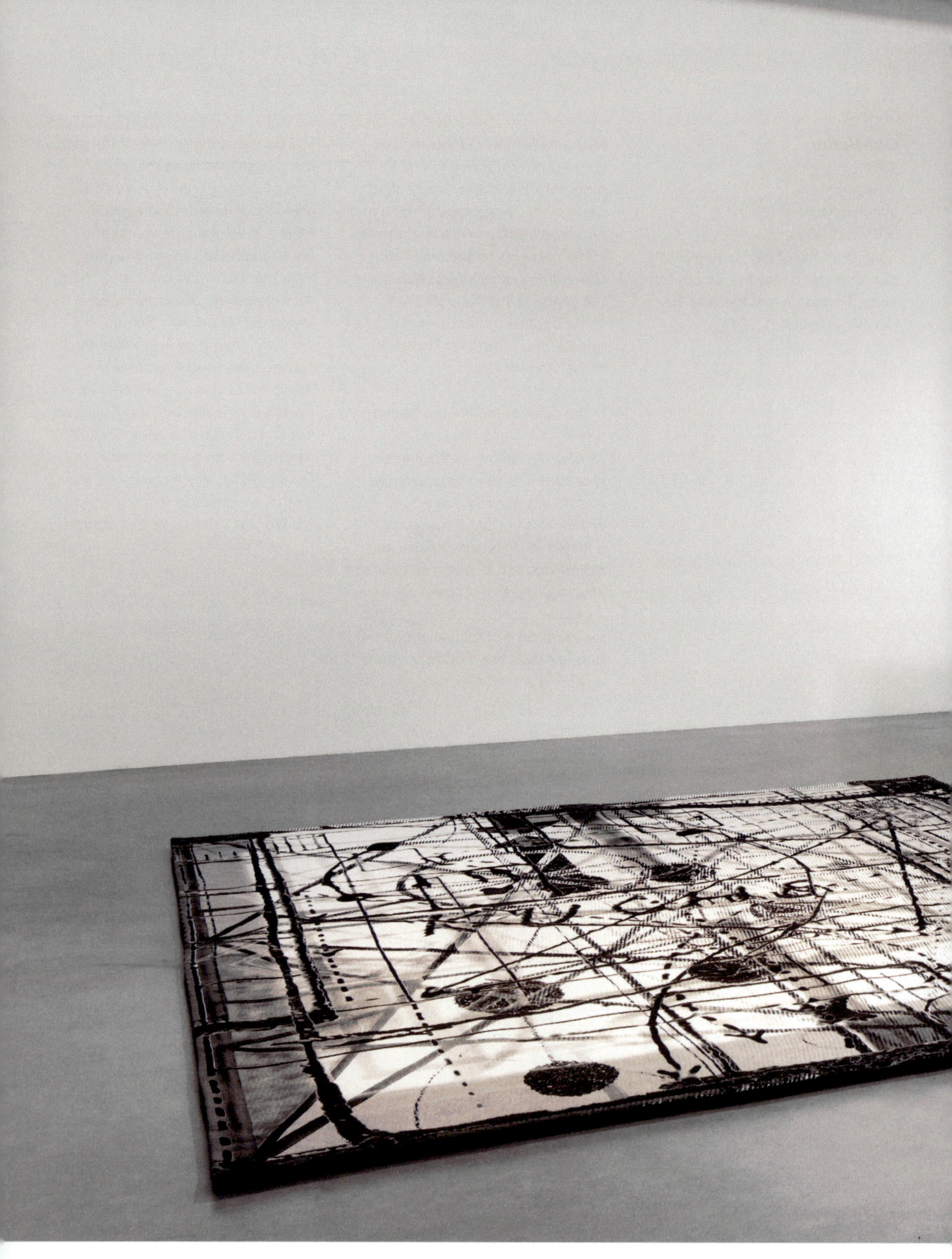

50   *Girl-Kultur,* 2019

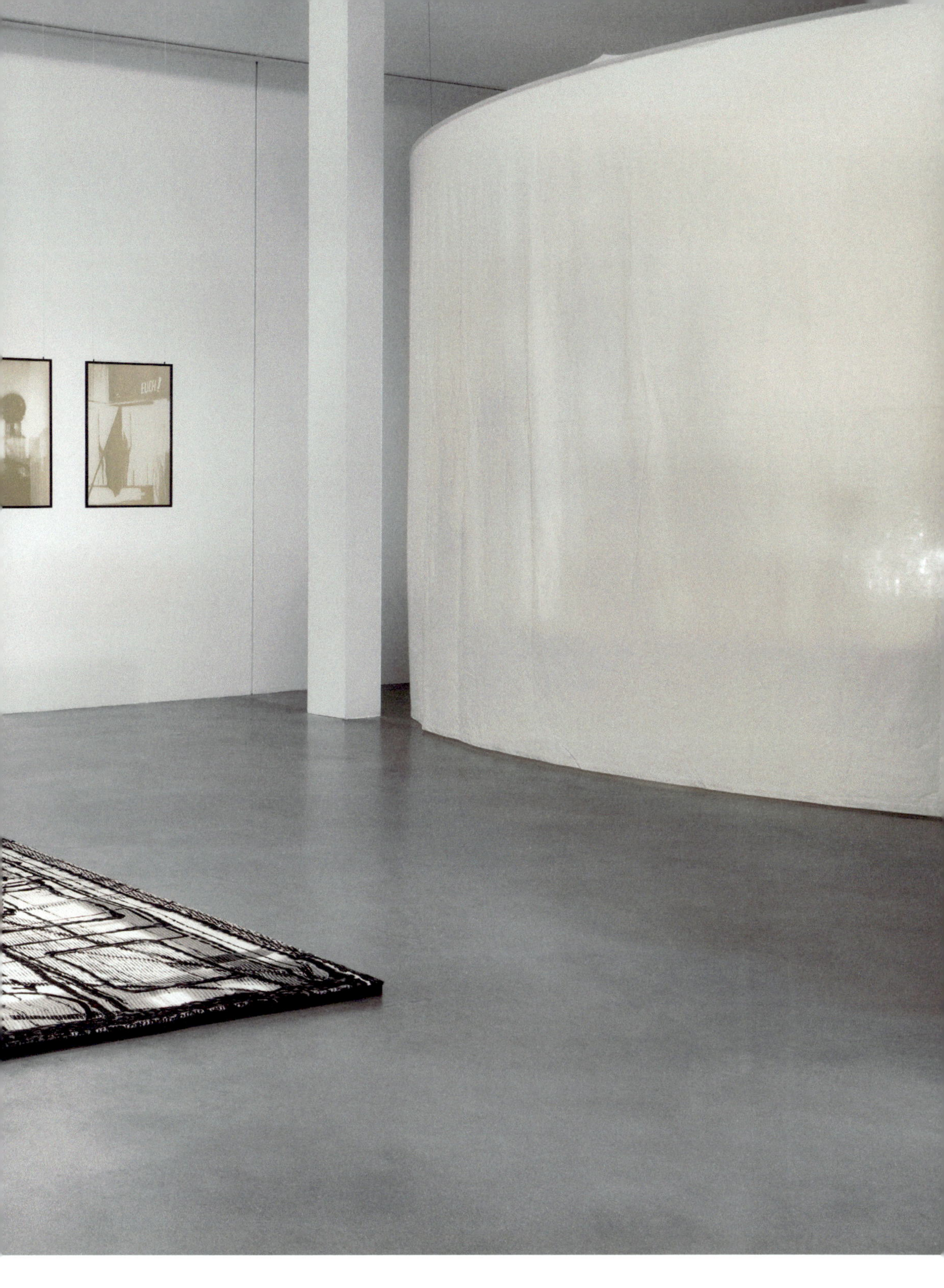

In a Mist, 2014 / 2015

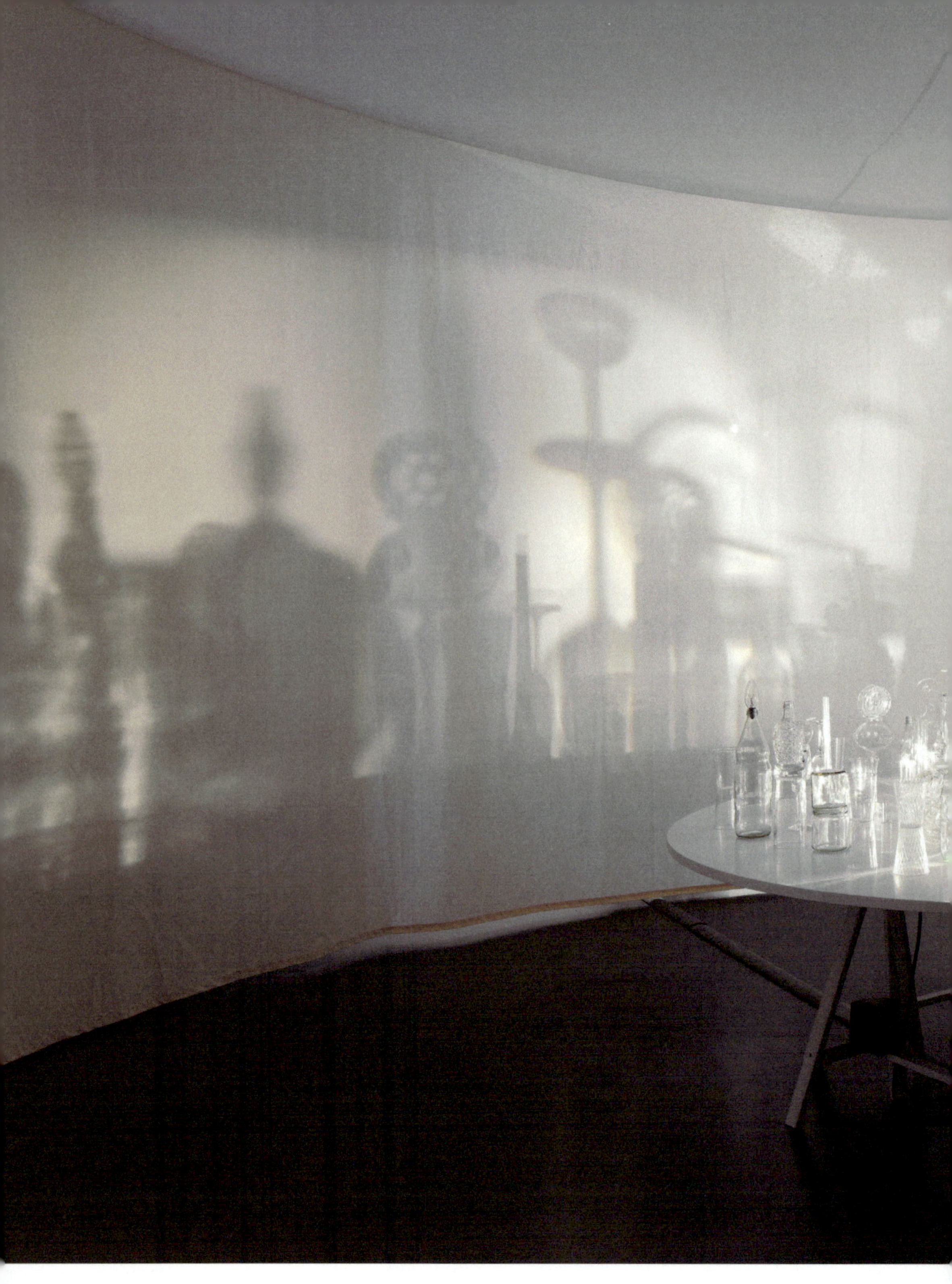

52   *Heimweh (Else Lasker-Schüler)*, 2012

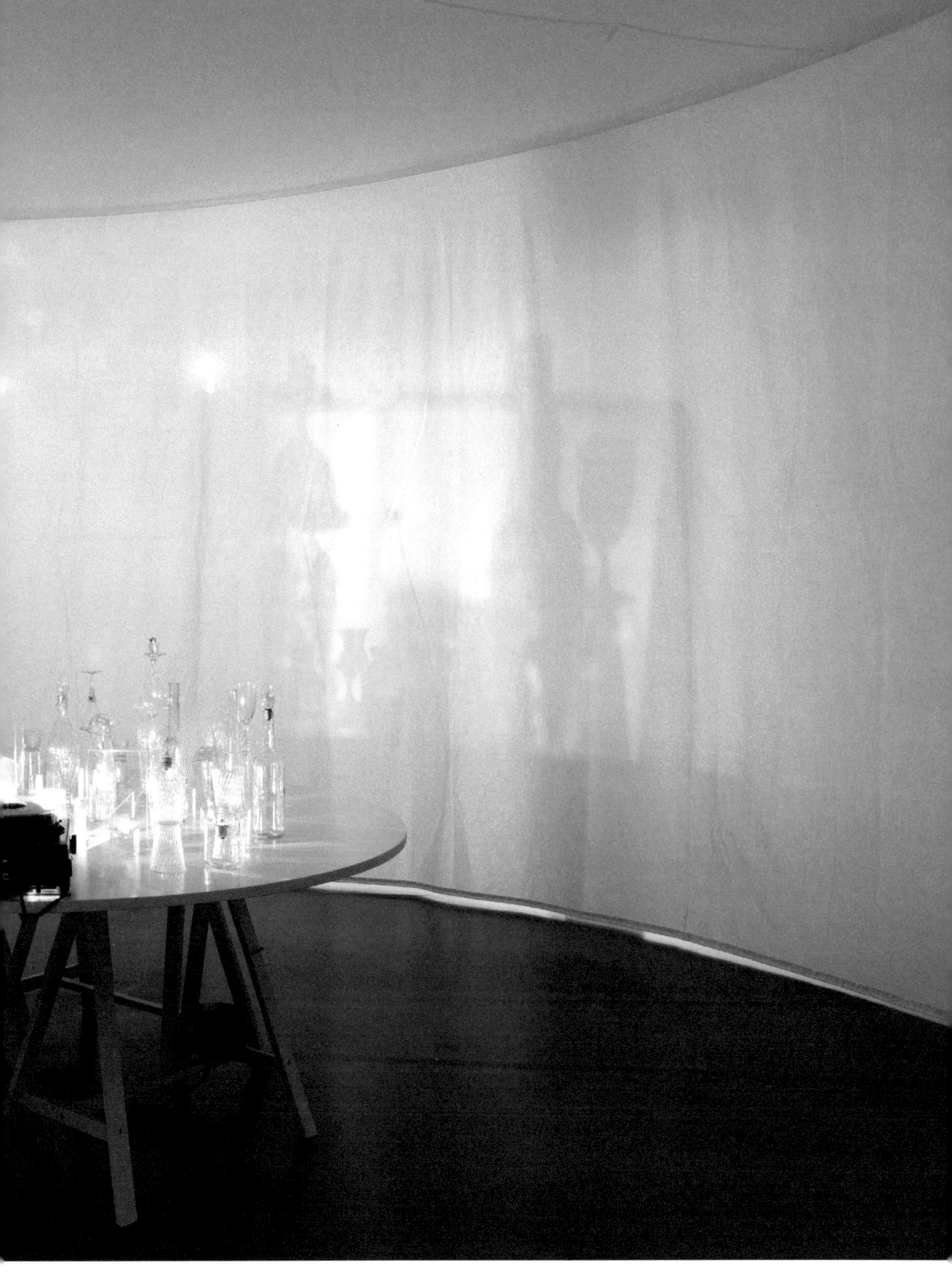

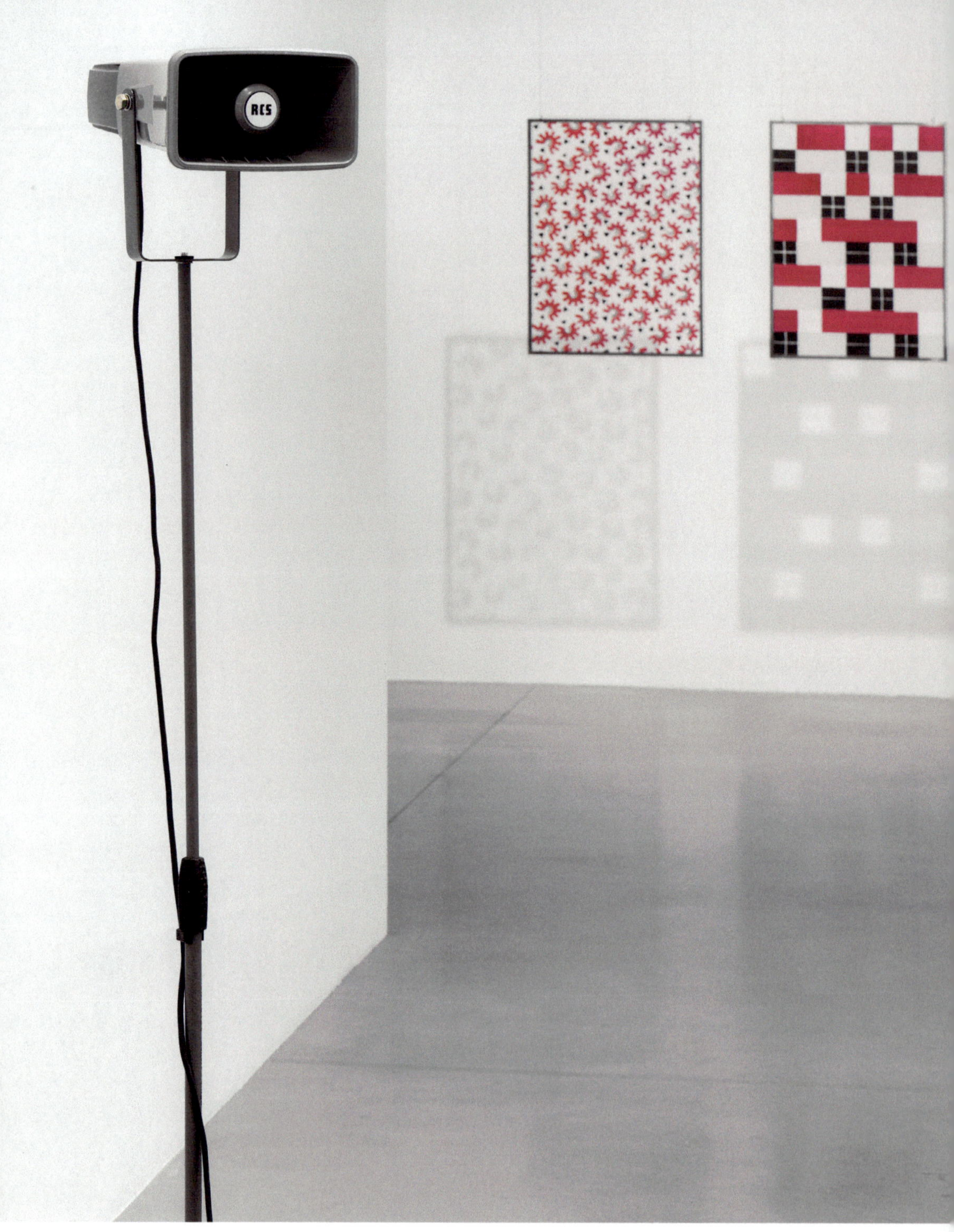

54   *Tania,* 2022 (Sound installation)   *In a Mist,* 2014 / 2015

In a Mist
2014 / 2015
Paintings on glass
Steel, etched float glass,
one-way glass
4 pieces,
each 78 cm x 58 cm

In a Mist is the title of a well-known jazz piece from 1927. Michaela Melián's paintings on glass of the same title, four of which are on view in this exhibition, deal with early artistic utopias and avant-garde movements from this period. The works translate not only the subject matter and motifs, but also various artistic processes such as textile printing, weaving, architecture, and stage design.

The two colourful paintings are adaptations of avant-garde textile works. One is a textile print by the Constructivist painter, designer, and theorist Varvara Stepanova. The design refers to the electrification of Russia, which was implemented according to Lenin's slogan "Communism equals Soviet power plus electrification" and was influential in visual art, architecture, and music at the time. The second painting interprets a weaving by the Bauhaus artist Anni Albers. The pattern recalls modernist building facades and thus addresses issues related to living and building like those that are dealt with in ***Girl-Kultur*** and the mural ***Tania***.

Two other glass works are made of etched one-way glass. The first shows a utopian urban landscape based on a photograph of Melián's installation Lunapark. A variation of this installation, ***Heimweh (Else Lasker-Schüler)***, is also featured in this exhibition. The second adapts a photograph of the stage design for Bertolt Brecht's didactic play *The Mother*, which premiered in Berlin in 1932, based on the novel of the same title by Maxim Gorki.

Heimweh (Else Lasker-Schüler)
2012
Glass and plastic objects, slide projector, motor, prism, screen, music track
Voice: Juno Meinecke
Music: Michaela Melián

The installation ***Heimweh (Else Lasker-Schüler)*** is a variation of the light and sound installation ***Lunapark*** (2012). Michaela Melián assembles transparent everyday objects on a round table. Cups, bottles, and plastic CD cases as well as precious glasses, carafes, and cut prisms form a varied, transparent table landscape.
A slide projector with a rotating prism projects the still life as flowing silhouettes onto the wall of the circular installation. The changing constellations recall the silhouettes of a city that is constantly changing in fleeting, fragile, cinematic movement.

László Moholy Nagy's *Licht-Raum-Modulator* from 1930 and his ideas from the Neues Sehen (New Vision) movement also appear in Melián's installation, as do the visions of the Gläserne Kette group of avant-garde architects and artists who saw the utopia of the "glass city" as the engine for a more humane society. A composition recorded with a glass harmonium can be heard, in which a recitation of Else Lasker-Schüler's poem *Heimweh* is embedded. Set to music in German as well as in phonetically memorised Arabic and Hebrew, aspects of being a foreigner and the experience of exile are processed.

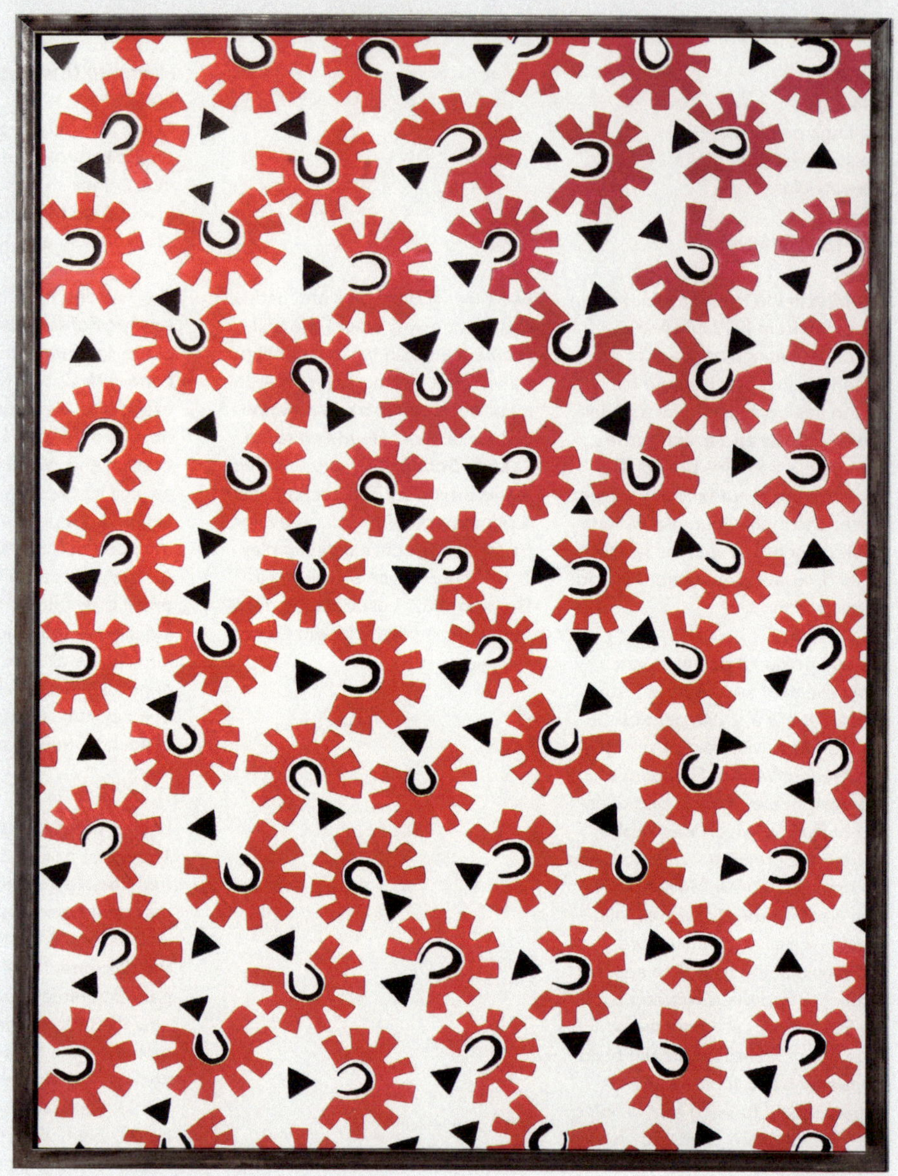

  In a Mist, 2014/2015

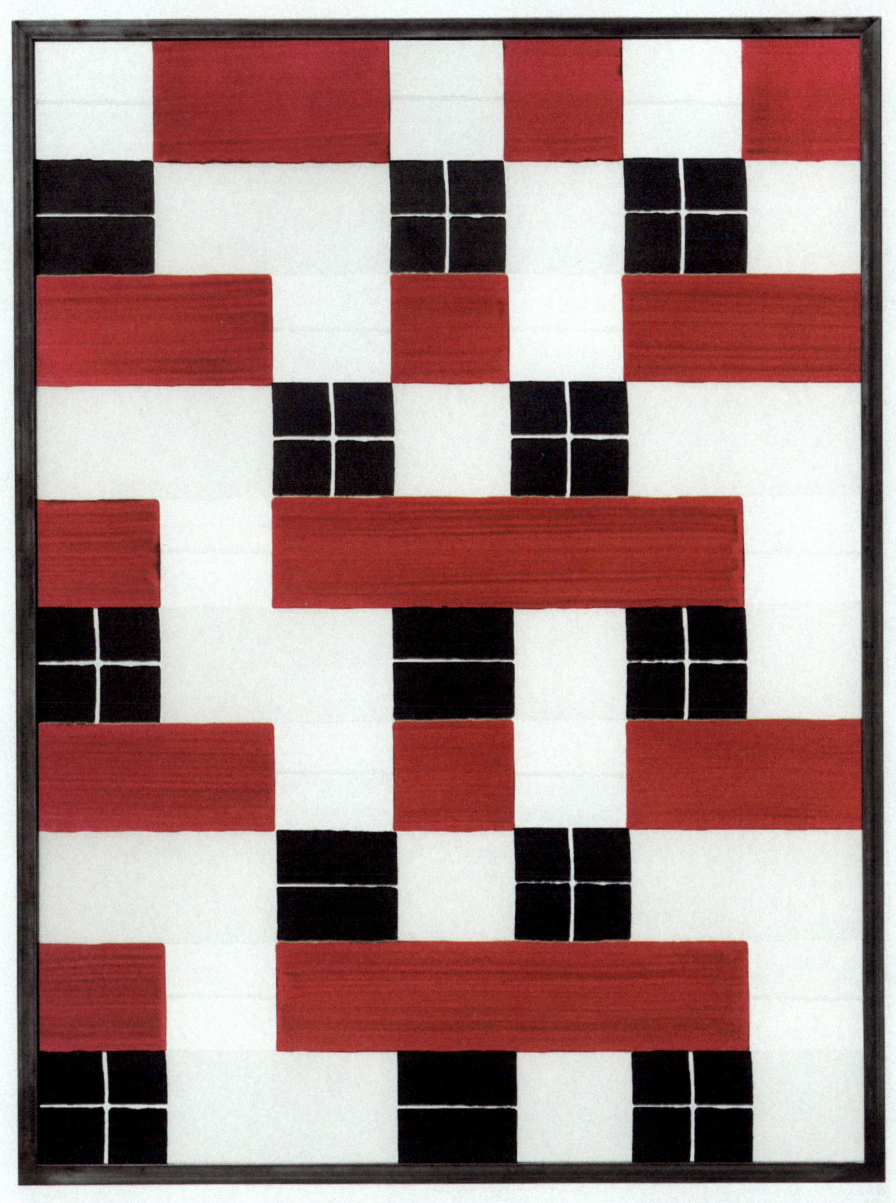

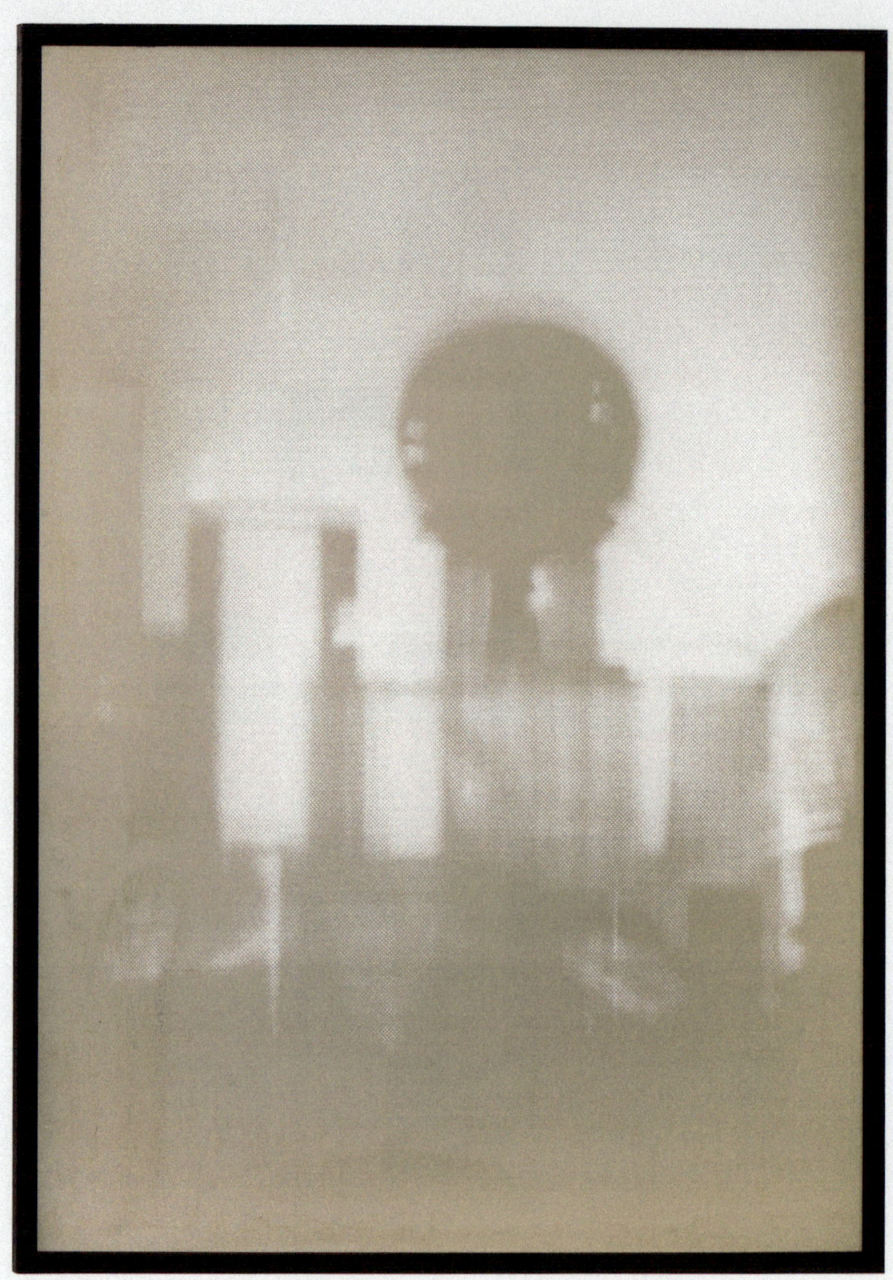

58   *In a Mist,* 2014 / 2015

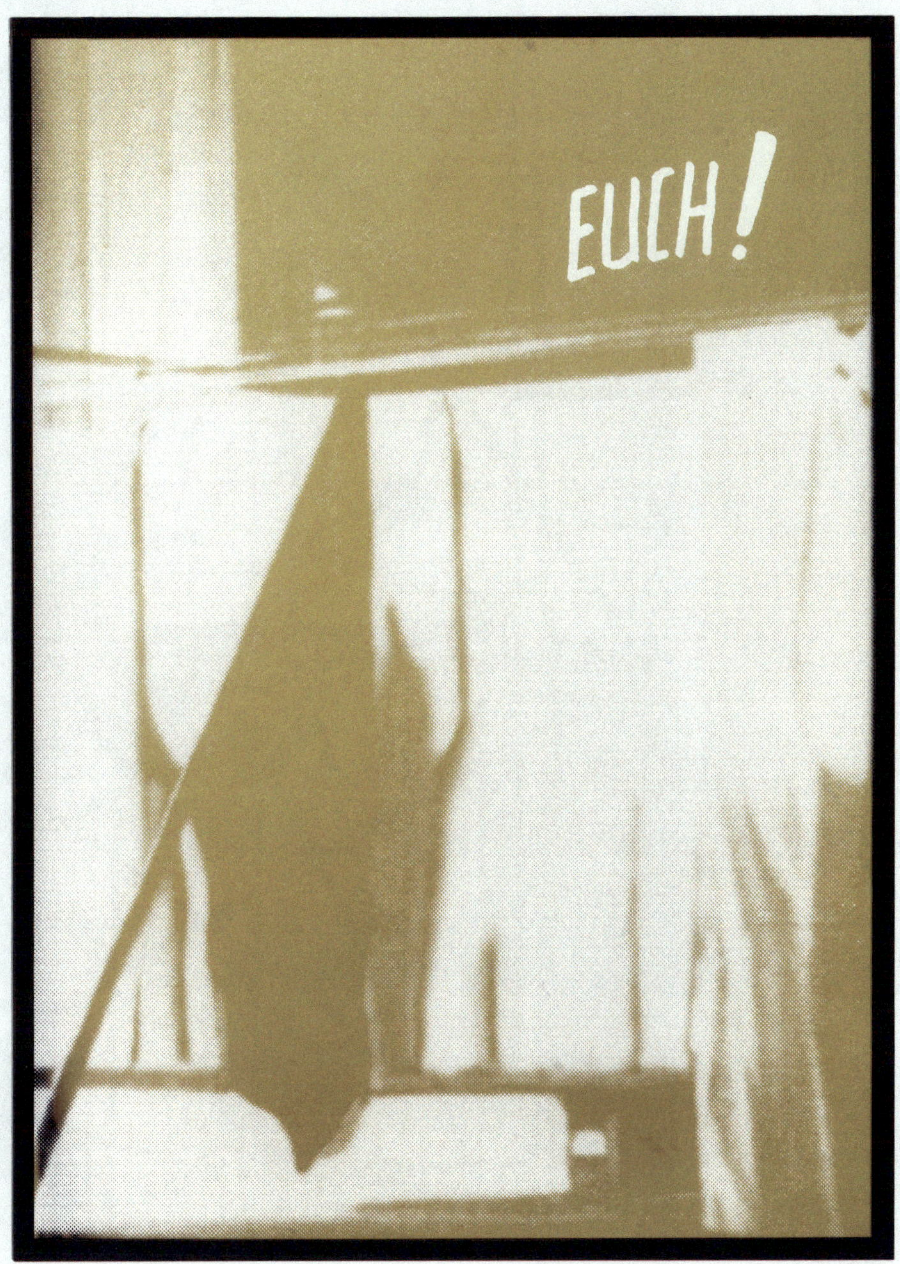
EUCH!

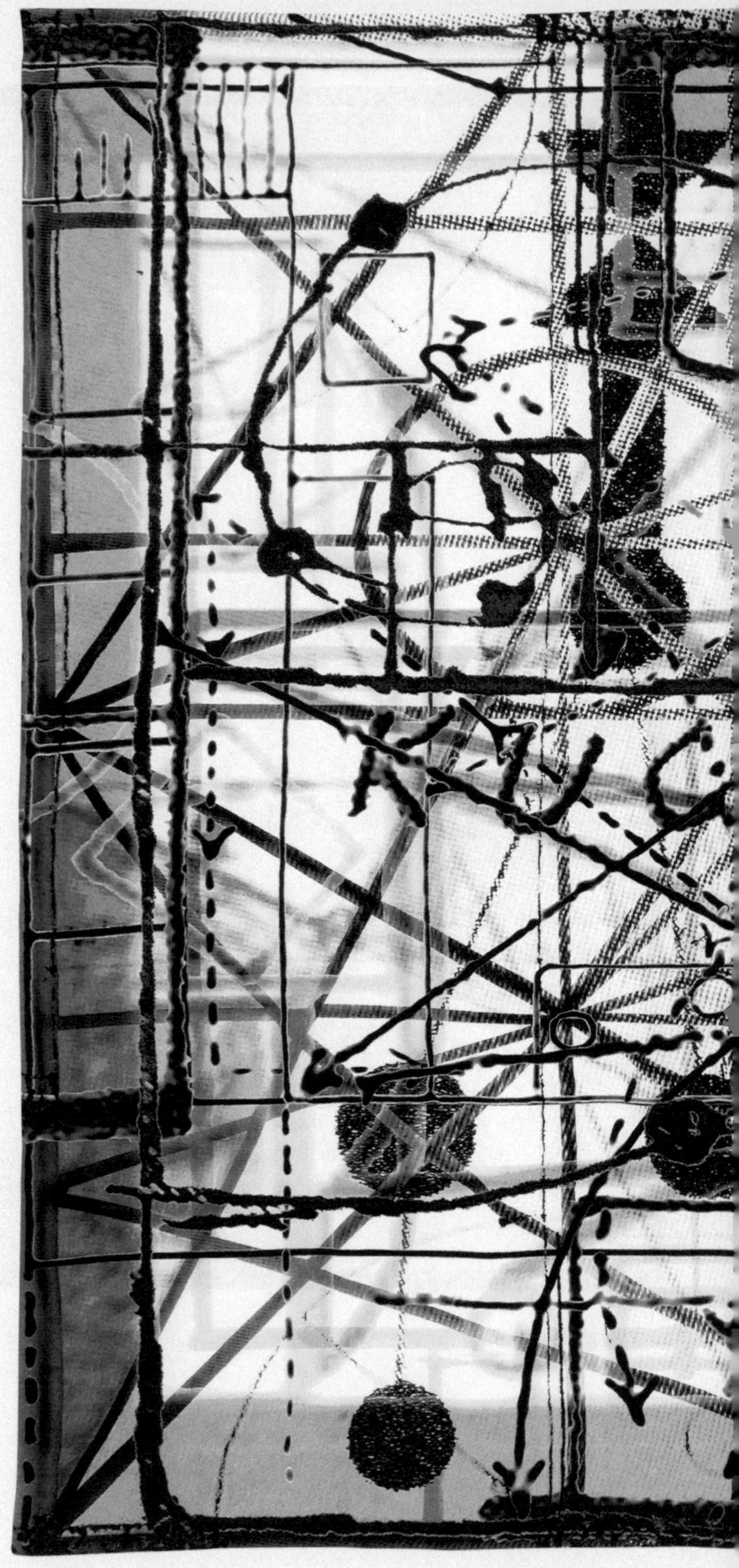

    Girl-Kultur, 2019

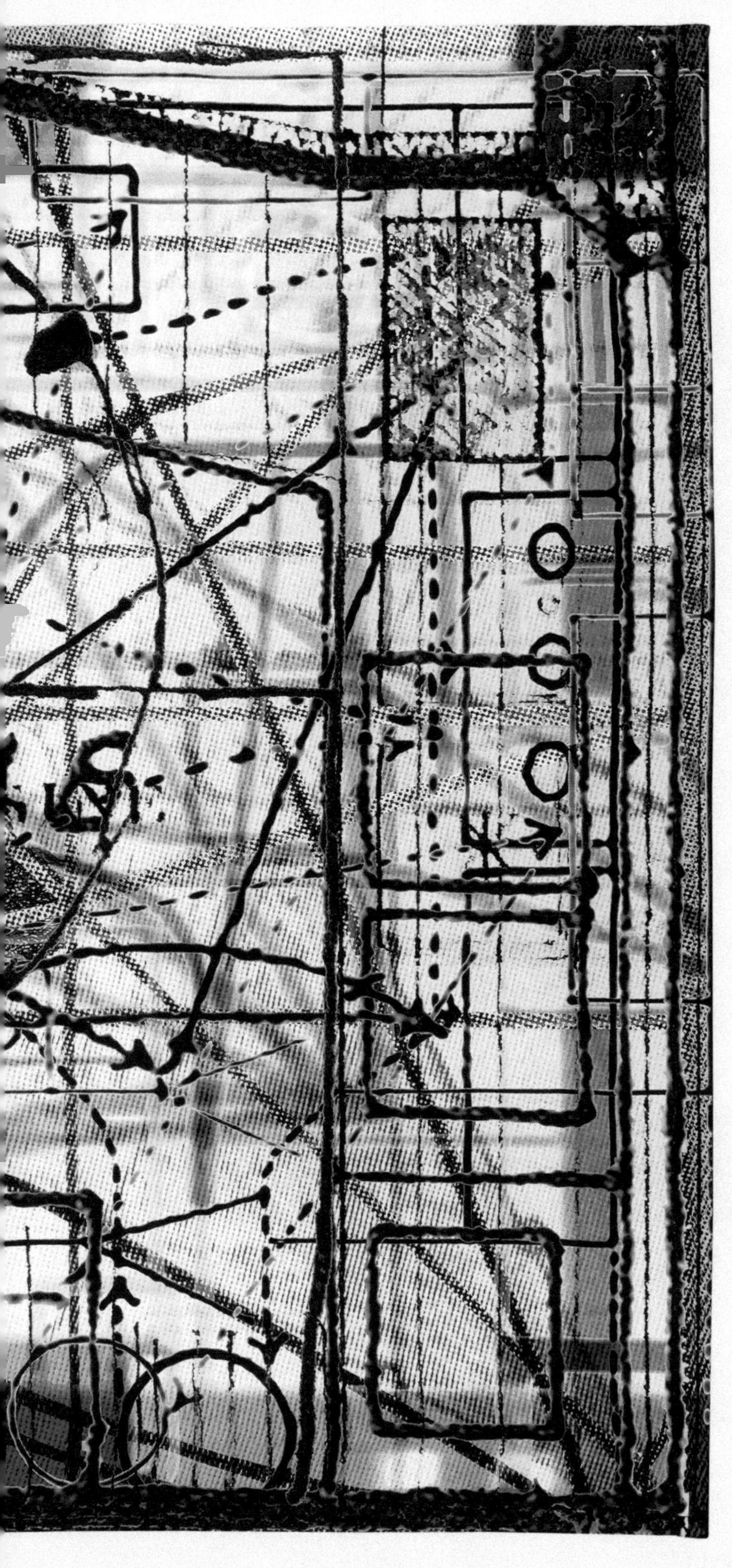

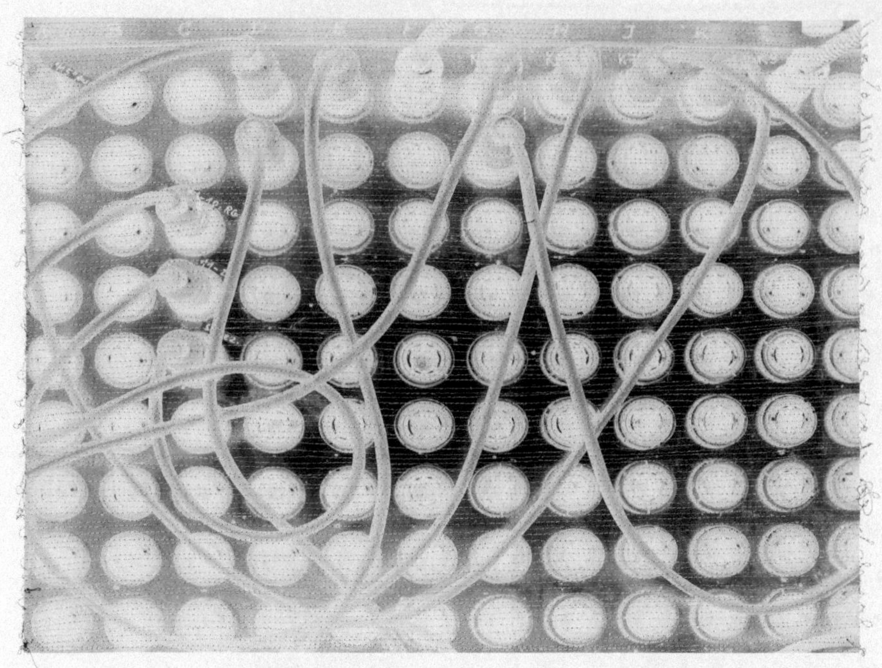

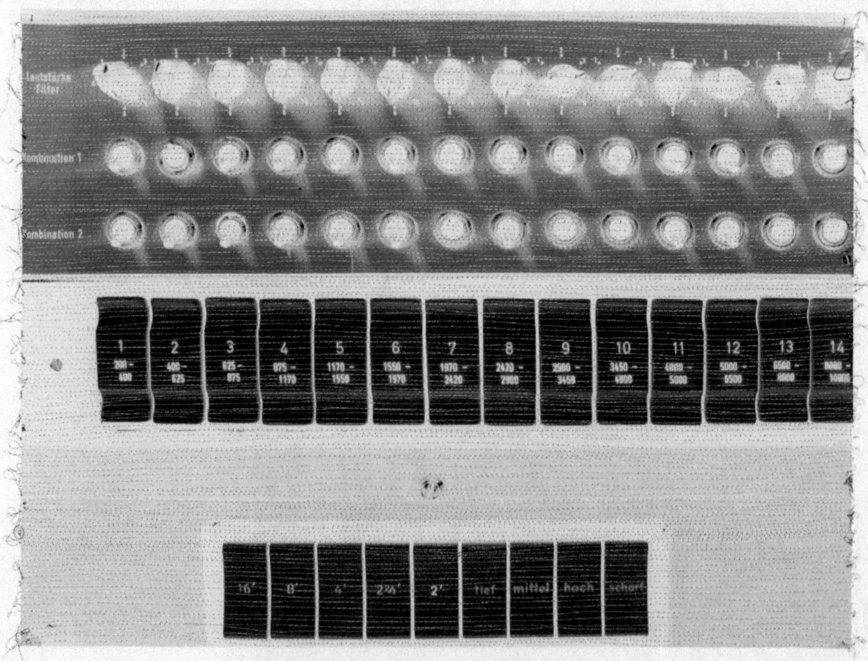

   Frequency Hopping, 2013

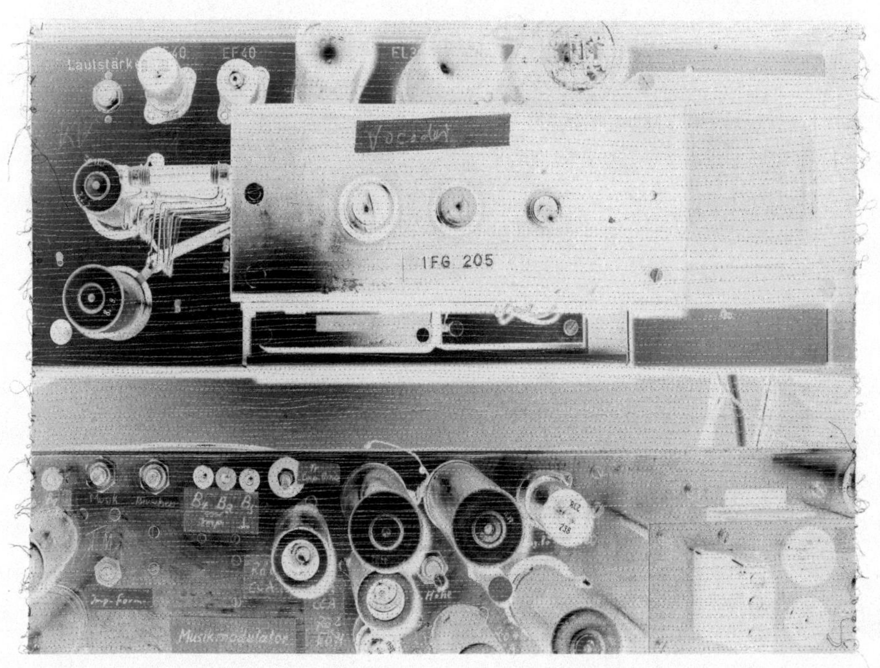

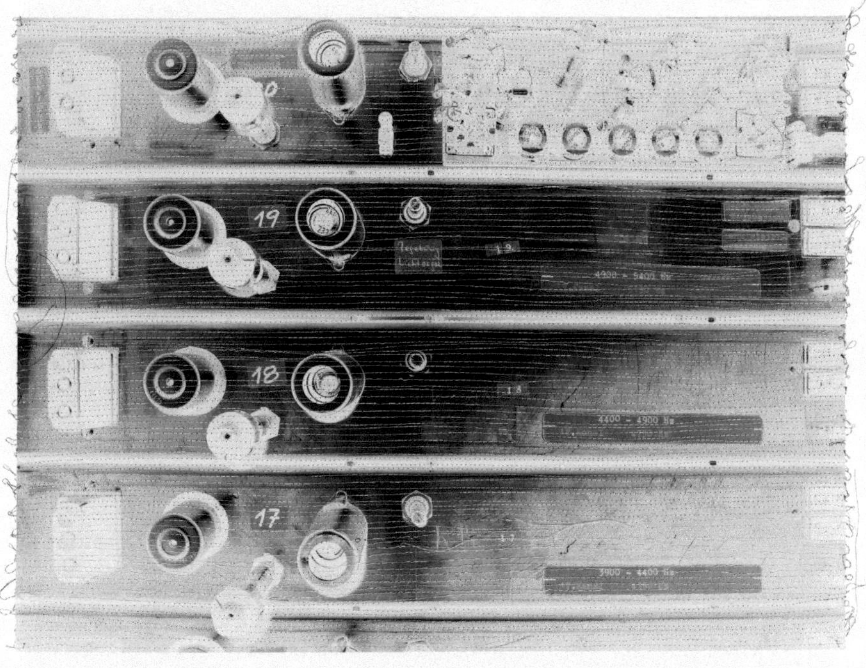

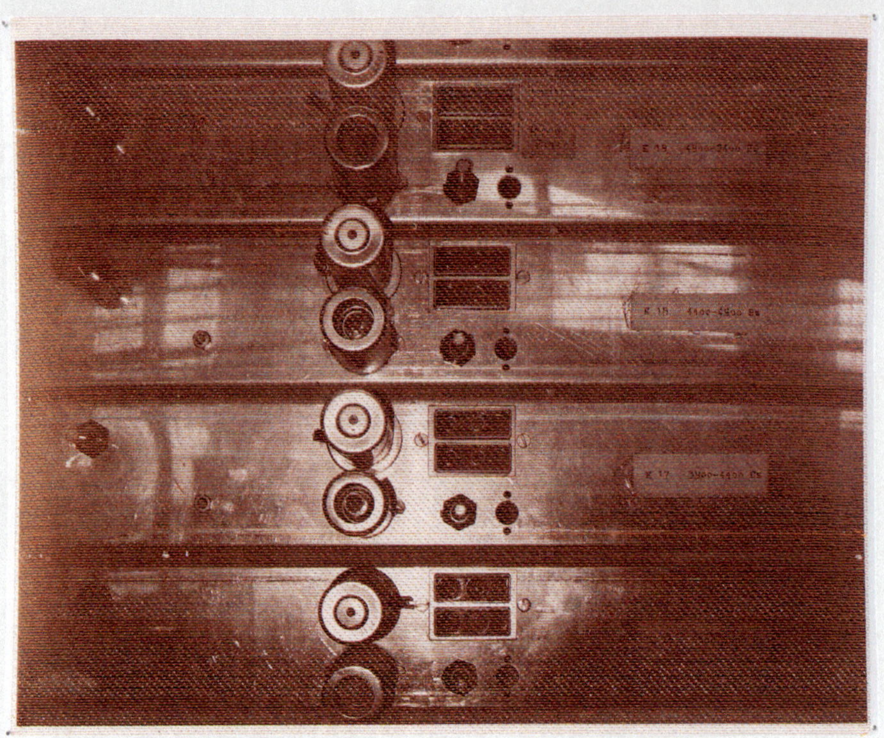

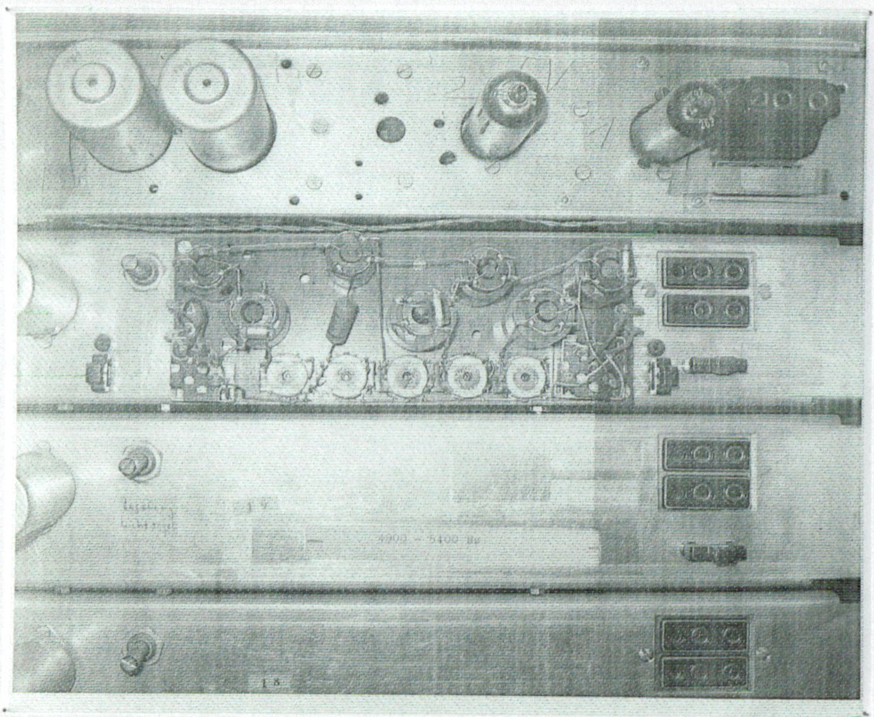

   Studio, 2011

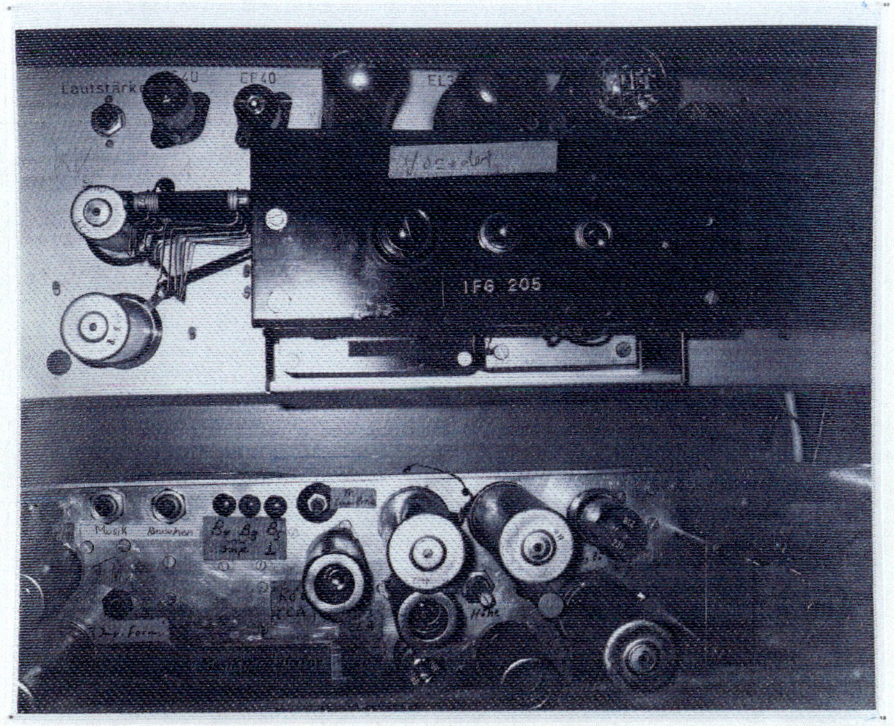
Lautstärke
EF40
EL3
IFG 205
Musik Brummen
RCA

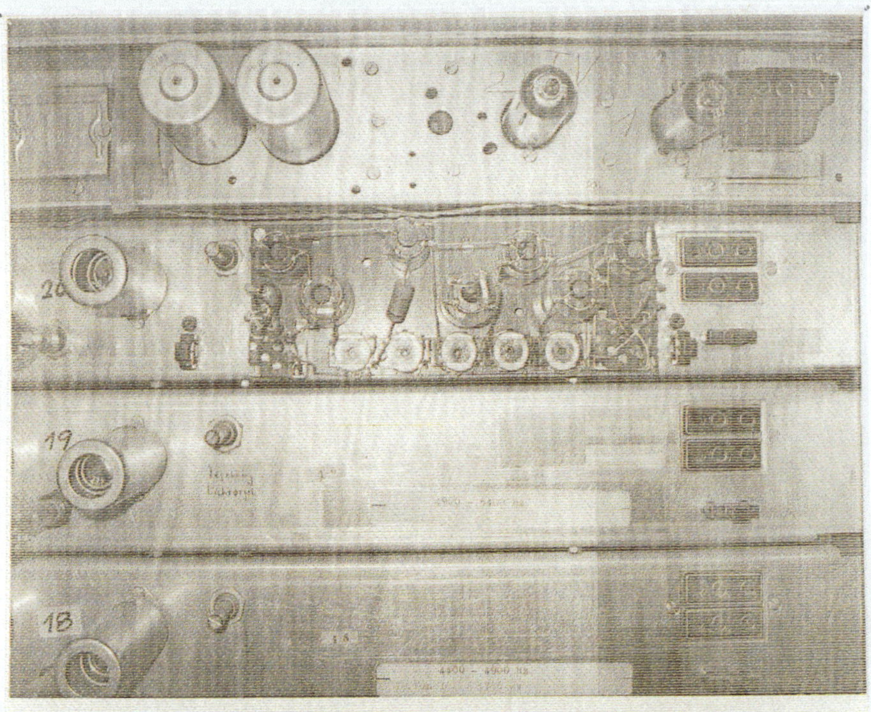
20
19
18

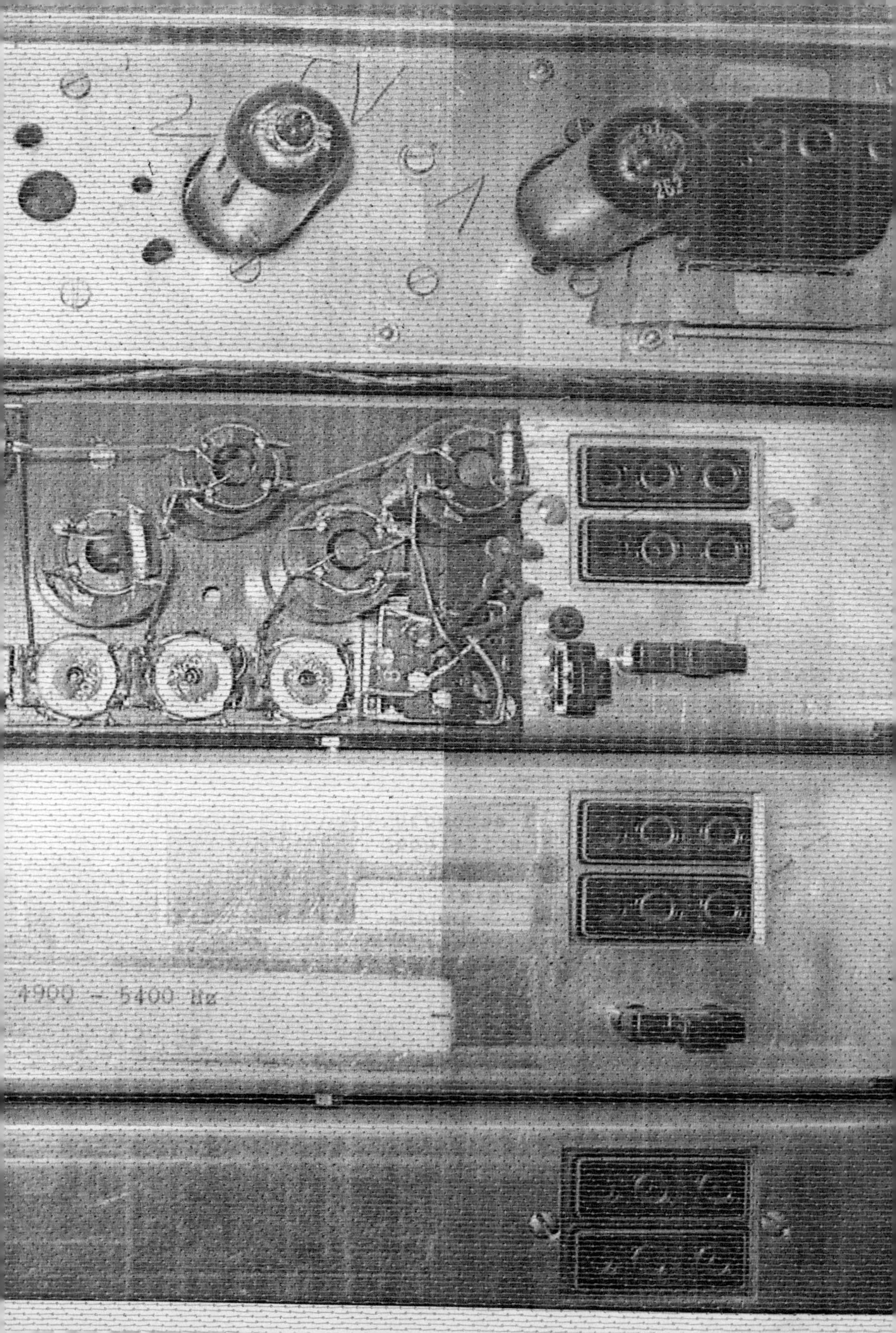

4900 – 5400 Hz

Navigating Berlin with a Street Map of Rio— A Walk About Town

Nadja Abt

We are on a walk with distractions. The kind that occurs when external stimuli are allowed to disrupt our musings–basically the opposite of walking through the city with noise-cancelling headphones.

Which brings us to the beginning of our story. I first met Michaela in person in 2018, during my time as an editor for *Texte zur Kunst*. At the time, I asked her if we could use her text **Electric Ladyland** for the December issue Noise/Silence. To be honest, I didn't even think of the issue's title when I started to reflect on Michaela's work at the KINDL – Centre for Contemporary Art, and so for a brief moment, I thought that I had "discovered" a common thread in the exhibition, namely noise and silence, that would pull my text together like an ingenious revelation. Thus the idea presented itself to me once more four years later as the conclusion of a sequence of associations in the exhibition space. The contextual links within the installation take us right into the heart of Michaela's working practice, because while the works are based on long research, while they have a political agenda and a soundtrack that sets the pace, they never veer into the realm of morality or didacticism, but rather remain poetic. Digressions are allowed, as in the stories they tell. One could say: the works help you think.

I would argue that all the works in this exhibition somehow blend silence with noise. The English word is most appropriate here, as it encapsulates a murmur, a din, loudness, buzzing, humming, clamour, interference, clatter, and much more. Silence certainly has a part to play, as the subject is women who resisted attempts to silence them.

In 2013, British writer Deborah Levy noted in her novel *Things I Don't Want To Know*: "To become a writer, I had to learn to interrupt, to speak a little louder, a then louder, and then to speak in my own voice which is not loud at all."[1]

I still consider this sentence to be an important guide, and in a figurative sense, it also applies in **Red Threads**: The first thing to catch your eye is the many horn speakers that fill the room in turn. I think of amplifiers, of demonstrations, of public address systems of any kind in public spaces, but also of governmental or institutional surveillance and announcements.

---

1 Deborah Levy, *Things I Don't Want To Know*, London 2013, p. 9.

I think of amplifiers, of demonstrations, of public address systems of any kind in public spaces, but also of governmental or institutional surveillance and announcements. Instead of the expected yelling, calm sounds emerge, andante, that is to say, in the rhythm of walking, which leads us into the exhibition.

Analogue musical instruments such as the cello, guitar, ukulele, accordion, and organ are layered with digital sounds and samples from old Latin American records. But this does not become apparent until later. Let us first go back again: Deborah Levy tends to be lumped into the genre of autofiction, which the literature industry has recently started promoting. This primarily describes authors who are read as female and who draw attention to larger, structural socio-political issues from their personal experiences. While its use has recently become somewhat inflated, the term does encapsulate something of great importance to the production of art that engages in storytelling. Stories do not depict "the" truth, and every story conceals multiple versions depending on the perspective from which it is told. This aspect of openness creates room for identification and interpretation. In this sense, Michaela does indeed work in an autofictional manner. The content of her stories is loud, the narrative style often quiet, but very precise. Storylines overlap or branch out, there is often a deliberate vagueness.

A handgun like the euphemistically named "Bullpup" (from Bulldog Puppy) rents the air with its rattle. Composed of colourful fabric, it falls silent and quietly talks to us about armed conflicts, terrorism, war, and the billions of Euros spent on the German army, which do of course benefit the German armaments industry in no small measure.

Revolutionary songs

As *A Song for Europe* by Roxy Music from 1973 puts it so well:
> These cities may change,
> But there always remains
> My obsession.

In 2004 Michaela sang these lines in her cover version of the song on the solo album ***Baden-Baden***. Obsession in the positive sense, engaging intensively with one particular thing over a long period of time in order to be able to continually re-evaluate it, as cities change, and to interlace horizontal and vertical storytelling. Take Michaela's long preoccupation with Tamara Bunke, alias Tania, for example, whom we encounter several times in the exhibition and whose various lives are re-traced in the mural that was created especially for the KINDL, on the flag, and in the soundtrack. As with the frontal portraits, for example, there are deliberate blurs, since this is not a painted copy of a photograph, but rather the verbal description of Bunke that Michaela gave to a composite artist of the Bavarian Criminal Police Bureau in Munich for wanted posters. Is it conceivable that the police artist somehow construed Michaela's facial features into the image, unable to separate the narrator from what is being narrated? The game of auto-fiction becomes apparent.

Tamara Bunke was born in Buenos Aires in 1937 to German-Jewish communist parents . The family had fled from Germany to South America in 1935. In 1952, they returned and settled in East Germany. From the time she began her studies at the Humboldt University in Berlin, there are various storylines surrounding Bunke, which I cannot discuss in detail here. A political activist in the GDR, she is soon trained as a secret agent in Cuba, adopting the nom de guerre Tania and operating under various identities, in Bolivia among other places, to spy on the upper classes there. After her role as a spy is exposed through her own fault, she joins Che Guevara as a guerrilla fighter, without his approval. In 1967, while crossing the Rio Grande, she is ambushed and shot. While she was celebrated as a partisan in the GDR, where schools and squares were named after her, in West Germany the pop-cultural appropriation of the revolution subsumed her biography into the image of a beautiful, solemn-looking woman wearing a beret. For **Red Threads**, two of Bunke's identities are particularly poignant. In Bolivia, she disguised herself as cultural anthropologist Laura Gutiérrez Bauer and conducted research on indigenous sculptures and musical styles. In the soundtrack of the exhibition, we can hear the rhythms of Latin American music from the 1960s and 1970s–a time when, for example, in neighbouring Brazil, the Tropicália movement around musicians such as Caetano Veloso, Maria Bethânia, and Gilberto Gil who, in resistance to the military dictatorship, established an anti-colonial, hybrid musical practice between traditional instruments and melodies with influences from psychedelic rock. It was the heyday of the so-called Música Popular, and the musicians of Tropicália radically expanded this paradigm.

For the soundtrack *Tania*, for example, Michaela used the final bars from the 1972 song of the same name by the activist Venezuelan singer Alí Rafael Primera Rosell, which celebrated the guerrilla. Elegantly, his voice sings a soft "Taaaania" to the sound of a French horn.

Matching this, Tamara Bunke was additionally disguised as the host of a radio program for women, a position she used to send coded messages to the fighters in the mountains.

Radio as an instrument of warfare, of political resistance, of the dissemination of pop culture, and finally also as an artistic medium in the form of radio plays takes on a central role in the artist's works. The motif of the sound wave recurs throughout the exhibition as a graphic notation, for instance in *Studio*, *Speicher*, and *Frequency Hopping*. The video installation *Speicher* is also a radio piece co-produced and premiered by the Bavarian public broadcaster Bayerischer Rundfunk.

Radio has the ability to reach people of different social classes both in the city and in the most remote villages. Radio has sparked revolutions. For example, on April 24, 1974, at 10:55 p.m., Portuguese radio played the love song *E Depois do Adeus* (Eng: And after the Farewell), which was the secret signal arranged to launch the military coup against the dictatorship of the Estado Novo. At around 00:20, the previously banned song of the anti-fascist revolutionary singer José Afonso sounded through the radio channels: *Grândola, Vila Morena*. To this day, it is the revolutionary anthem of the Portuguese holiday on April 25, the day of the Carnation Revolution.

Even more popular internationally is a song originally sung in the early 20th century by Italian working-class women in protest against disastrous working conditions in the rice fields in the region around Bologna. Over time, the women's original lyrics were overwritten by the fighters of the Resistenza, preserving the tune of *Bella Ciao*.

In her soundtrack, Michaela performs a kind of female reappropriation, in which *Bella Ciao* is slowed down by several times and mixed with other revolutionary songs, such as *The Internationale*, the anthem of the Cuban Revolution, and the aforementioned South American sounds. It is hardly possible to name them all because the artist works with up to 80 separate audio tracks. Instruments that have already been recorded are digitized and distorted. Rhythms that are consciously recognized or perceived are interlaced with soundtracks subconsciously absorbed by the brain, which tap into our musical memory in their layered texture. In this context, music is the art

form most capable of functioning as a mental time machine that can trigger a wide variety of emotions, something that the soundtrack in the film **Speicher** noticeably takes advantage of, for example. In the catalogue, Jan Verwoert comments on **Speicher**: "In contrast, the attraction of immaterial contemporary testimonies is often undiminished precisely because they wear out less quickly in use. Music, for example, is sometimes able to almost instantly evoke the hopes and promises of the future of past centuries."[2]
To this day, the recognition factor of *Bella Ciao* is still so high that the first five chords strummed on the guitar are enough to conjure up the song and hundreds of associations of rallies with chanting or baying protesters in one's ear and mind. A mass of people striding in 4 / 4 time–which in turn reminds us that music does not only mean movement in resistance, but also fascism. This ambivalence, which could be characterized as an inner uncertainty, is recreated in several other of Michaela's works.

Ticking bombs and rattling guns

Take, for example, the combination of the **Mossberg Model Bullpup** rifles made of fabric and the **Briefmarke** drawn in black ink on the opposite wall of the first room. The latter shows the logo of the Red Army Fraction, founded in 1970, with an automatic firearm and five-pointed star, without, however, mentioning the Red Army Fraction by name. The logo has seared itself deep enough into decades of German history to be instantly recognized by multiple generations (I would say up to and including Millennials). All it takes is these gestures by the artist, highly abstract in fabric, sound, and ink, to reveal the tragic tapestry of protest, terrorism, and the arms lobby from 1970 to the present.
To illustrate, another small digression, which will again bring us to South America: Like many young people in Germany in the mid-to-late 1970s, my mother became passionate about the RAF. The flashy iconography, in the form of the red star with a machine gun as a sign of resistance against fascism, against the Nazis who after the war were once again installed in their high posts, and guerrilla warfare was subtly papalized in images. Che Guevara and the terrorists of the RAF had become icons of a leftist youth. It was during this time that my mother applied for a job as a flight attendant with the German airline Lufthansa. She was accepted and began her

---

2 Jan Verwoert, "Zurück zur Zukunft", in: Brigitte Reinhardt, Stella Rollig and
   Bart van der Heide (Eds.), *Michaela Melián. Speicher*, London 2009, pp. 57–78, here: p. 57.

training at the end of 1977, in the middle of the so-called German Autumn, when on October 13, a Lufthansa passenger plane 737-200 named Landshut was hijacked by four Palestinian terrorists and taken to Mogadishu. The operation was intended, among other things, to force the release of Andreas Baader, Gudrun Ensslin, Jan-Carl Raspe, and other RAF members. This kidnapping represented a crucial turning point for West Germany in many ways. With the successful liberation of the hostages, the police unit GSG9, founded in 1972 specifically for anti-terrorist operations, became known nationwide. After Baader, Ensslin, and Raspe were found dead in their prison cells five days later in the wake of the failed operation, the first generation of the RAF attained a kind of mythical hero status among young leftists. They were revered, in a somewhat glamorized fashion, until the 1990s—thanks in part to Stefan Aust's bestseller *The Baader-Meinhof Complex* (first published in 1985, now in its fourth revised edition). As a direct consequence of the Landshut hijacking, my mother was required to "search for bombs" before every flight. None of the budding flight attendants had ever seen a bomb before, so they listened for a ticking sound in the seats. Her profession had thus moved uncomfortably close to her idols, and the sound of the German Autumn and its traces are still firmly imprinted in the emotional memory today.

It was during the storming of the Landshut that the GSG9 deployed the submachine gun MP5 of the German gunsmith Heckler & Koch for the first time, with great media coverage. The same model is featured in the centre of the RAF star and reproduced on Michaela's postage stamp.

A brief temporal detour. Forty-one years later in Brazil, on March 14, 2018, Rio de Janeiro City Councillor and Chairwoman of the Women's Committee Marielle Franco lost her relentless fight against the Polícia Militar's indiscriminate killings in the favelas. As she travels in a car with her driver, the two are gunned down in a hail of bullets in the open street. Since the investigation quickly pointed to the upper circles of politics, the murder is still not completely solved. The murder weapon was a German Heckler & Koch MP5.

When I stand in front of Michaela's work **Briefmarkenset 10, 20, 33, 45**, my first question is: What might the generation after me possibly associate with postage stamps, in a digital world of e-mail, in which the RAF no longer exists and terrorism has become a vague term under which is used with questionable frequency? And yet urban guerilla icon iconography is more prevalent than ever, e.g. the olive drab military zip jacket and frontal shots used in the media appearances of Ukrainian President Volodymyr Selenskyj. I would even argue that Selenskyj has crafted a kind of revival of that iconography which in 2022 once again demarcates the so-called "good" from the so-called "evil".

The history of the media's use of images and their pop-cultural marketization, which Michaela has so accurately portrayed, seems more topical than ever.

And thus I am already completely immersed in the meanderings and the varying versions of history, and thereby also the numerous versions of true events. My walk leads to the mural *Tania*, created especially for the exhibition. The painting shows different places and episodes from Tamara Bunke's life–or rather those that tie in with her life, as a kind of fictional continuation of her biography. Here, too, we can witness the poetic realization of the research that I described earlier. The stamped dots are reminiscent of digital pixels and not only produce a blurring effect, but also illustrate the various possibilities of non-linear narrative strands. The dots draw my attention to the analogue elements in Michaela's work. Hand-stamped, hand-drawn, hand-sewn, hand-played instruments, and music created by manually plugging jacks into old synthesizers at the Siemens Studio for Electronic Music. In the process, analogue action is fed back into gadgets again and again, digitally altered and churned out anew–deconstructed, in other words. A feminist approach, indeed: Manual labour = women's labour. Women's work = poorly or unpaid work. Poorly paid work = often monotonous work = reproductive work.

Machine clatter

In the 1976 short *SCUM Manifesto*, feminist filmmakers Carole Roussopoulos and Delphine Seyrig sit across from each other at a small table. In voice-over, we hear Seyrig dictating Valerie Solana's *SCUM Manifesto* (1967), while Roussopoulos taps it out on a mechanical typewriter. The aggressively hammering sound is just as present as the actual text. In the catalogue for the exhibition *Defiant Muses*, Ros Murray writes about the filmmakers: "The typewriter in SCUM is used as a prop to draw attention to women's work as a form of reproductive labour, the two reproducing Solanas in a way that says much about reproduction. Ironically, perhaps, most of Solanas type-written work was lost because it was burned by her mother, along with her other possessions, after she died. In what seems like a move that anticipates this particularly destructive form of reproductive futurism, Roussopoulos and Seyrig opt for a form of technological reproduction that allows them to stake a claim in alternative, anti-patriarchal forms of expression."[3]

In Michaela's work **Studio**, the typewriter is replaced by the sewing machine. With white or coloured sewing thread, it rattles across the black-and-white photographs from the Siemens Studio for Electronic Music. The close-ups show control knobs on mixing consoles in an aesthetic reminiscent of early sci-fi movies. Unlike Roussopoulos and Seyrig, the artist's chosen language is quiet: We do not hear the rattling, but we do see the holes punched by the sewing needle, while the thread passes over the paper like waveform audio tracks. Here, technical reproduction with the machine not only represents a critique of underpaid wage labour performed by women, but it is also a very specific feminist overwriting of the console as a tinkertoy in the still male-dominated world of electronic music–which is of course not to say that there were no women there at all. Pioneers in the field were–among many others–Johanna Beyer, Éliane Radigue, and Clara Rockmore.

In my attempt to trace the central themes of *Noise* and *Silence* in the exhibi-tion, I want to show that in Michaela's works, one is always inscribed in the other. They may be silent gestures, but the white noise or clamour of history always resonates. Silent in the way of Deborah Levy, i.e. in her own unique style and always pushing against silence, when the biographies of women take centre stage. As the American writer and activist, Audre Lorde once said: "Your silence will not protect you. But for every real word spoken, for every attempt I had ever made to speak those truths for which I am still seeking, I had made contact with other women while we examined the words to fit a world in which we all believed, bridging our differences."[4]

As with Lorde, Roussopoulos, and Seyrig, Michaela's **Red Threads** is about a political-feminist relating and making visible, "to make some noise".

<hr>

3   Ros Murray, "Cutting Up Men? Delphine Seyrig and Carole Roussopoulos's Playful
     Forms of Video Activism", in: Nataša Petrešin-Bachelez and Giovanna Zapperi (Eds.),
     Defiant Muses, Exhibition catalogue Museo Nacional Centro de Arte Reina Sofía 2019,
     pp. 102–133, here: p. 112.
4   Audre Lorde, "The Transformation of Silence into Language and 'Action'" (1977),
     in: Roxane Gay, (Ed.), *The Selected Works of Audre Lorde*, New York 2020, pp. 9–14,
     here: p. 10.

Soundtrack

We've reached the end of our walk, and I sit down in the **Mannheim Chair**, oversized sound boxes that function like listening swings. Surrounded by sounds from **Speicher** and **Music from a Frontier Town**, I look out the large windows at Berlin and hear the soundtrack to the city. "These cities may change", I think. The sounds mix with the voices of other visitors, the squeaking of the swing chains, beats from **Tania**, and the voice of Juno Meinecke, who recites Else Lasker-Schüler's poem *Heimweh* (Homesickness) in the installation of the same name. Am I now listening to about 300 audio tracks at the same time?
If you listen to a lot of music, you may wake up with a soundtrack in your ears to start the day, or you may deliberately steer your day or your work with the help of a certain soundtrack.
The works then turn into notations of a mood, and their effect can change depending on the soundtrack. It follows that no matter how many times we go to **Red Threads**, we'll never see the same exhibition.
How clever of her, I think to myself, and listen quietly.

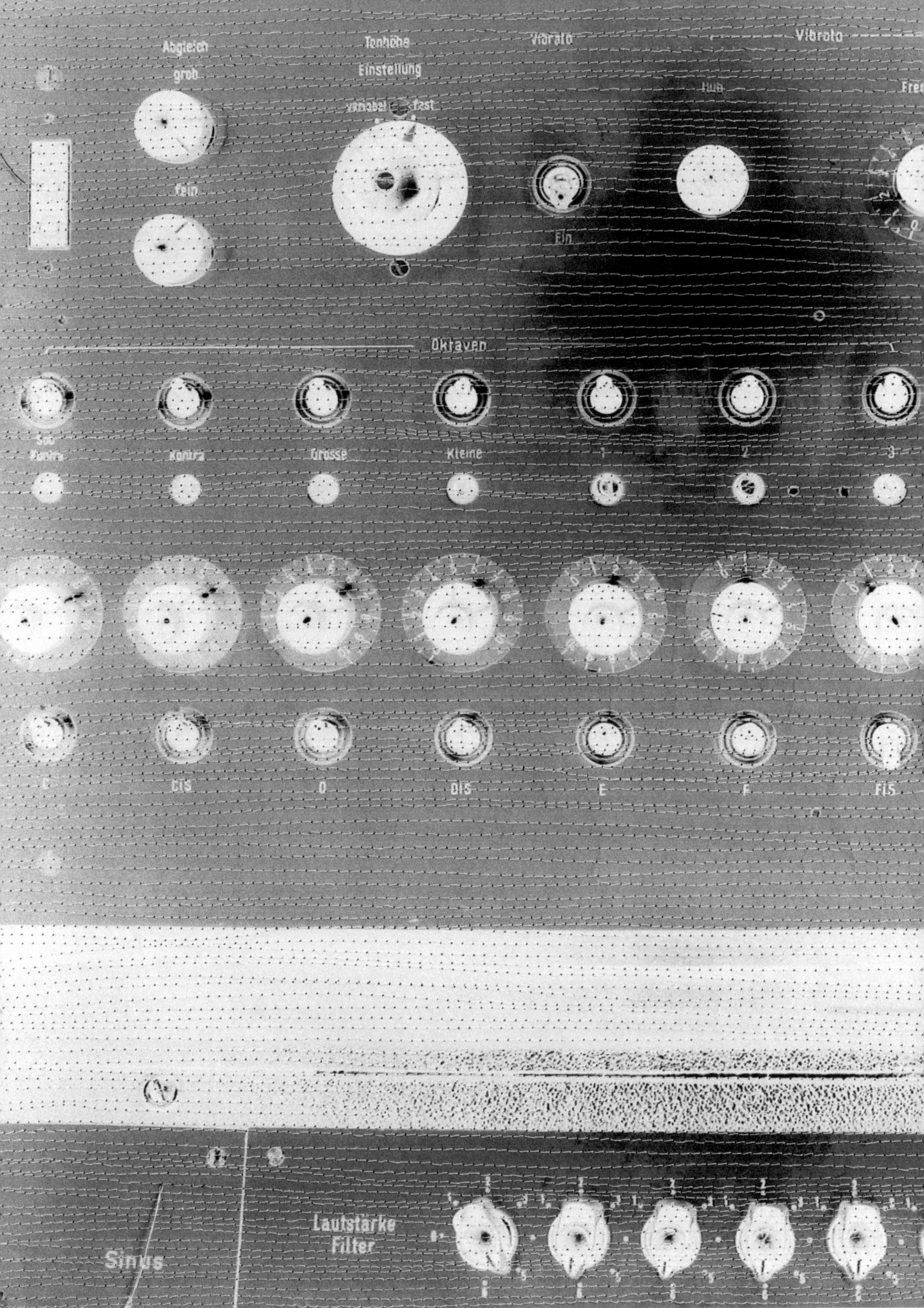
Abgleich
grob
fein
Tonhöhe
Einstellung
variabel fest
Vibrato
Vibrato
Ein
Frei
Ein
Oktaven
Sub
Kontra
Kontra
Grosse
Kleine
1
2
3
C
CIS
D
DIS
E
F
FIS
Lautstärke
Filter
Sinus

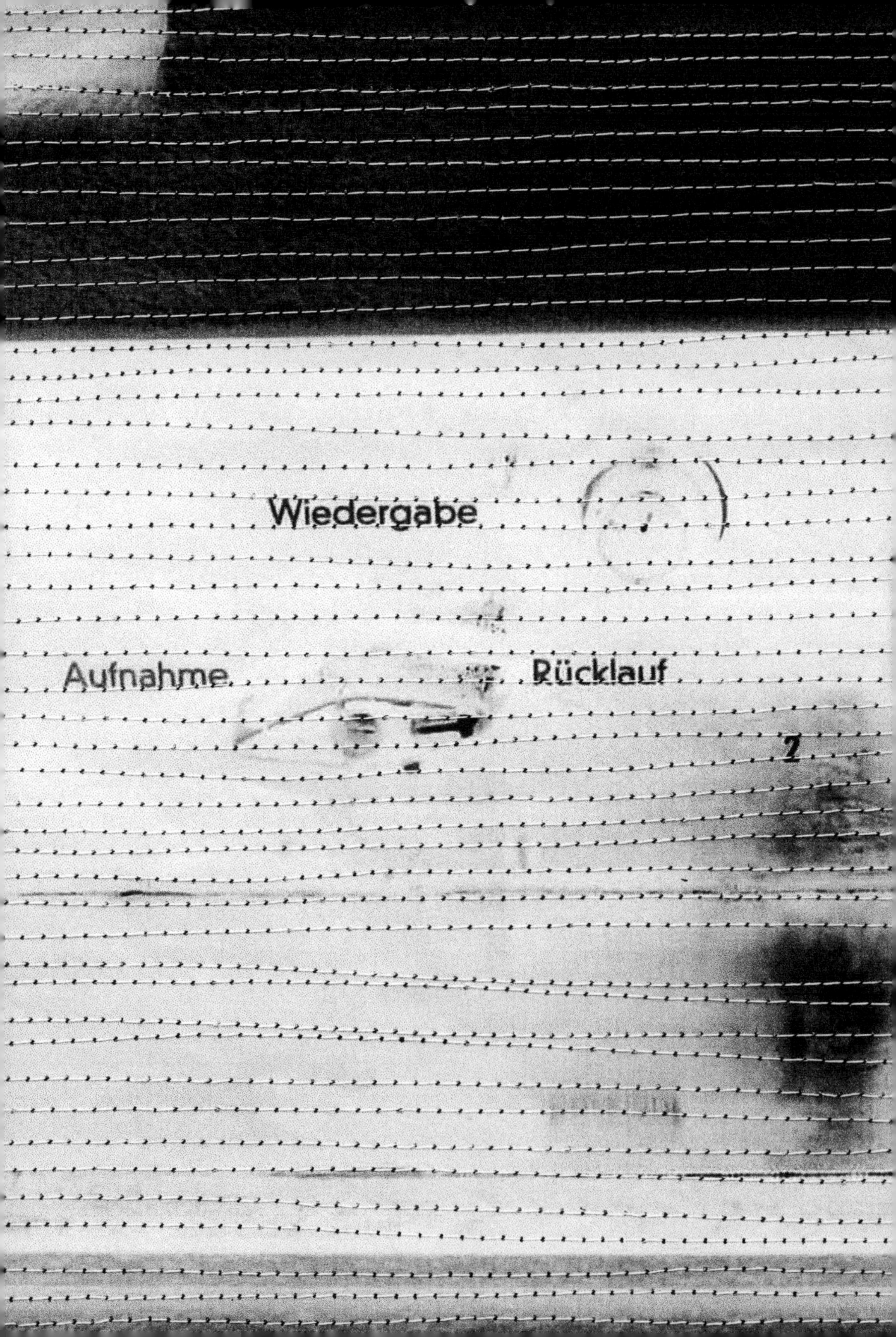

Wiedergabe

Aufnahme   Rücklauf

2

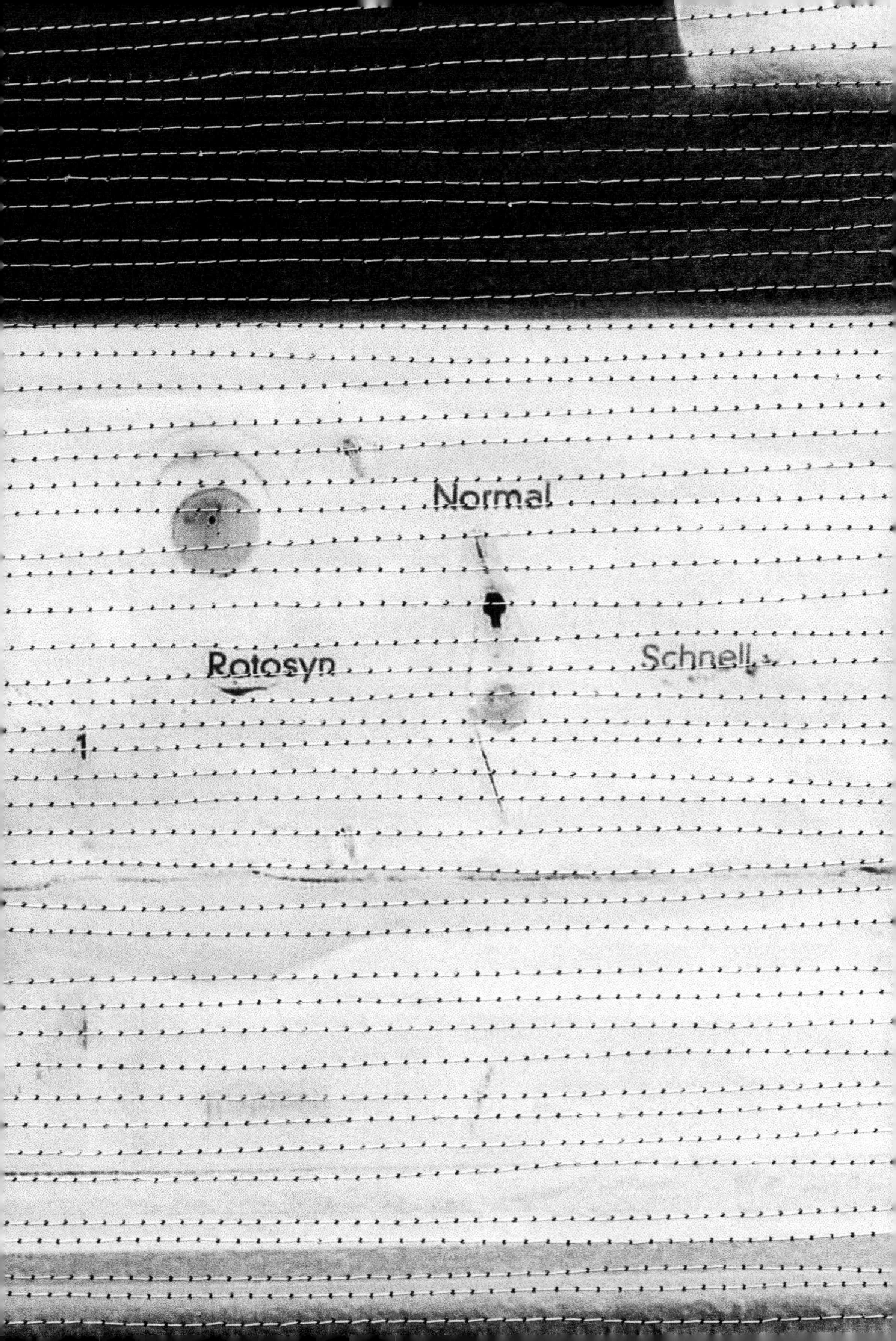

Normal

Rotosyn

Schnell

1

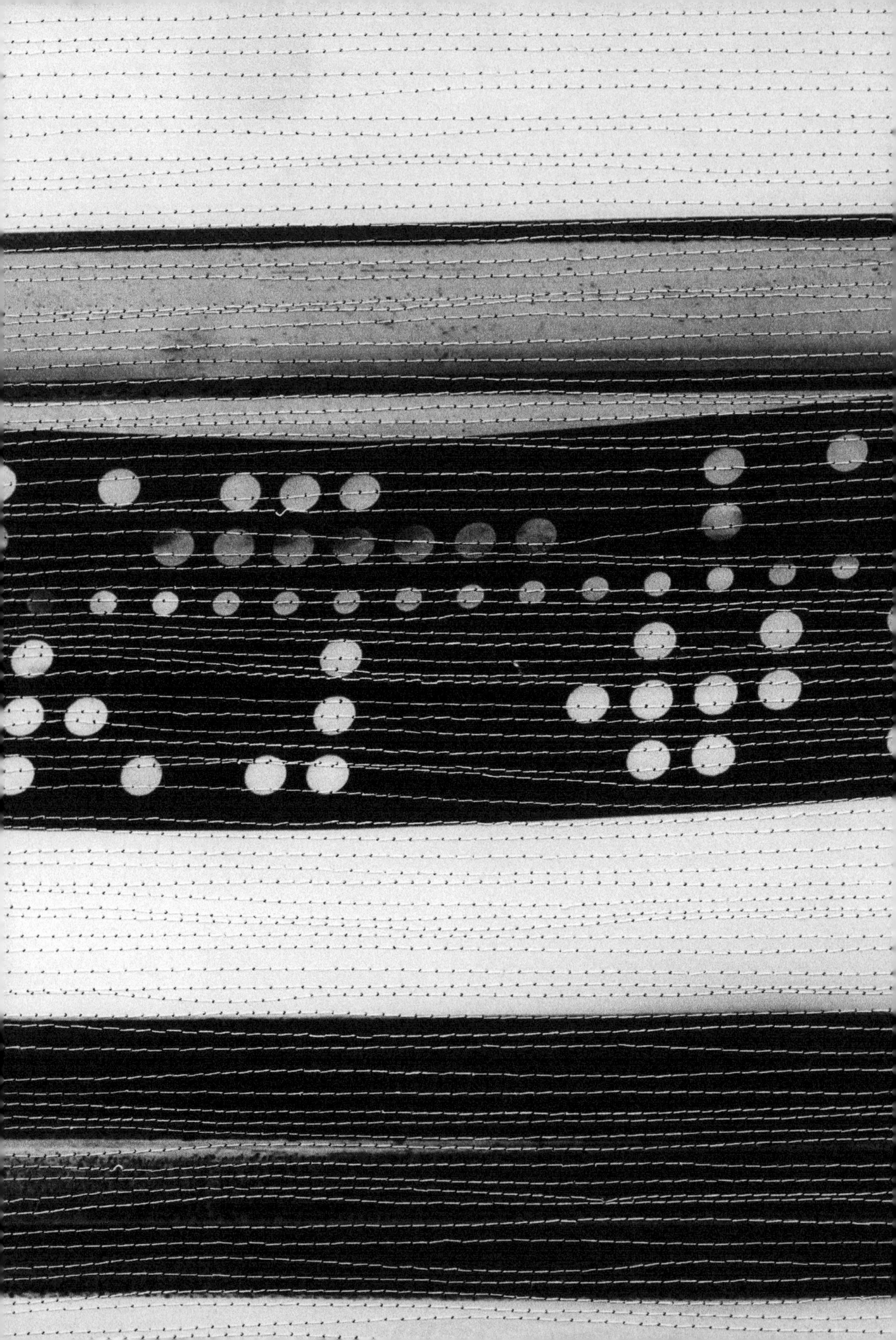

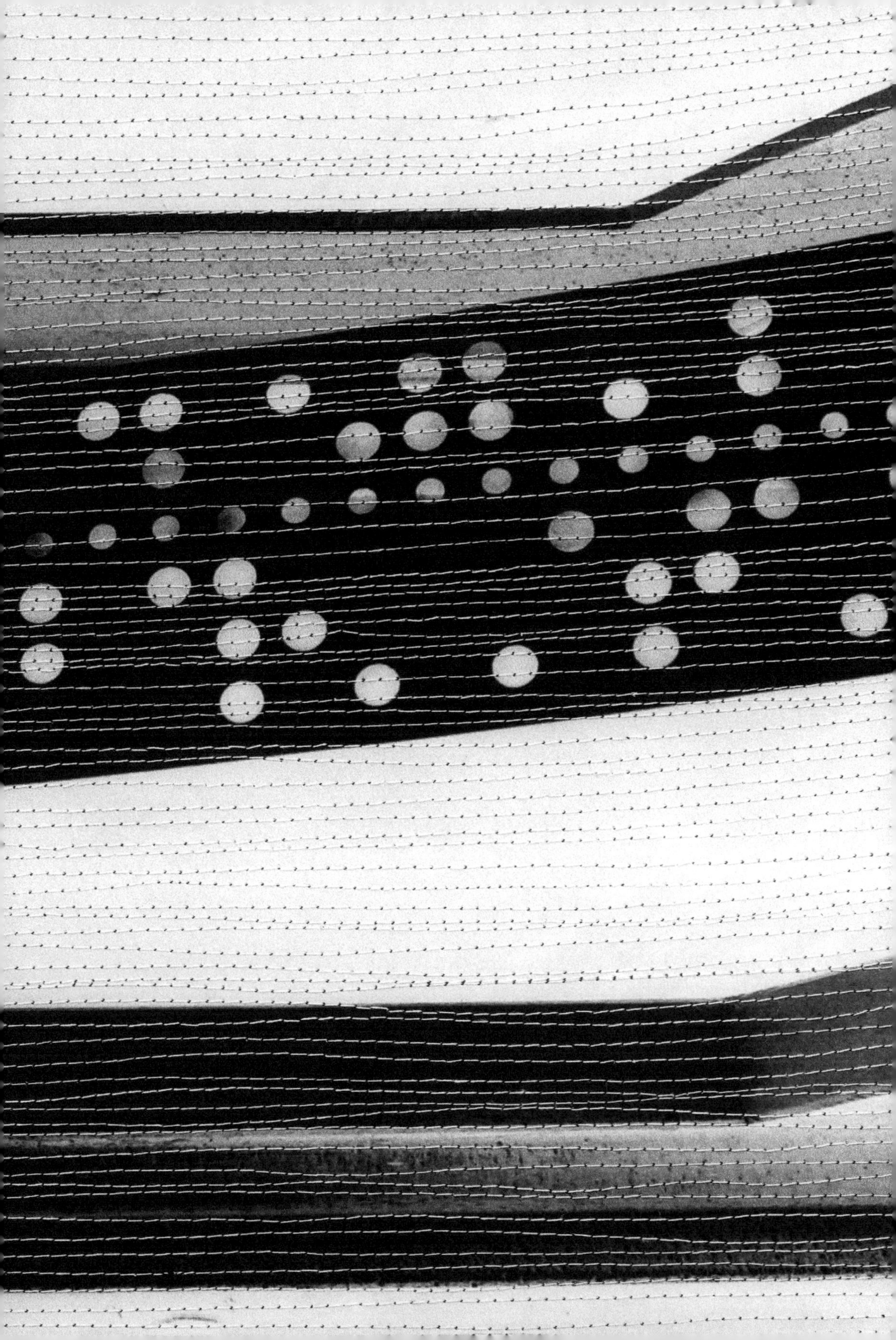

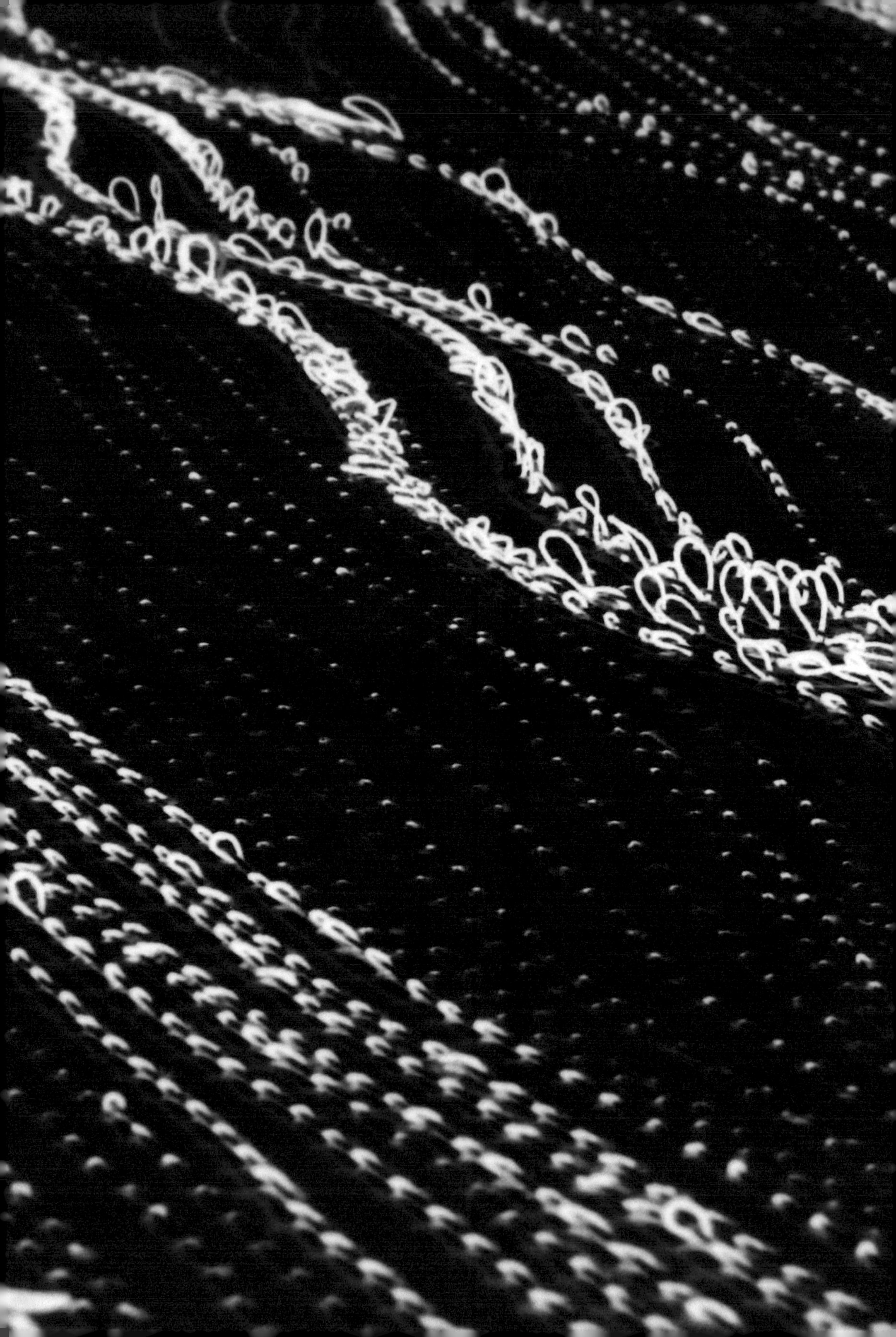

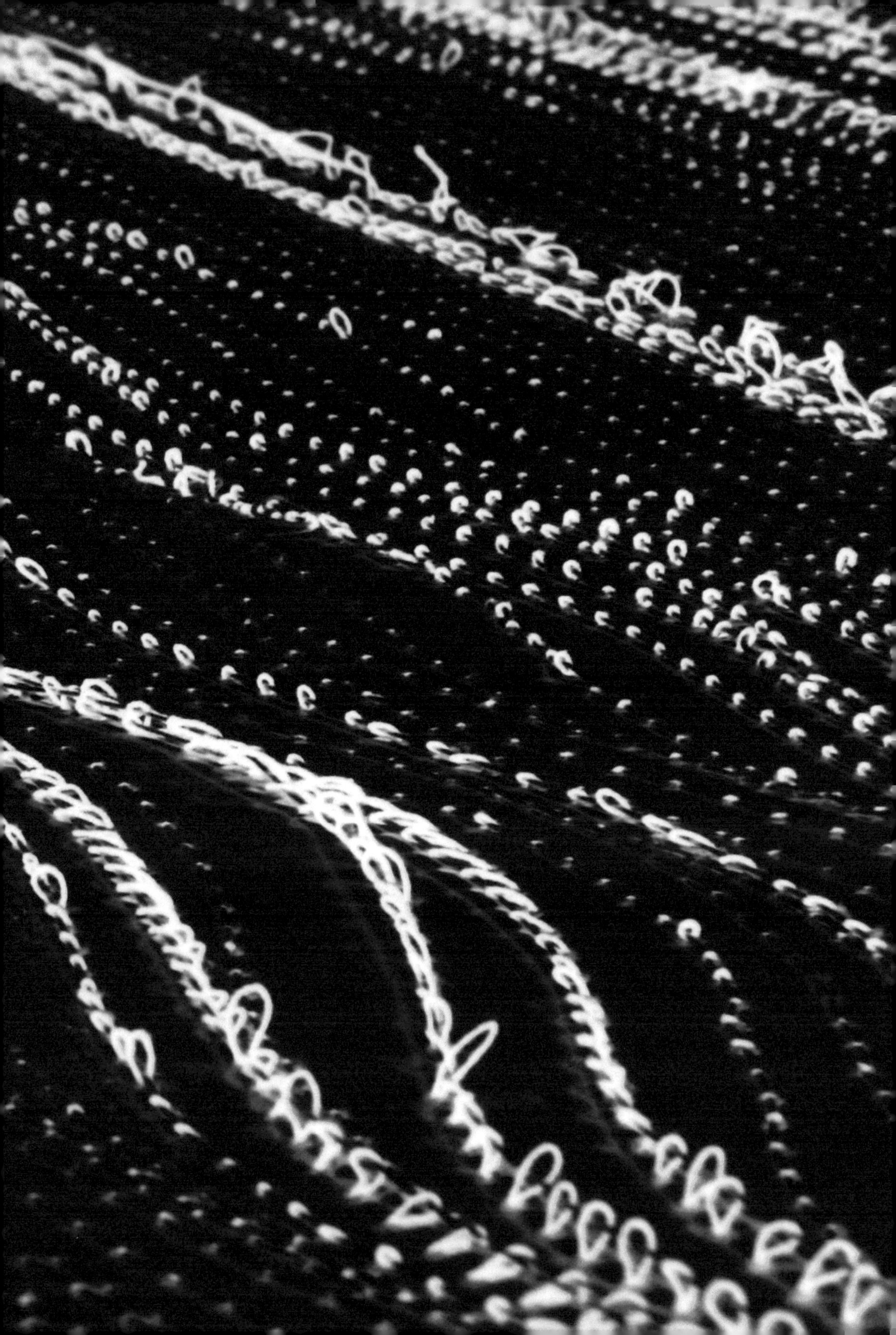

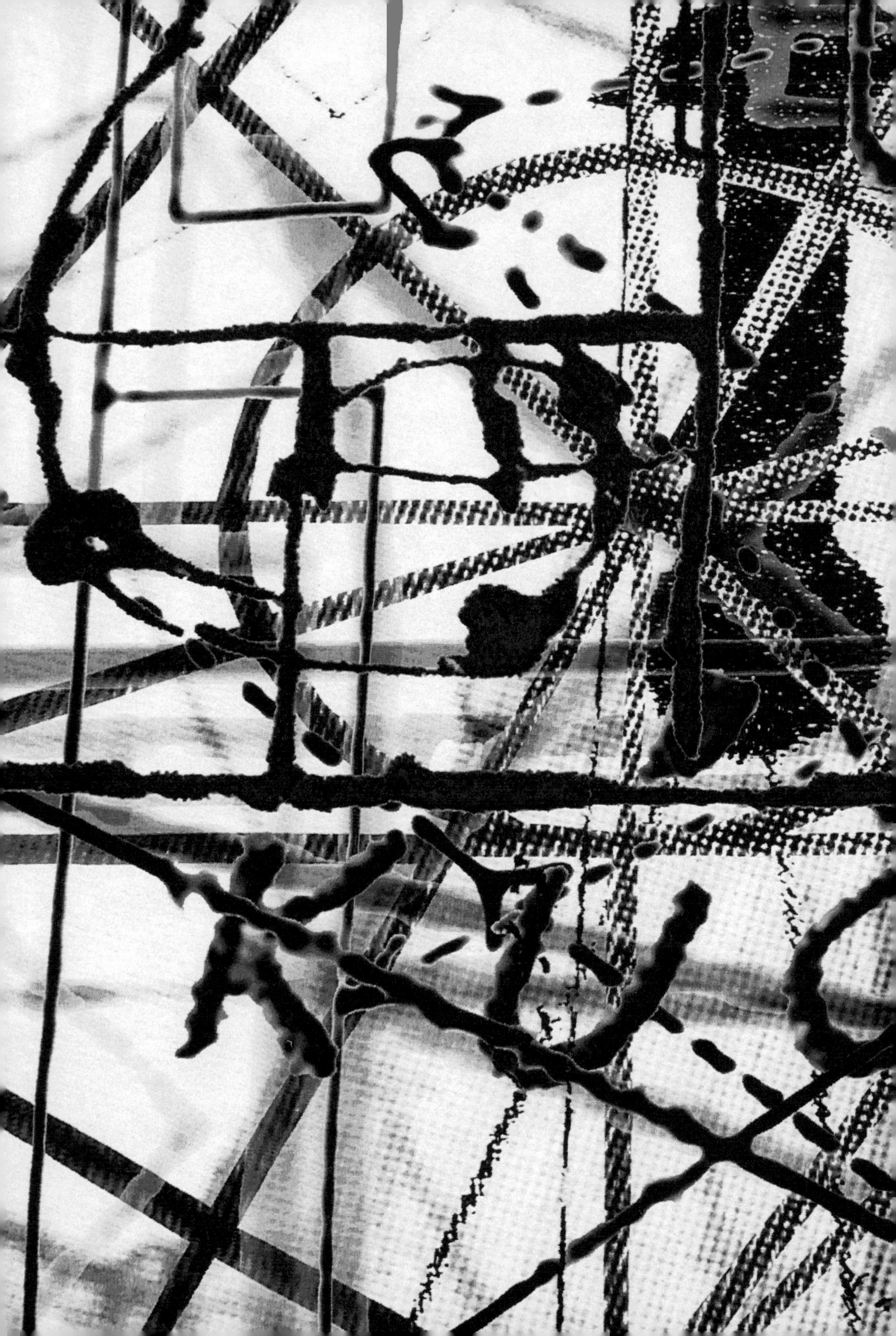

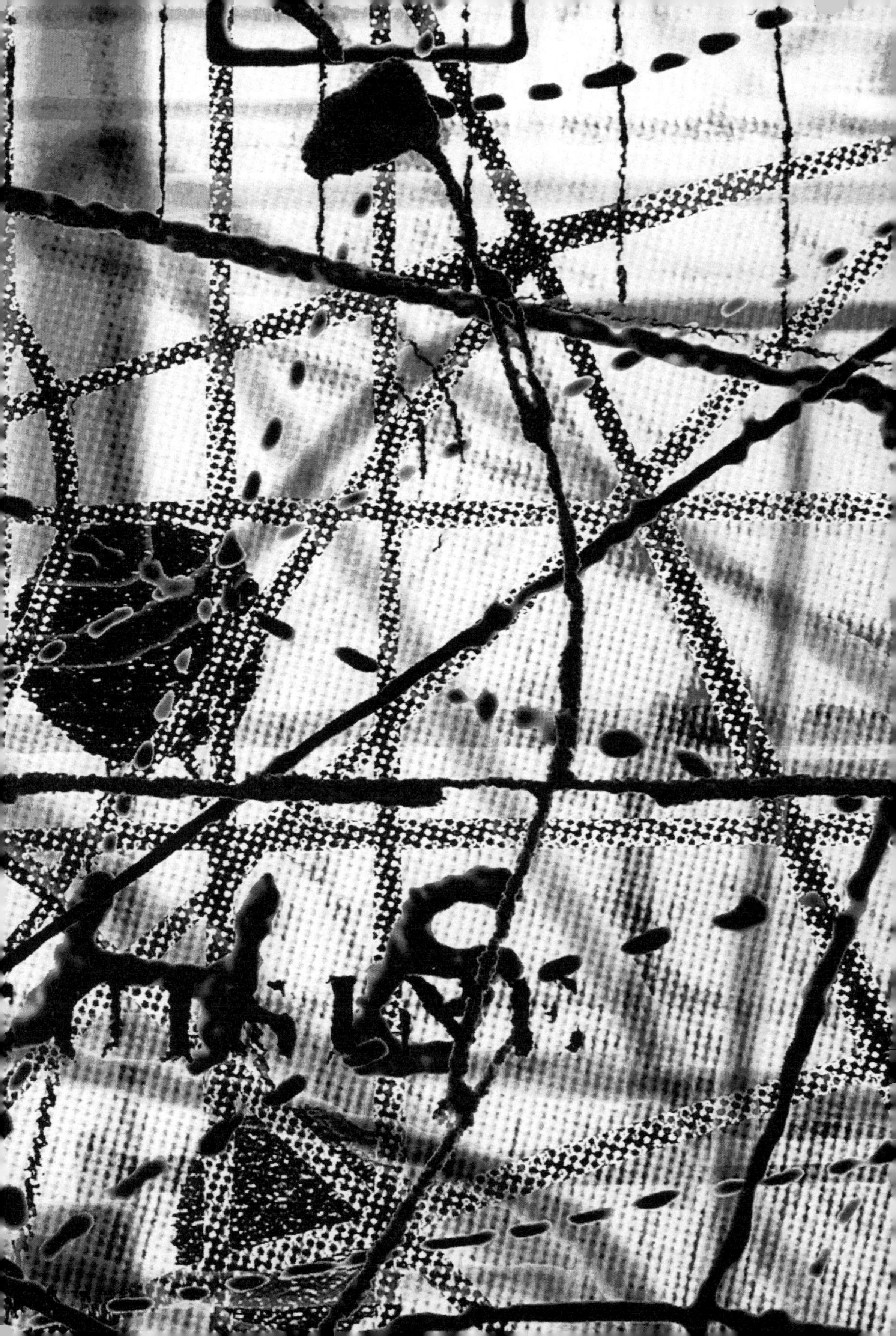

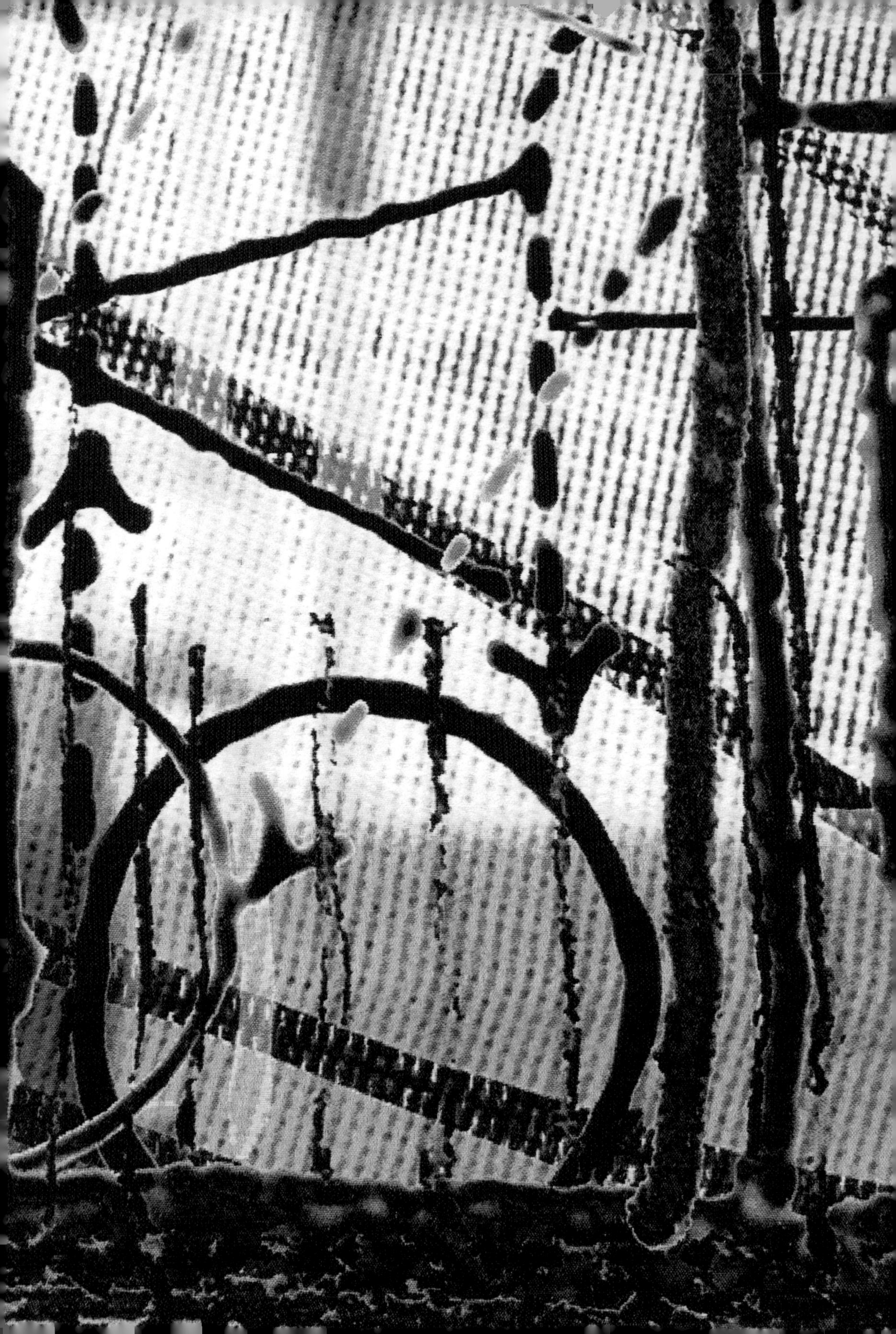

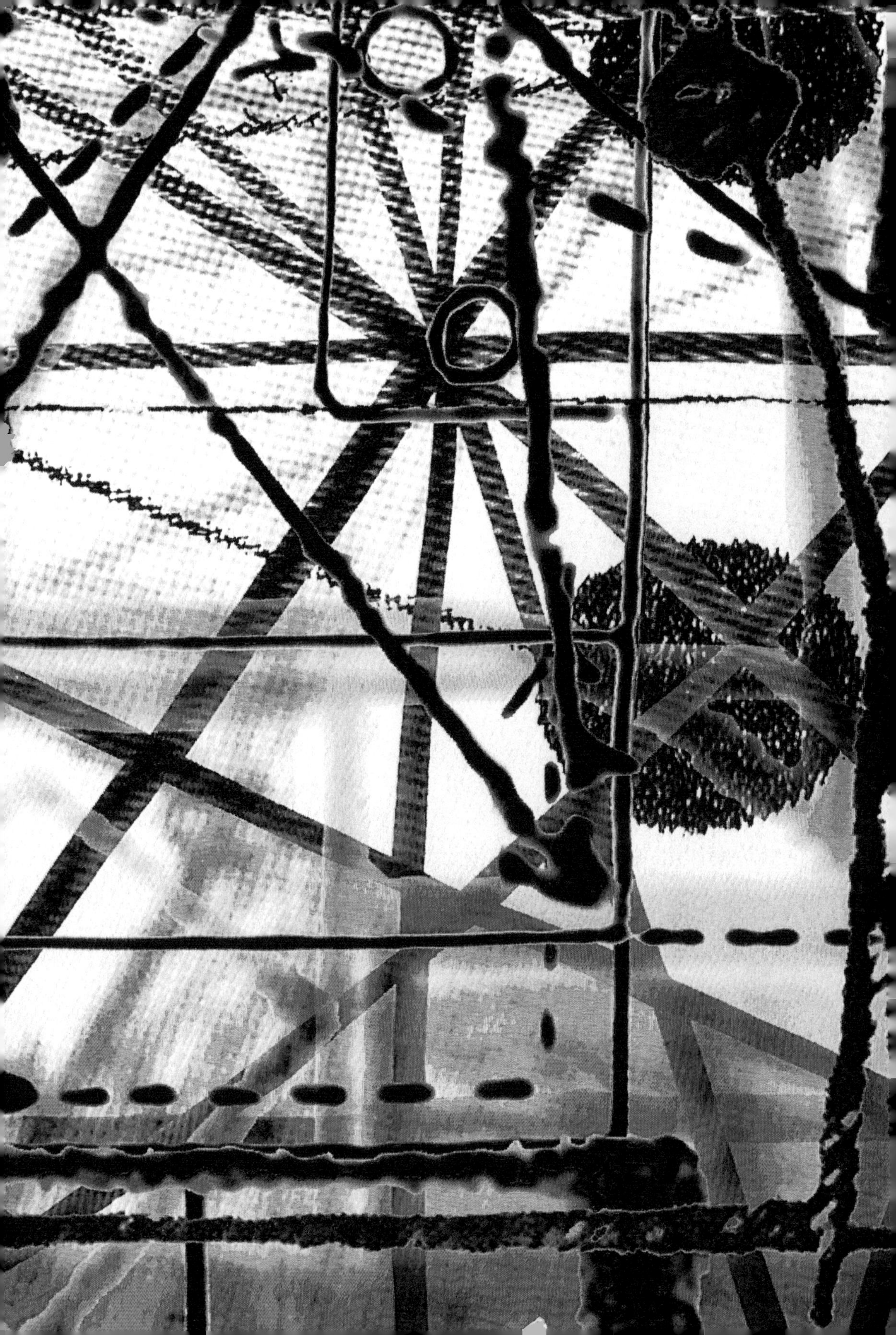

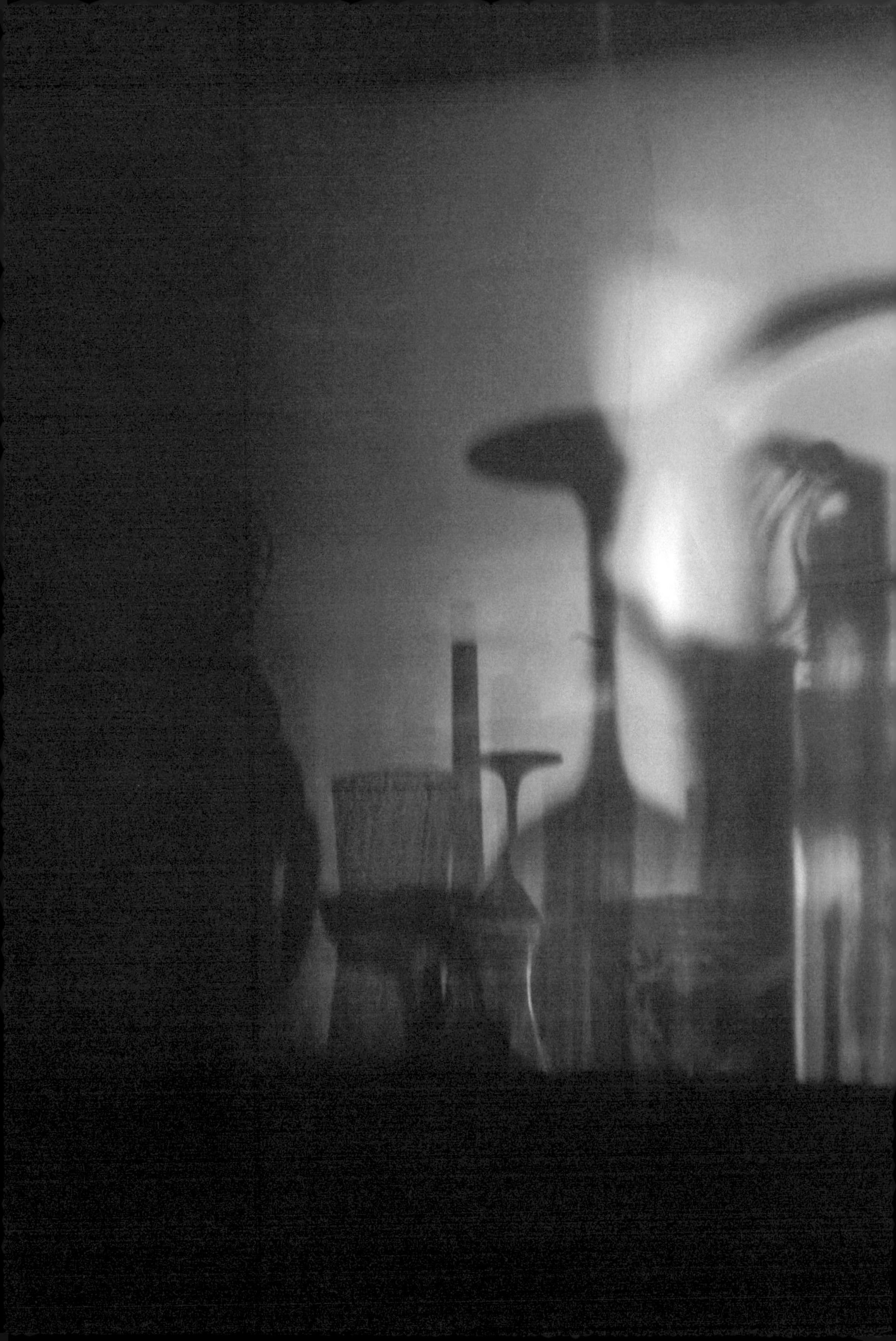

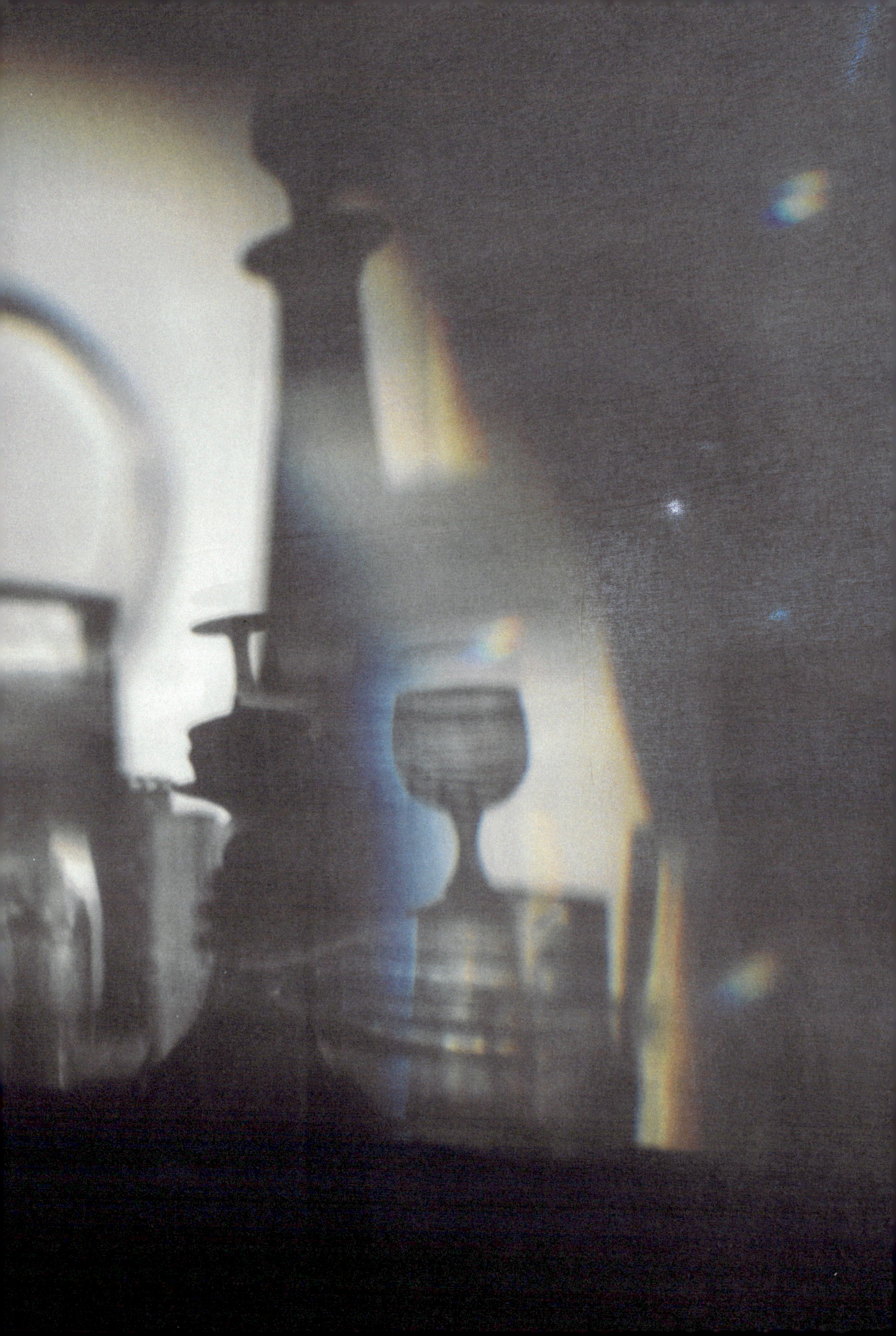

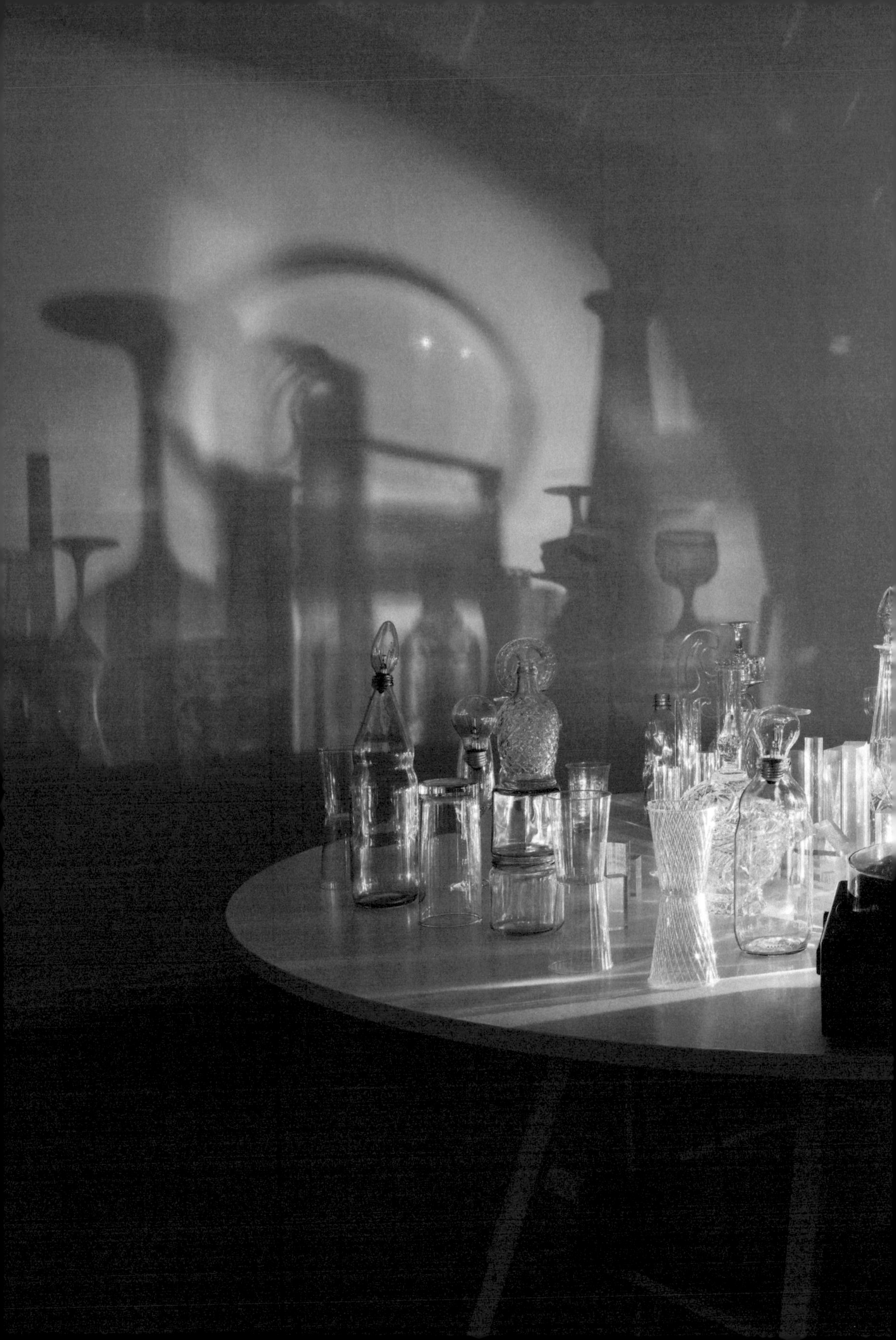

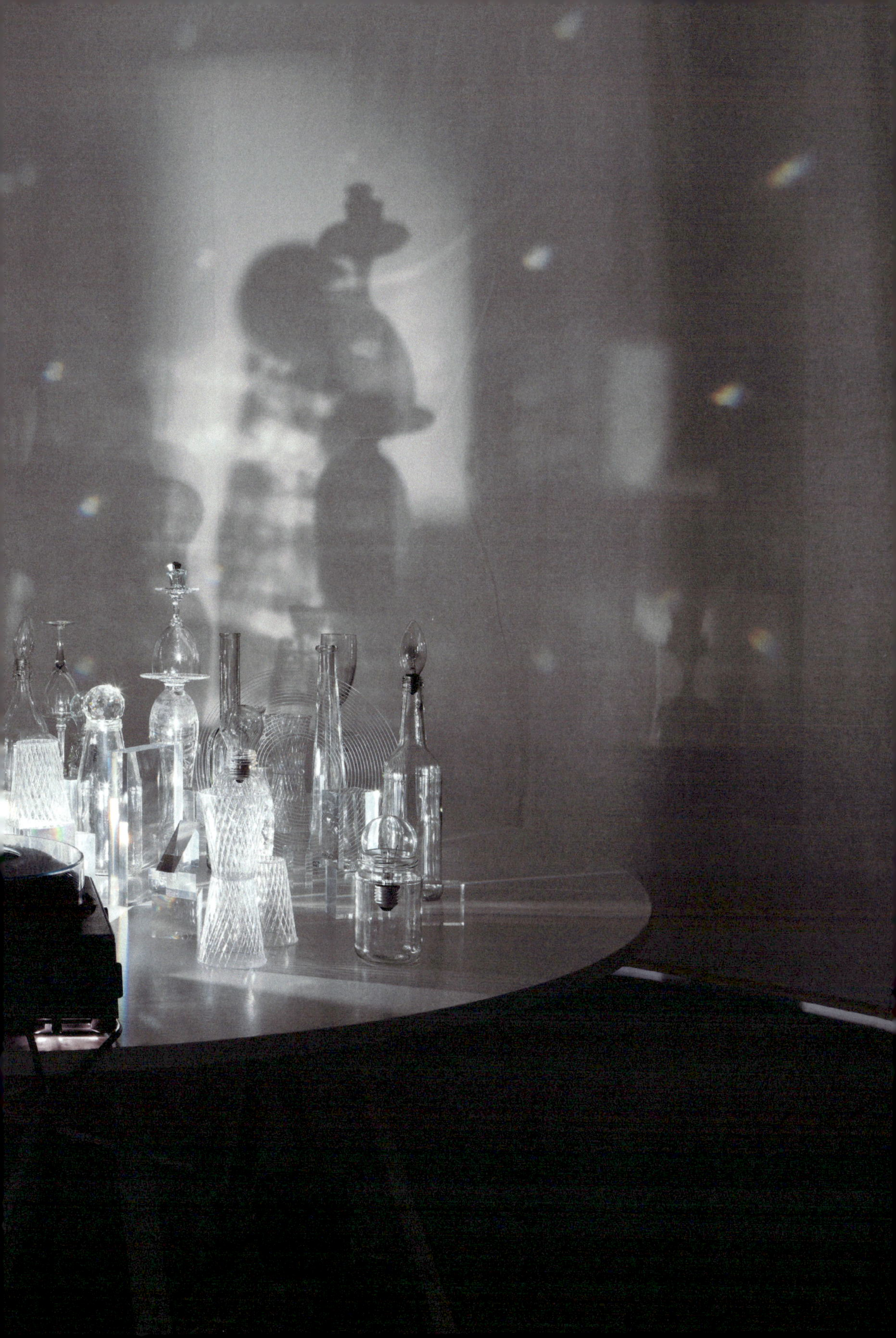

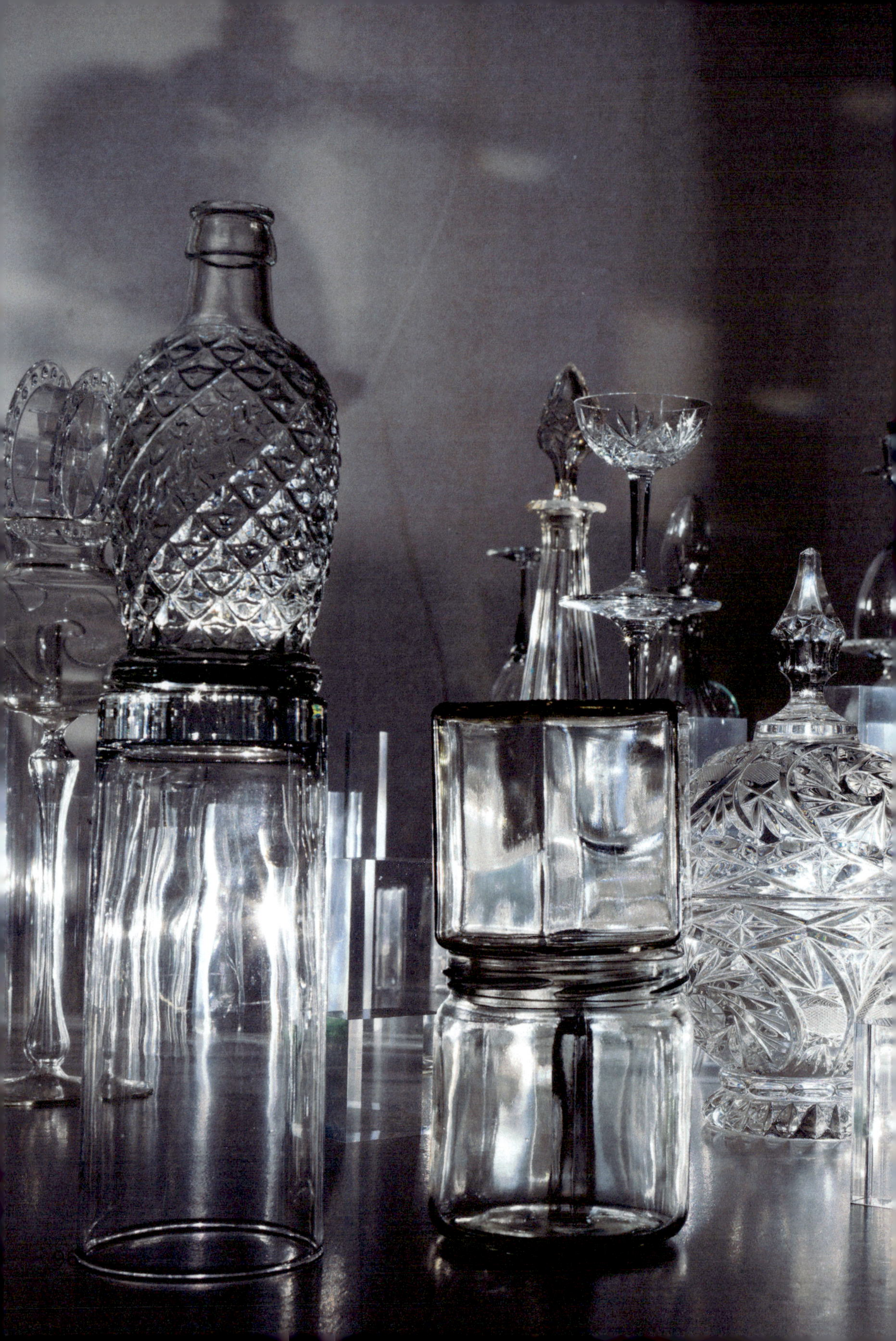

Stories, Myths, Ironies, and Other Songs: Recorded, Directed, Revised, and Produced by Michaela Melián[1]

Hanne Loreck

Michaela Melián seeks out kindred spirits in her artistic work. Not exclusively, but predominantly, she finds female companions. Some of them are prominent, such as the weaver and Bauhaus artist Anni Albers (1899–1994) or the poet Else Lasker-Schüler (1869–1945), some are marginal figures in history or only part of their life's work has been handed down, others were unknown before the artist "saw" something in them and picked up their trail. Researching their respective works, attitudes, ambitions, ideas, and materializations, Michaela Melián forges an affinity with them by making them like herself. In this elective kinship, however, the artist does not mirror herself, but instead of a (narcissistic) replica, she assembles a crystalline, faceted image, like her installation with sound ***Heimweh (Else Lasker-Schüler)*** (Homesickness) (2012) presents in a pictorial-spatial mode: Light circles above transparent objects, while brilliant lights flare up and shadows flit across a cylindrical projection screen. The result is not something closed, but something open, mobile, but also fragile. The light itself is refracted prismatically and "conjures up" a transient city silhouette from the loose arrangement of everyday plastic beakers and precious nostalgic cut glass vessels. But the prismatic does not merely pertain to the optical; as a metaphor, it can be applied to sonic and phonetic moments, which almost always constitute an essential part of Michaela Melián's work.

Lauren Fournier has recently updated the concept of "autotheory".[2] In her study, the Canadian theorist and curator cites female artists and literary figures who contextualize the everyday life (of a woman, partner, mother, migrant, and so on), its routines and setbacks, with considerations in the realm of art theory, philosophy, and social policy, and who conceive and articulate both their lives and their aesthetic-theoretical production as reciprocal interweaving. The term "interweaving" is meant to evoke knits and

---

1   I draw my title from the publication Quinn Latimer and Adam Szymczyk (Eds.), *Stories, Myths, Ironies, and Other Songs: Conceived, Directed, Edited, and Produced by M. Auder*, London 2014.

2   Cf. Lauren Fournier, "Autotheory as Feminist Practice", in: *Art, Writing, and Criticism*, Cambridge 2021.

fabrics as structure and quasi-materialization as well as the effect, the impact that one mode of knowing has on the other field of knowledge and vice versa. This construction touches on Michaela Melián's practice insofar as the self is here understood relationally from the very outset and certainly not as a given self-sufficient entity. It even seems as if the earlier production was highlighted by the more recent reference, and both were given an additional dimension in the actualization out of a very specific present-day concern. Such futurity was inherent in the historical artefact, whether intentional or unconscious, but can only be realized in a self-less practice like that of the artist.

What can be said of the explicitly written knowledge forming of the writer, literary theorist, and philosopher Hélène Cixous (* 1937)[3] can be applied to Michaela Melián's process as well, though it must be expanded to include an audiovisual practice: "Cixous subverts [...] an understanding of theory as a 'theory of something' that has an object or tries to produce one, and yet writes about it from a distance."[4] This is how the artist and media theorist Annika Haas sees it in the context of Cixous's so-called "ant theory"—a theory that "does not set up a theory" but rather recalls a childlike observation. This ant theory becomes a method of "relating 'things to things'",[5] so that they follow one another like characters that always incorporate the preceding character and refer to one that follows, which interlink despite and by way of the gap, despite and by way of the distance. Haas can/not make out an I, which already looks at itself from the outside, since the memory goes back to a time when language does not yet provide an I as a controlling or meta-function of semantic inclusion and attribution or as a discourse. From Cixous's point of view, however, we do not stop at what could also be understood as a rhetorically adequate anecdote. In terms of biographical thinking, the philosopher and artist Eva Meyer, who in turn listens to Hannah

---

3   Cixous is born into an old Jewish maternal line from Osnabrück and grows up
    in Oran / Algeria surrounded by a variety of languages including German, French,
    Arabic, Yiddish and the Low German dialect of her mother's home town.

4   Annika Haas, "Ihre erste unterbrochene durchgängige Linie. Hélène Cixous'
    Ameisentheorie", in: id., Jonas Hock, Anna Leyrer and Johannes Ungelenk (Eds.),
    Widerständige Theorie. Kritisches Lesen und Schreiben, Berlin 2018, pp. 235–243,
    here: p. 236. Why correlate Cixous with Michaela Melián? The artist expressed
    her appreciation for the philosopher and writer in the wonderful review of
    Cixous' loving epitaph for her mother Eve (1910–2013) "*Mother Homer is Dead ...*,"
    March 13, 2020, in: Michaela Melián, "*Muttersprachen. Michaela Melián über
    Hélène Cixous' 'Meine Homère ist tot ...'*" (Mother tongues: Michaela Melián on
    Hélène Cixous's 'Mother Homer is Dead ...'), online: https://www.textezurkunst.de/
    articles/melian-muttersprachen/ (last retrieved 18.6.2022).

5   Haas, ibid, p. 237.

Arendt, takes us back to where it remained for a woman "to become a 'mouthpiece' for events, to transform something that has happened into something that has been said. This is achieved by repeatedly telling and re-telling, in reflection, one's own story to oneself and to others."[6] Even though the pre- and retelling interests me spatially and temporally, not least because it implies posteriority, and it also reminds me of Cixous's interrupted line, of the before and after as positions that can never be clearly determined, what is at issue here is the inherently unique aspect of the story. Such inherent uniqueness in the sense of having or possessing is radically questioned by Michaela Melián's approach. Her own inherent uniqueness shares in the partial identifications, which in turn can be not only human but also non-human. There is a thing, a historical moment, a biography, a technology—and along with these "aspects", there is the well-known canonical reception, such as that of the architecture of the Weissenhof Estate in Stuttgart (**Girl-Kultur**, 2019) or the far less well-known story of the Siemens Studio for Electronic Music, established in 1959 and now exhibited in the museum (**Speicher**, 2008). Updated, i. e. designed for the present and the future, however, every research primes a political desire for other stories that allow alternative conditions or indeed another story to be imagined. One must, of course, be on guard in order to find the material–a military expression that stands for high, even heightened vigilance and allows me to connect to Michaela Melián's most recent work which she devised for the exhibition **Red Threads**. **Tania** orbits the biographical-political narrative of Tamara Bunke (1935–1967), born in Argentina, raised in East Germany, educated in Cuba, and perished in Bolivia, a leftist icon of the liberation struggle and anti-imperialist revolution in Latin America. But Tania–her political code name–was not just one. The young woman had to acquire alternative biographies in her training as a guerrilla in Bolivia and as a Cuban secret service agent, for example, to be able to act completely naturally and unsuspicious, habitually and linguistically, in every public encounter as the ethnomusicologist Laura Gutiérrez Bauer. Remarkably, this is not the first time that Michaela Melián has variegated the figure of Tania; since 1991, she continues to reassemble her in different facets and to publicize her in different ways; thus, for example, a flag has recently been added to the already existing symbolizations of Tamara Bunke. The fact that her estate was archivally processed in Berlin between 2013 and 2015 was a site-specific catalyst for tracing also Tania in 2022 as a "red thread".

6   Hannah Arendt quoted from Eva Meyer, "Was heißt biographisches Denken?" (What is biographical thinking?), in: id., *Autobiographie der Schrift*, Basel and Frankfurt a. M. 1989, pp. 41–64, here: p. 45f.

Michaela Melián is certainly not aiming at the biographical in general, and biographical components may in fact sometimes just come her way, namely when things, facts, and aspects are involved that could not have been expected at all, but instead—very much in keeping with Cixous's ant theory—arise from observation and can be developed out of the material itself (such as the story of Elsbeth Büchle, who in 1928 posed as a nameless model with a Mercedes sports car in front of the Le Corbusier House at the Weissenhof Estate and turned out to be a Laban dance teacher, physiotherapist and breathwork practitioner with her own studio; **Girl-Kultur**). And there is not only the concrete case of individual biography, especially since the artist decades ago has opened up a field that presents "specific" rather than "arbitrary" elements: An imperative of remembrance concerning the National Socialist past, the achievements of socially and feministically committed women whose significance has been ignored or minimized by historiography (e.g. Bertha Pappenheim, Bertha Benz, Hedy Lamarr) as well as historical periods and institutions of critical-progressive thought and artistic action—such as Russian Constructivism with its notable presence of women artists or the Bauhaus, which admitted women to a previously unheard-of degree but deemed them responsible for textiles (**In a Mist**, 2014 / 15). The artist also has her eye on the contemporaneous New Objectivity along with its architectural-ergonomic innovations for the motion sequences in the kitchen. Spatially implemented at the time of the Bauhaus, everyday care routines were to be simplified and accelerated–with the problematic side effect of institutionalizing the housewife, a female subject who runs the household and organizes the family—and stays at home to do so, as indicated by the very word housewife. In **Girl-Kultur**, a digitally woven large-format tapestry, Michaela Melián addresses these pros and cons simultaneously by layering the various historical studies of motion sequences in technical diagrams to the point that the intention of economization appears broken in the exemplary tangle of lines and so-called progress does not result in a perfectly organized image.

Nevertheless, such elective affinities should not only be seen aesthetically; they also result from solidarity with the exponents of socio-political upheavals. Despite various ambivalences towards revolutions and even their downright failure, their utopian quality still sparkles today if you retrieve it from the uniform and disarming flow of art and cultural history, as Michaela Melián does. Appropriated and formally reinterpreted, the old critique of capitalism and hierarchy can resonate again today. One such hierarchy that Michaela Melián implies to counteract it in her artistic practice can be found in the classical devaluation of applied versus so-called free art, of handicraft or production art versus painting or sculpture. When a textile print by the Soviet painter, designer, and theoretician Varvara Fyodorovna Stepanova (1894–1958)[7] and a fabric pattern by the Bauhaus weaver and textile theorist Anni Albers (1899–1994), both from 1929, are reproduced and consolidated in a glass painting with artisanal expertise, as it were, the historical artists become building blocks of their own work biography, and the appreciation of their work transcends the aesthetic and leads into a retroactive solidarization with the ideological context that they once intended to materialize through their choice of design media. Even though the two artists were not activists, they pursued their goals through forms, design, teaching, and programmatic writings. When Michaela Melián also reproduces a photographic image of the material part of her installation ***Heimweh (Else Lasker-Schüler)*** on one-way mirror glass for ***In a Mist***, she includes herself in these aesthetic approaches, creating a bond with the producers and their concerns.

Michaela Melián compiles and samples. ***Tania*** (2022) is even technomaterially composed of many small stamp impressions. What looks like a continuous line from a certain distance disintegrates into small black and grey squares when viewed up close. Tamara Bunke's "Biocomic", transferred to the free-standing wall banderole in a dense episodic patchwork without beginning or end, on the one hand, follows the socialist-communist mural tradition with its public didactic narratives. On the other hand, the procedure itself, the small-scale, mosaic-like stamping, speaks to that which is as incomplete as it is legendary, which constitutes the transmission of the protagonist's vital records and is moreover characteristic of historiography in general. Stamping is repeated elsewhere in Michaela Melián's work: A cliché or printing block that can reproduce an image multiple—theoretically infinite-times and stands for a reductive view of something or someone, being given or denied the stamp of approval as a mark of official recognition, or drawing food stamps, which may not be in current colloquial use but remains synonymous with unemployment and destitution—all these are associations that can be made here. It is precisely these voids, the incomplete, the omitted, that prompt us to critically analyse such gaps and to fill them with new research results, but also to supplement them figuratively

---

7   Stepanova worked with her fellow artist Lyubov Popova for the First State Textile Factory
    near Moscow on designs for fabric patterns and clothing.

and fictionally, in the spirit of Donna Haraway's "speculative feminism". 'Or, to put it another way: only as the myth of Tania does Tamara Bunke's biography appear coherent. This way, it is held together by so-called character traits such as determination, consistency, (self-)control, solidarity, and courage, but above all, by Marxist-Communist conviction.[8] Michaela Melián does not judge the certainly controversial realpolitik of the armed struggle. Instead, she introduces a figure in decided indecision, with an opaque accumulation of references and scenic multiplication. Donna Haraway frames the figure as a materialist-semiotic ensemble: "Figures collect up hopes and fears and show possibilities and dangers. Both imaginary and material, figures root peoples in stories and link them to histories. Stories are always more generous, more capacious, than ideologies [...]. I want to know how to inhabit histories and stories rather than deny them. I want to know how critically to live both inherited and novel kinships, in a spirit neither of condemnation nor celebration. I want to know how to help build ongoing stories rather than histories that end. In that sense, my kinships are about keeping the lineages going, even while defamiliarizing their members and turning lines into webs, trees into esplanades, and pedigrees into affinity groups."[9] It can be a year or a place that connects the two. Of course, the aesthetics and themes are always guided by partisanship, not dogmatic partisanship, but an audible and discernible nonetheless. Albers and Lasker-Schüler were of German-Jewish origin and had to go into exile to escape Nazi persecution. The poet and draftswoman Lasker-Schüler, however, also imagined and presented herself in male form as Prince Jussuf of Thebes, and in her famous correspondence between her*him and the Blue Rider in the form of Franz Marc, writing and image intertwine to form a union. Michaela Melián's multimedia practice combines musical composition with a pictorial visual as well as a spatial arrangement.

Likewise, the paths of discovery are not linear, but intersecting: researching in archives, analysing the finds, observing, associating, abstracting, fantasising, and inventing. They describe different relationships to a theme, a task (whether chosen or set) that are expressed in the prepositions: about,

---

8   Cf. Eberhard Panitz, *Der Weg zum Rio Grande. Ein biographischer Bericht über Tamara Bunke (The Road to Rio Grande. A Biographical Report on Tamara Bunke)*, Berlin 1973.
    Bunke interpreted for Panitz and colleagues of the writers' delegation of the Central Council of the communist Free German Youth (FDJ) during their visit to Havana and Cuba in 1961.
9   Donna Haraway, "Introduction. A Kinship of Feminist Figurations", in: *The Haraway Reader*, New York and London 2004, p. 1.

to, from ... We encounter this same mix on the side of artistic techniques when, to cite just one example, Michaela Melián draws, stamps, or sews the contours of figures, objects, or buildings, or even fashions them from steel. What creates the comparable visual impression of a line nevertheless plays into a respective different material, cultural, and gender-political dimension: This is precisely what is articulated in **Red Threads**. In the fairy tale, "red like blood" stands for pulsating life, but without the red of the revolution, "the blood" will pulse differently. Exactly how can be inferred from Cixous's concept of "feminine writing" to a feminine way of multimedia production. According to the philosopher and woman of letters, female writing rushes along the margins of discourse[10] and produces effects such as pluralization, resulting in the formation of an "ambiguous polyphony"[11] (English "equivoice"; French "équivoix"). This kind of writing–in Michaela Melián's case, audiovisual composing–does not emanate from the author-artist, but from the power that "brings forth the Other and is brought forth by Others".[12] In a subtle way, this gives us an idea of what the relationship Melián–Tania or Melián–Weissenhof is like. The materials bring forth the artist and the artist brings forth her figures. There is also something to be said about rushing along —a rapid movement where much happens to pass the gaze without prior arrangement, and much happens to the gaze itself, in a sense. The speed of perception seems to me just as significant as the margin, that very specific place. It is only just part of that which has been handed down, it articulates its outermost boundary, but it frays into hitherto ignored knowledge: Where marginalization prevails, the question of its economies is especially valid, of symbolic capital as well as of social hierarchy. This area „emerges/exists always in the dissimilarity that runs 'in' us and between us. Elsewhere, Cixous also speaks of a 'non-closed mix of self/s and others'",[13] Naomie Gramlich and Annika Haas comment.

10 Cf. Naomie Gramlich and Annika Haas, "Situiertes Schreiben mit Haraway, Cixous und Grauen Quellen" (Situated writing with Haraway, Cixous and Grey Sources), in: *Zeitschrift für Medienwissenschaft*, 20, 1/2019, pp. 38–52, here: p. 44.

11 Cf. Hélène Cixous, "The Laugh of the Medusa" (1975), in: Esther Hutfless, Gertrude Postl and Elisabeth Schäfer (Eds.), *Hélène Cixous. Das Lachen der Medusa. Zusammen mit aktuellen Beiträgen*, Vienna 2013, pp. 39–61, here: p. 46.

12 Elisabeth Schäfer, "Hélène Cixous' Life Writings–Writing a Life. Oder: Das Auto- / Biographische ist nicht privat" (The auto/biographical is not private), in: *Jahrbuch für Medienphilosophie*, 3, 2017, pp. 81–98, here: p. 84, quoted from Gramlich and Haas, "Situiertes Schreiben", p. 44.

13 Gramlich and Haas, „Situiertes Schreiben" (Situated writing), p. 44; ibid quote Hélène Cixous, "Preface", in: Susan Sellers (Ed.), *The Hélène Cixous Reader*, London 1994, pp. xv–xxiii, here: p. xvii.

For her first engagement with the figure of Tania in the context of an exhibition with the eloquent title **Subjekt, Prädikat, Objekt** (1992), Michaela Melián got a police sketch artist from the Bavarian State Office of Criminal Investigation to draw Tamara Bunke according to her dictation. Now the portrait, which was created in the manner of a facial composite, is taken up again by her. While after 30 years, Tania once again becomes the main subject of a work of art, her function has changed. Then an idol of the left, she is now a little-known historical protagonist of armed revolution and the socialist-communist liberation struggles in Latin America. Remarkably, however, her life is much better researched today, and new facts and details have transformed the myth into a more real, but in turn also more ambivalent, image of the activist.[14] What is becoming visible and audible today is a kind of exhortation: like a ghost, Tania should haunt us, her conviction should inform our critical stance in a hypercapitalist and socially extremely unjust age.[15] On the other hand–and I perceive this as a deliberate articulation of the ambivalence or conflict—a gun made of fabric defuses the killing in combat; a gun as sofa or beanbag, **Mossberg Model Bullpup** (1993), is more content in an internalized form of resistance and struggle, almost in an interior design version–and displays the same scepticism towards gun violence as it does towards traditional gender attributions. But there is also the representation of the public. It lies in the loudspeakers distributed overhead, so-called pressure chamber loudspeakers used for warning messages on public transport systems. In their appearance, they are reminiscent of megaphones and the public address systems ubiquitous in socialist states. However, Michaela Melián does not broadcast propaganda or political indoctrination. Her composition combines indigenous sounds—Tania used the cover identity of an ethnomusicologist recording vanishing musical traditions in Bolivia—with melodies of internationally popular proletarian, partisan, and protest songs. Only now and then does a briefly highlighted sequence of notes, the distant memory of one of the songs, rise up from the fabric of instrumental sound, including Inca flutes. The specific space constituted by this acoustic blend merges with the uncounted, visually interwoven scenes on the Tania mural. To spot persons, landscapes, places, and architectures in Cuba and the GDR and to follow Tania's life like a film, one is best seated on the velvet rifle ... Inside and outside, private or public,

14 Cf. Walter Reinthaler, "Tamara Bunke, kubanische Revolutionärin" (Tamara Bunke, Cuban Revolutionary), online: https://www.bilderreisen.at/portraets/portraets-cuba-bunke.php (last retrieved on 18.6.2022).
15 Cf. Avery F. Gordon, *Ghostly Matters. Haunting and the Sociological Imagination*, Minnesota 2008.

soft weapon or war, more feminine connotations of the former, mostly masculine understanding of the latter. There remains the dichotomy represented by the choice of means between (self-)defence and pacification.

For Michaela Melián, intervisual, intersonic, and intertextual references are not intended to create an autobiographical intimacy, but they do temporarily and situationally support what can be called the biographical if we consider this to be the lives of Jewish artists forced into exile, the conditions of their survival, and the responsibility to never forget German history. Even without the focus on her predominantly literary and discursive genealogies, Michaela Melián's artistic strategy is one of reminiscent, citational reference—"Citation as Relation" is the title of one of Lauren Fournier's chapters on autotheory. In other words, the multimedia artist Michaela Melián assembles an aesthetic-theoretical "family" for herself, which, of course, unlike the bio-ideological model, is based on kinship in spirit and by no means in blood.

(right)
Girl-Kultur, 2018
Installation view Staatsgalerie Stuttgart, 2019

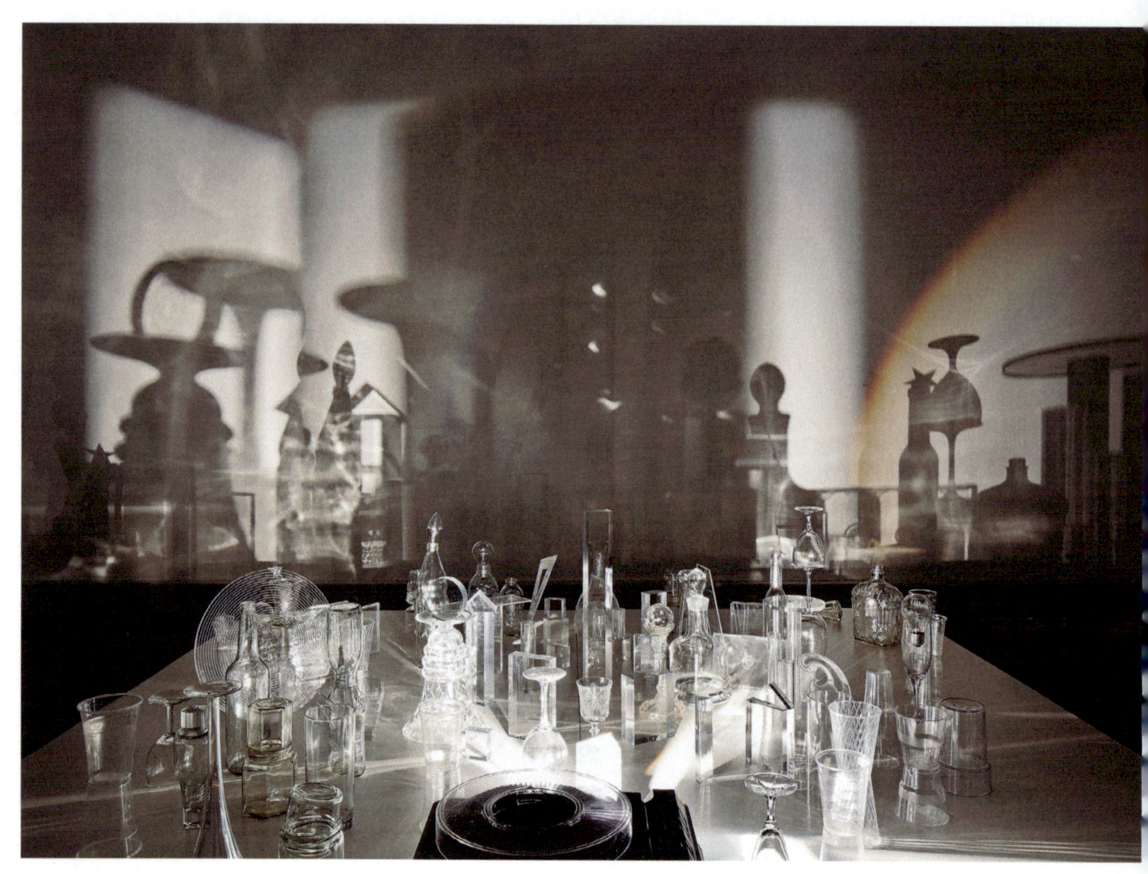

Lunapark, 2011
Installation view Badischer Kunstverein, 2014

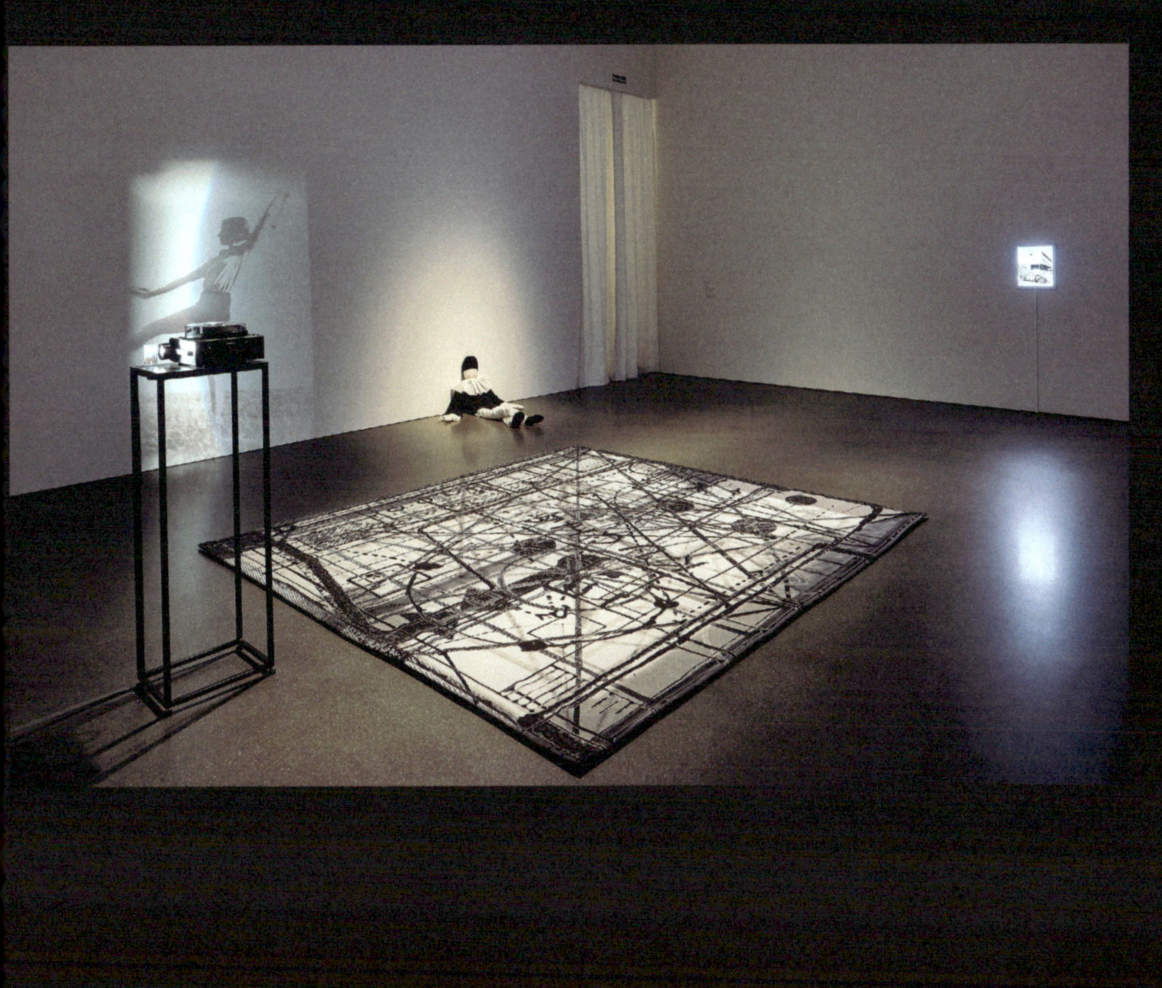

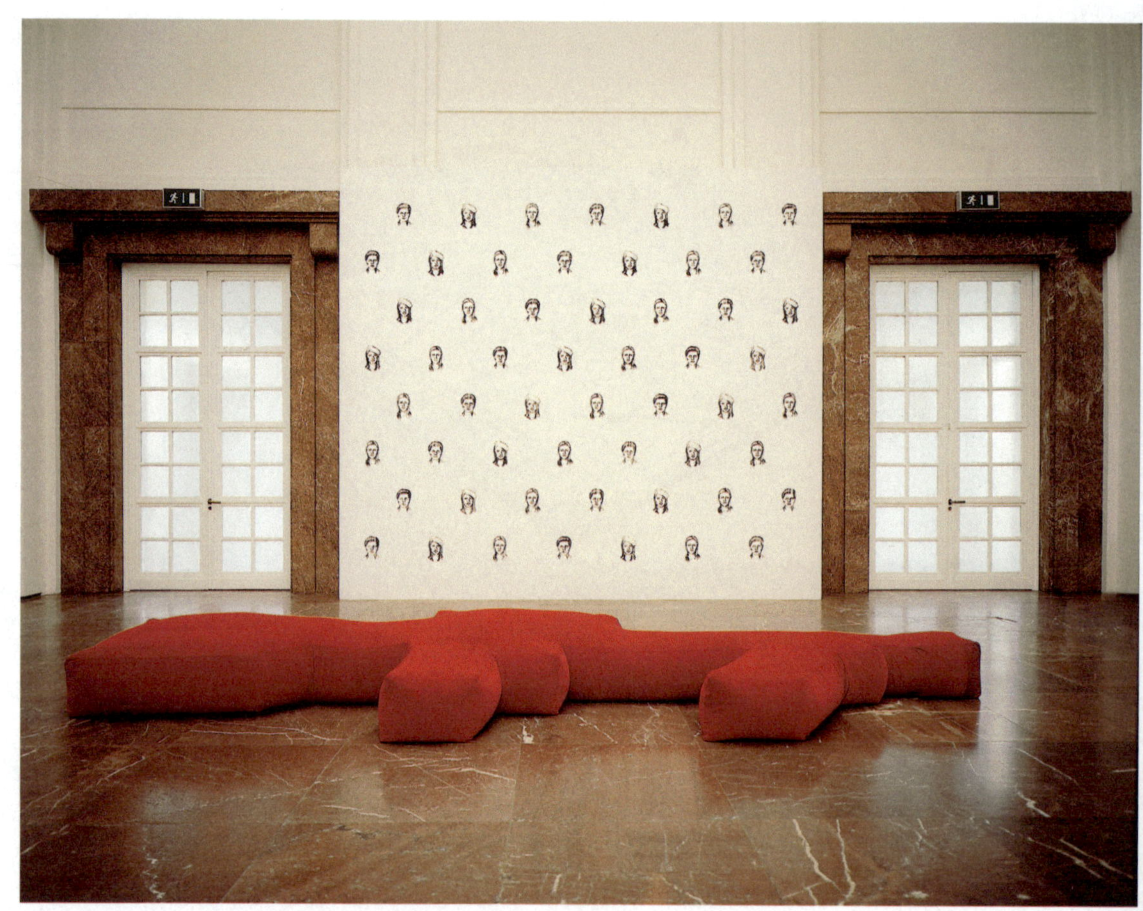

Declaration of Independence: Mossberg Model Bullpup, 1993 /
Goldman Bunke Moorman, 1994
Installation view Haus der Kunst München, 1994

Artist Talk:
Michaela Melián in Conversation
with Joanna Warsza[1]

JOANNA WARSZA: Dear Michaela, back in 1989, a pivotal year for the re-organisation of the Eastern-Western European dichotomy, you went to the Munich police and asked them to have a sketch made based on various sources of a person you were particularly interested in and who is also a red thread of this exhibition: namely Tamara Bunke / Tania. Who is Tania, a woman born in Argentina, socialised in the GDR, working in Cuba, a female counterpart to Che Guevara? Why is she so important to you?

MICHAELA MELIÁN: I first learned about Tamara Bunke, aka Tania, from the organisers of a concert I played with my band F.S.K. in East Berlin in 1989, just a few days after the opening of the Wall. I was surprised because we in the West knew nothing about her, we only knew Che Guevara. Even though there is such a close connection between the stories of these two people, they were remembered separately and differently in the two parts of Germany. That intrigued me, which is why I devised the exhibition *Subjekt, Prädikat, Objekt* (*Subject, Predicate, Object*) more than 30 years ago. And now I have revisited this theme for the KINDL exhibition **Red Threads**.

Who, then, was this Tania? Let's start with a short biography: "Tania" was actually called Tamara Bunke. Her parents were active in the communist resistance in Berlin before they fled from Germany to Argentina in 1935. Tamara Bunke was born in 1937 in Buenos Aires. The family lived in a German-Jewish neighbourhood, where German emigrants had been settling for many decades. From 1945, they were joined by fascist Germans who came to Argentina via the so-called ratline. Che Guevara's father had an office in the same neighbourhood. In 1952, when Tania was 14 years old, the Bunke family returned to Europe, to the GDR. At first, they lived in the newly founded Stalinstadt (today Eisenhüttenstadt), later in Berlin-Prenzlauer Berg. After graduating from high school, Tamara studied Romance languages and literature at the Humboldt University in Berlin. It seems, however, that she was always homesick for Argentina, she didn't like life in Germany, she wanted to get away and applied to leave the country. When Che Guevara visited the GDR with a Cuban delegation in 1960, Tamara accompanied him on his tour of the country as his translator. From then on, she was determined to go to Cuba to work on the revolutionary transformation of society there. How exactly she organised her departure for Cuba in 1961 is not entirely clear. At any rate, she flew from Prague to Havana with the ticket of a dancer from the Cuban National Ballet who had defected to the West. I have read many times that this departure was also interpreted as a defection.

---

1   The conversation took place on 11 May 2022 in front of a live audience at the KINDL – Centre for Contemporary Art in Berlin.

In Cuba, Tamara immediately joined the revolutionary People's Militia and wore their uniform with the beret. Her activities focused on the literacy programme and the advancement of women, but she also worked as a translator. Around 1963, she was probably recruited by Che Guevara for the Cuban secret service, with the aim of spreading the socialist revolution to the South American continent. She received intensive military and intelligence training, including several months of travelling through Europe under different identities–to South Tyrol, Hamburg, Frankfurt, Munich, West Berlin and Prague. Finally, in 1964, the Cuban secret service planted her in Bolivia as an agent under the guise of the ethnologist Laura Gutiérrez Bauer, in order to provide strategic support for the underground struggle that Che Guevara wanted to launch there with his troops. Tania / Laura lived undetected in La Paz as a researcher on indigenous culture. She loved the music of South America, the folklore as well as the popular hits, and could play the guitar and accordion herself. This love of music opened many doors for her. She even managed to penetrate the entourage and family of President René Barrientos, that is to say, the highest social circles. She used the tape recorder and the camera she needed for her agent work to document the music culture of the High Andes. And she regularly hosted a radio programme for rural women. These broadcasts then included coded messages for the guerrillas. Meanwhile, Che Guevara's underground fighters marched through rugged jungle terrain in the Andes and tried in vain to recruit the rural population for their struggle. For them, Tania was one of the few contacts to the outside world. When Tania was unmasked in March 1967, she joined the 60 or so fighters as the only guerrillera and marched with Che Guevara's detachment for five months until, while crossing the Rio Grande with some of the guerrillas, she was ambushed and shot dead. The Commandante Che Guevara and the rest of the detachment were tracked down and captured a few weeks later, in early October, by the Bolivian military with the support of the CIA. Except for five who managed to escape, all of the guerrillas were executed.

J: You have made a quasi detective-work about Tania, but as you said in the brochure accompanying the KINDL exhibition her portrait can only be made from "unreliable narrations, forged documents, cover identities, projections, and suggestive documentation, and constantly eludes understanding." How did you trace her, which kind of sources did you use, and in which form? You have portrayed Tania in a number of sound pieces, but also in a mural at the entrance to the exhibition. And those threads, both the sound and the visuality, accompanied by meticulous research, always make a strong substance of your work. In fact, as an artist, you both studied the cello and painting. Therefore, your exhibitions can be experienced in space and in the acoustics. Can you talk about your multilayered portrait of Tania in the composition and the wall painting?

M: I started working on the exhibition by producing the music, that is to say before I decided exactly which works would go into the exhibition. For this, I compiled a collection of international protest songs from the labour movement, including *Bella Ciao, Guantanamera, Wir sind die Moorsoldaten*, the *Internationale*, the national anthem of the GDR and the Cuban *March of the 26th of July*. I recorded the melodies and the accompaniment of the pieces with the synthesiser to be able to fill the individual tracks with sounds of instruments I cannot play myself and then to complement these tracks once more with analogue instruments played by myself. From this material, I then developed a composition in such a way that only fragments of the musical pieces can be heard in very different instrumentations. These fragments often overlap, but many people will still recognise the popular songs. The whole composition is based on a sample from the song *Tania / Eres guerrilla y flor*, (Tania / You are Guerrilla and Flower) very well-known in Venezuela, from the second album, published in 1974, of the singer Alí Primera, whose songs were declared part of Venezuela's national heritage in 2005. Here, Primera sings quietly in a high, thin voice, delicately accompanied by the echo of a horn that shortens the melody, a drawn-out, wistful "Taaaniaaaa". In addition, there are a lot of samples from archive recordings of indigenous Andean music, great rhythms created with various percussion instruments and melody fragments played on the siku (pan flute). With their unique sound, these archive recordings always bring their own specific space into the composition, the movement, the location, the ambience of the musicians and also the temporality of the historical recording. I always try to combine different layers in my compositions, including digital and analogue recording processes that are preserved in the sounds. In that sense, then, the piece **Tania** is a densely woven stretch of music. In the exhibition, the piece is heard in its entirety every hour; it lasts 9:30 minutes. Distributed among the 16 loudspeakers arranged in the room, each instrument has its assigned place. Then, only fragments of the piece can be heard, in ever-changing intermediate mixes, sometimes half a minute, sometimes three minutes long, interrupted by short pauses. These fragments of the piece wander through the room, from one loudspeaker to the next, guiding visitors through the exhibition with their ears, leading them around the circumference of the mural. With its sounds and the way it is installed and played, the composition thus defines this exhibition space.

J: Speaking of the wonderful mural, one of the main pieces of this exhibition, which uses a similar method of different traces and bits and pieces. Can you guide us just a little bit inside this piece? How it echoes both South American murals, but also socialist mosaics, the best-known of which include *Aus dem Leben der Völker der Sowjetunion* (*From the Life of the Peoples of the Soviet Union*) on Karl-Marx-Allee, where Bunke's parents lived.

M: When I first entered this exhibition space on the second floor of the KINDL, I immediately noticed these windows overlooking Berlin, especially the former East Berlin. And so I had the idea of picking up this theme Tamara Bunke / Tania again, this thread, after 30 years. The historian Isabel Enzenbach did some research for me and gathered all the new information that has emerged over the past 30 years. She went to the Stasi archives, for example, because Tamara Bunke was allegedly also assigned by the Stasi to spy on Che Guevara as an informer. Today, in addition to the publications from the GDR, there is a lot of material including academic papers, documentaries, journalistic articles, literary works and biographies, from Cuba, Bolivia, Germany and the USA, among others. Time and again, the authors in the texts of the most diverse provenance come to the conclusion that Tamara was in love with Che Guevara and that this is why she became a guerrillera. But this cannot really be deduced from the available facts. Speaking of facts: There are no personal effects of her except a few old photos, a blank diary, some letters and the photos she took herself while with the guerrillas. Anything published about her in the GDR has been controlled and formulated mainly by her mother. There are other versions of this story told in Cuba, still others in Bolivia, Chile, Peru and so on. In South America, Tania is a public figure and revered as a heroine. As there are no direct personal testimonies from her since her unofficial departure from the GDR, this has opened the door to speculation.

When I was combing through the material compiled by Isabel Enzenbach, I didn't take notes, I drew them. I ended up with 250 drawings of this complex— that is, people, architectures, landscapes, topographies, and so on—which I then collaged into a huge drawing, corresponding in size to the free-standing wall at the centre of the exhibition space.

It was clear right from the start that the mural was to go on this wall, which is the first thing you see when you come out of the elevator into the exhibition space. Only the edges of the wall had to be rounded so that the drawing could run around the wall as if it were a loop without a beginning and end. I did not arrange events chronologically in the collage but rather wanted the multiple links between the individual drawings to take effect. For example, in the middle of each of the two sides of the mural I placed this pole with public speakers and the cables extending out from Havana in all directions: acoustic information transmitted to the public through these public speakers, and the power cables and telephone lines that form a kind of network which we are, so to speak, right in the middle of. I took up this motif directly for the installation here in the exhibition. Alongside indigenous architecture and works of art from the Museo Nacional de Arqueología de Bolivia, we find the Karl-Marx-Allee or the Brandenburg Gate, Tamara's apartment in Havana, schools named after her in the GDR and Cuba, a mountain of harvested potatoes from the Andes or Tamara as a dancer in Treptower Park, all amalgamated into one image.

Next to a drawing of Tamara Bunke as Tania in uniform is Patty Hearst, who adopted the nom de guerre Tania after being kidnapped by and later joining the radical left-wing Symbionese Liberation Army (SLA); in the picture, she is seen robbing a bank with her kidnappers. Tamara Bunke, in turn, got her fighting name from the Moscow schoolgirl Zoya Kosmodemyanskaya, who called herself Tania as a partisan. Zoya Kosmodemyanskaya committed arson attacks on SS bases during the Second World War and was hanged at the age of 18. The drawing was made after a photo, very famous especially in the East, in which Kosmodemyanskaya is forced to wear a kind of placard on her chest that says "arsonist" while being led away by SS men for execution. In the GDR there were a lot of institutions named after Zoya Kosmodemyanskaya, and there were postage stamps commemorating her.

And here we come full circle again because some of the early works that can be seen in this exhibition are drawings of stamps, which of course never existed in this form. Postage stamps accompany social discourse, they represent cultural appreciation and literally bring them into circulation. They are cheap but can become collectors' items at the same time.

J: It's a kind of an affective archive, a kind of mental map of your 30 years of research. Can you speak a little bit about the techniques because it's something of a mural but maybe also of a mosaic, and how was it actually made?

M: I had realised some murals with this technique before, the translation of a drawing into small square dots. Viewed as a whole from a distance, the mural looks as if it were made of small square mosaic stones. The closer you get, however, the more the drawing dissolves into individual pixel dots, so to speak, and you can see that the small squares have been stamped onto the wall. To create the mural, my drawings were projected onto the wall using a projector and then the stamping was done using the projected lines as a template. The entire set-up team helped with the transfer to the wall. The translation of my drawing is therefore teamwork, which is also reflected in the result, because everyone held the small stamp differently, applied the paint to the wall at a different speed, sometimes with more, sometimes with less pressure. Of course, an association with the murals and mosaics at Alexanderplatz in Berlin, for example, is intentional, but with the decisive distinction that the *Tania* mural does not formulate a mission, a message, but rather functions like a data storage medium. Each dot, each pixel carries information that is stored next to other information and relates to it. This also corresponds to the process that precedes the mural: I read, watch films, browse the internet, listen to music, have conversations, collect, arrange and reject. And in the same way, when transferred to the wall, the originally fine drawing inevitably becomes abstracted, simplified, more perforated, more open.

J: Back in the early 1990s, you went to the Munich police and asked them to make
a memory drawing of Tania based of the sources you had. However, for this
kind of police database, only "male" facial features based on racist stereotypes
were available. And it's a like with the revolutionary memory where Che Guevara
is so well remembered, while she is not. Can you speak a little bit about this
encounter with the police and these male facts and threads, and how to contra-
dict them in the memory work?

M: I started collaborating with the police sketch artist of the Bavarian Criminal
Police Bureau (LKA) in Munich when I read an article about him in the *Süd-
deutsche Zeitung*, around 1989/90. Just like me, he had studied at the Academy
of Fine Arts in Munich, only much earlier. I contacted him and his department
then agreed to collaborate with me as part of its public relations effort. At the
time, the police sketch artist of the LKA had started to make scans of his existing
composite sketches in the course of digitisation and had used these scans to
develop a simple computer programme that allowed one to very quickly click
together individual facial features to create a portrait. The newspaper article had
showcased this programme and reported that many police stations in the
Schengen area worked with these hand-drawn face fragments.
I started from the premise that any portrait naturally always represented a projection of the person producing it onto the person being portrayed. And at
the same time, from a feminist perspective, I am critical of the artist's signature
of male genius expressed through the hand. Or in other words, men formulate
the canon of art history by drawing, painting, or sculpting women. How can the
idea of what someone looks like be translated into language and this description
then be fed through a system, through a machine, to create a portrait of that
person?
That the police computer's programme had been provided exclusively with
drawings of male facial features I only learned when I sat down for the session
with the police sketch artist. At the time, this was explained to me as follows:
violent crimes with unknown perpetrators were a male domain, whereas female
perpetrators were more likely to be found in domestic, private, family or
terrorist environments. These facial features, charged with attributions, give
the portraits a somewhat hard and androgynous quality. But then Eve is already
sculpted out of Adam's rib in the biblical narrative.
I selected twelve female figures who had been largely omitted from the historical
canon of art, politics, literature, or music. Based on photos of these women,
I formulated a description, which the police sketch artist of the LKA used to
create the respective portraits.
The first drawing created in this way was the portrait of *Tamara Bunke aka Tania*.
In her case, I had used the iconic photo with the beret, taken before she
joined the Cuban secret service as an agent, from the book *Tania La Guerrillera*,

published in East Berlin in 1973, as a model. At that time, I had to search for books in libraries and second-hand bookshops to find suitable photos of the women, because there was no internet as we know it today. Shortly after the fall of the Berlin Wall, the only material I had on Tania was the East German books. For these publications, Tamara Bunke's story had been adjusted to present her as a female counterpart to the western idol of Che Guevara for the youth of the GDR. In the 1970s, this probably worked for a while, except that there were no T-shirts with Tamara, but schools and kindergartens were named after her.

J: Let's go into memory work. One of your most poignant projects in the public space is *Memory Loops*, a counter-memorial, an acoustic monument in Munich, realised in 2010. How would you yourself describe this monument to the victims of Nazism, of the regime, with around 300 tracks that link to the personal or concrete stories connected with the sites in Munich? Can you speak about *Memory Loops*, but also wider, how do you think contemporary art can contribute to the memory work, in Germany and elsewhere?

M: In contrast to the previously discussed works, *Memory Loops* is a commissioned work. In 2008, I was invited to take part in the City of Munich's competition *New Forms of Remembrance and Commemoration. Victims of National Socialism 1933–1945*. What interested me about the invitation was the fact that the tender did not specify a location for which the memorial was to be designed. I had the feeling that this competition was only an ideas competition and that perhaps it was not really about realising a project. Since I live in Munich myself, I knew that although there had been repeated efforts and serious proposals for many years to get an appropriate memorial in Munich, nothing had ever come of it. And so I proposed the audio memorial *Memory Loops*, which does not require a fixed place in the urban space. *Memory Loops* is an acoustic memorial that covers the whole city with its audio tracks. You can listen to it anywhere in the urban space with your mobile phone because the audio artwork is deposited on the internet on a drawn topography.

In my concept, I proposed to evaluate interviews with contemporary witnesses that can be found in private and public archives and to produce them anew with young speakers. To do this, I wanted to work with experts in the city and get their advice on which relevant source material could be found in which archives. The jury then agreed that *Memory Loops* should be realised, one of the reasons being that this project would not be another "wreath-dropping site". But immediately a media shitstorm ensued, because some politicians and journalists wanted a visible memorial, they could not imagine that dignified remembrance work could be accomplished with a mobile phone. It is important to mention that in 2008, mobile phones and the internet were generally seen only as communication tools and not as a technology that could be used to make art.

Nor were the devices and possibilities back then comparable to the smartphones
and powerful internet of today, 14 years later. But for what I had envisaged,
the level of technology was sufficient. It was about a robust website that could
play 24 hours of audio material on a well-thought-out and designed interface.
All of this was only possible, however, because Bayerischer Rundfunk, the local
public broadcaster (which of course has a significant perpetrator history of its
own during the period in question), co-produced the project. This meant that,
on the one hand, I was able to use sources from their archives, and at the same
time, I was able to use their recording studios to record the voice tracks with
the actors and the children.

Because in **Memory Loops** there is not a single original sound track, everything
was newly recorded and produced. We worked out the manuscripts for the
texts with a research group of students of Jewish and contemporary history.
In the end, it was like a big film production, with a total of 120 people contrib-
uting.

J: What is a monument, what is a memorial, what is a counter-memorial, what
is a para-monument? How do you place this **Memory Loops** project, this
immaterial acoustic public sculpture within this grammar of remembrance in
the public sphere?

M: I would put it this way: a counter-memorial aims for a different kind of remembering–and that's why **Memory Loops** is a counter-memorial because it really
delegates the work and the responsibility of remembering back to the public.
Here, only those who wish to remember and who give **Memory Loops** of their
time will remember: you have to listen. To understand what reaches us through
the ear, one has to take one's time.

You can also see it as a para-monument, first of all, because it's invisible and
doesn't function in the same way as sculptures that inhabit the urban space
as placeholders for memory, which I may walk past for years and not know
what they were built for. **Memory Loops** also includes material that deals with
memory processes. In Munich, for example, there are no *Stolpersteine*[2] on public
ground because there were reservations against them from parts of the Jewish
community. For that reason, they only exist in the city where they have been laid
on private property. I have compiled a dialogue from interviews I found in the
radio archives from the perspective of the various parties, the descendants of
 the victims, politicians and local residents. This soundtrack, a short radio play
of a few minutes, is an example of a para-monument because it comments on
the concept of a monument or of remembering. This is how I would describe
a para-monument: an existing monument becomes the starting point for a work
by being reworked in some way.

<hr>

2   Literally "stumbling stones or blocks": Commemorative brass plaques embedded
in the pavement in front of the last address of choice of victims of National Socialism.

J: Now at the end, let's speak about softness in your exhibition. In its centre stands a sofa. A very soft piece of furniture, and yet it's a weapon. And apparently it spent 30 years in the depot, what is it and where was it all these years?

M: The **Mossberg Model Bullpup** (1993) was first shown at the Friedrichshof of the former Muehl commune in Austria in an exhibition on the theme of art and utopia. After the commune had dissolved and Otto Muehl was imprisoned, a symposium and an exhibition were organised there. For the room where the communards had held their action-analytical performances until just a short while before, I designed this sofa in the shape of a machine gun, made of red velvet–previously there had only been the smaller weapons as part of the works on **Tania**. I was familiar with these action-analytical performances from the Academy of Fine Arts in Munich. When I was a student in the 1980s, members of the Muehl commune, who presented themselves as a artists' group and some of whom lived in Munich, used to turn up occasionally to show film documentations of their performances in the large auditorium of the Academy, trying to recruit new members. I particularly remember the performances in which a large red velvet mattress was the centrepiece, which was then beaten and slashed by the performers, who were supposed to free themselves from their bourgeois background. That's what I had in mind when I designed this huge velvet mattress in the shape of a weapon–about 10 times the size of the original weapon and five times the size of the mattress in the film. A year later, the large **Mossberg Model Bullpup** was shown at the Haus der Kunst in Munich, in front of the central wall in the great hall, above which there used to be the speaker's platform specially built for Adolf Hitler.
It is always important to me that visitors can sit down, because that way they spend more time in the exhibition listening, getting involved, looking more closely. For this reason, I have developed a number of sculptures for exhibitions that can also be used to sit on, such as the **Mannheim Chair** (2015), which is also shown in this exhibition.

J: In the softness of the sofa, one can read the discourse about demilitarisation through art. And how can art be useful in all this introduction of an anti-imperial mindset, for example, would you have some kind of a closing statement around those? How do you feel, all these years you've been performing something, which maybe could be classed as what the Polish philosopher Ewa Majewska calls "weak resistance", i.e. the softness of resistance?

M: From the very beginning, I have been thinking about what art can do and what I myself would like to see in exhibitions. I would say for me that everything we do has political relevance, even though art certainly cannot actively change the course of the world. It can however be a voice in a discourse or a process. In a way, I would say, I am trying my hand at a different kind of history painting, unfolding something multi-layered and complicated. And in this aesthetic and mental space, the viewers can wander around and relate to what they see.

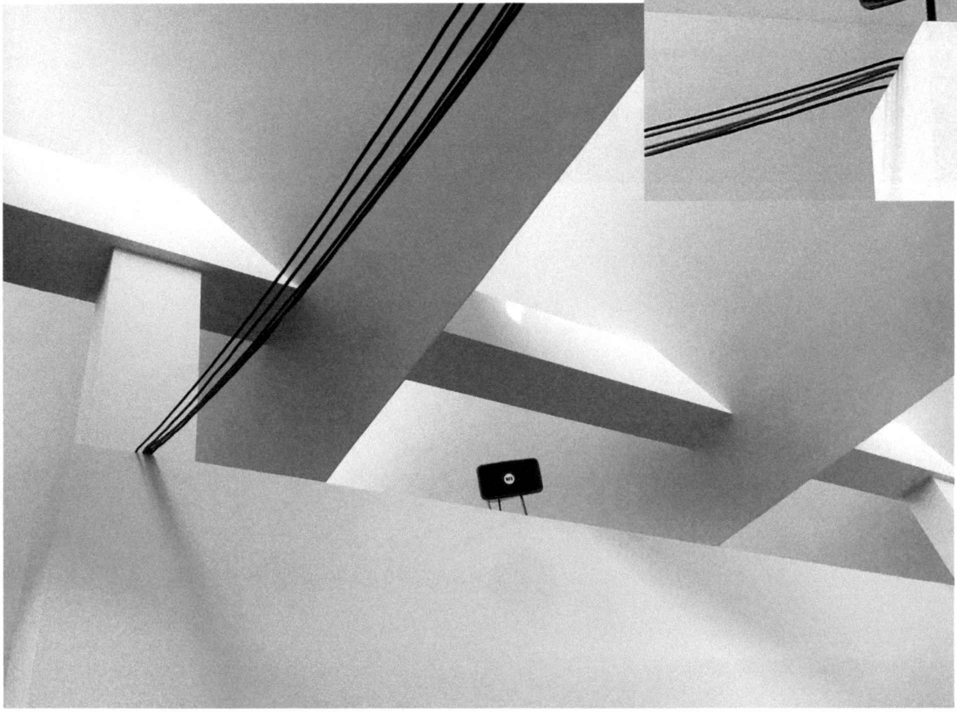

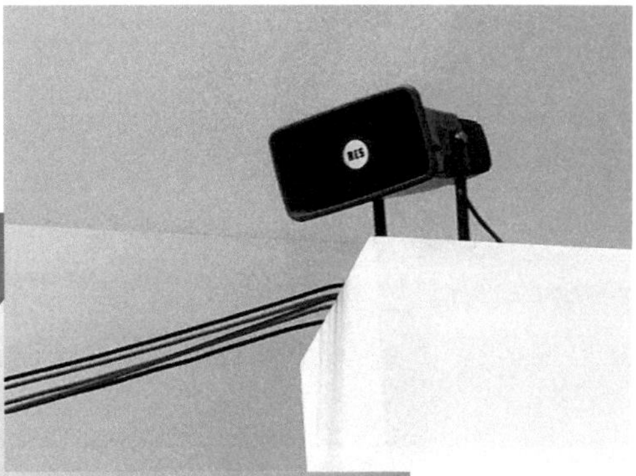

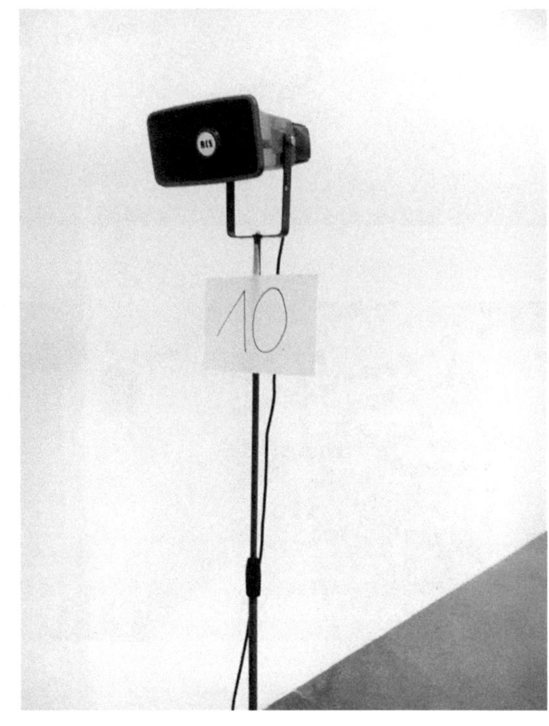

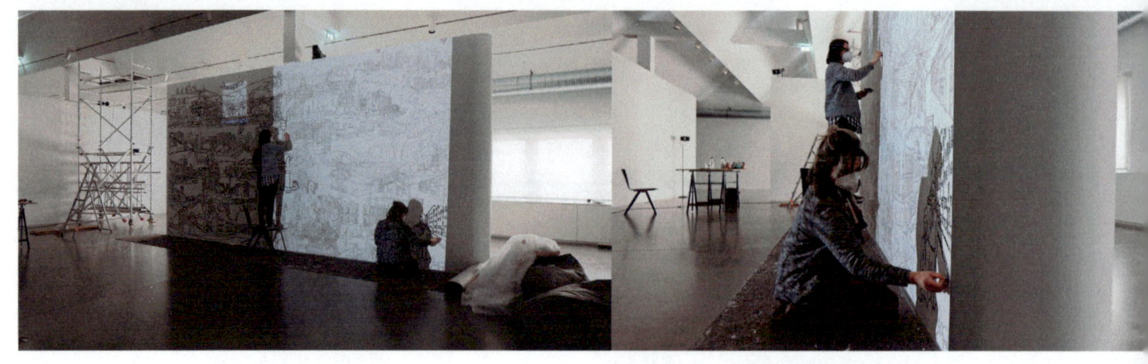

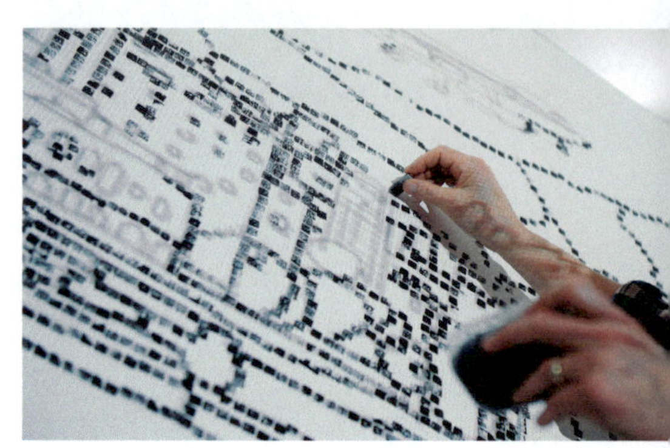

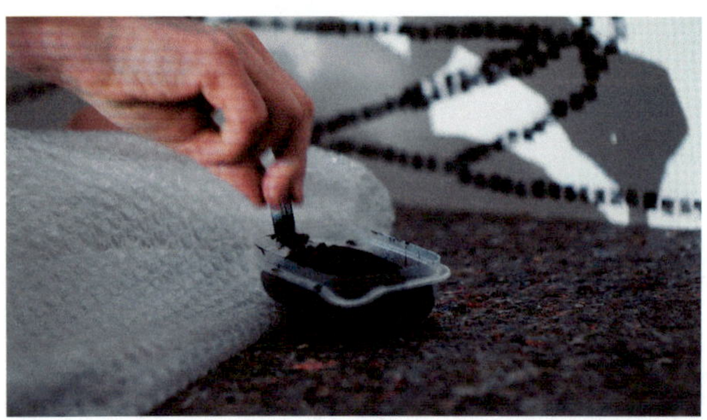

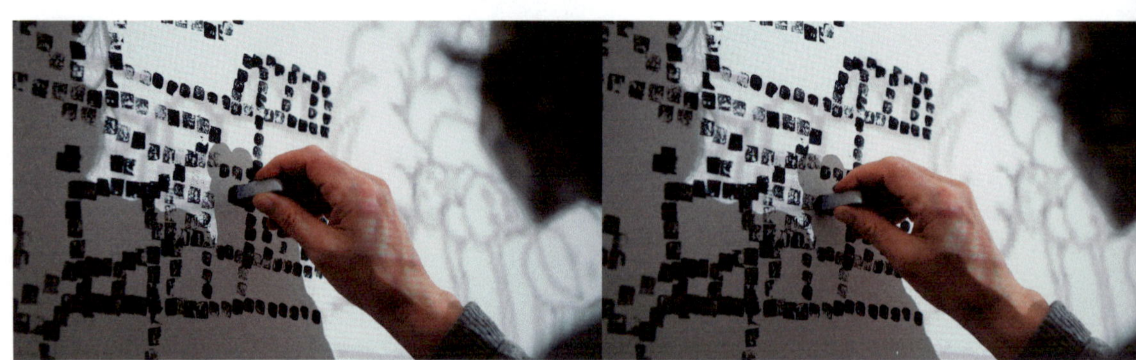

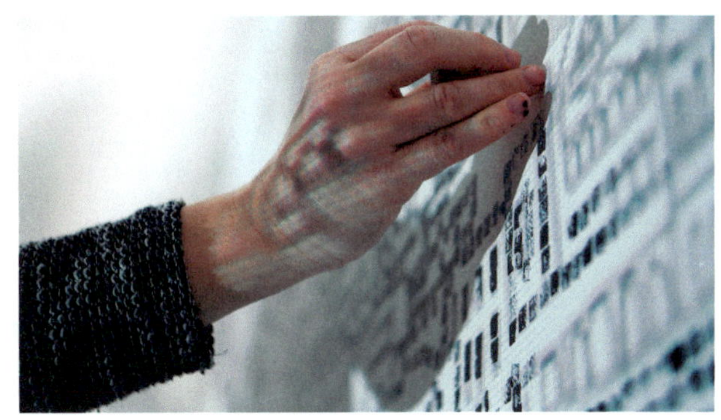

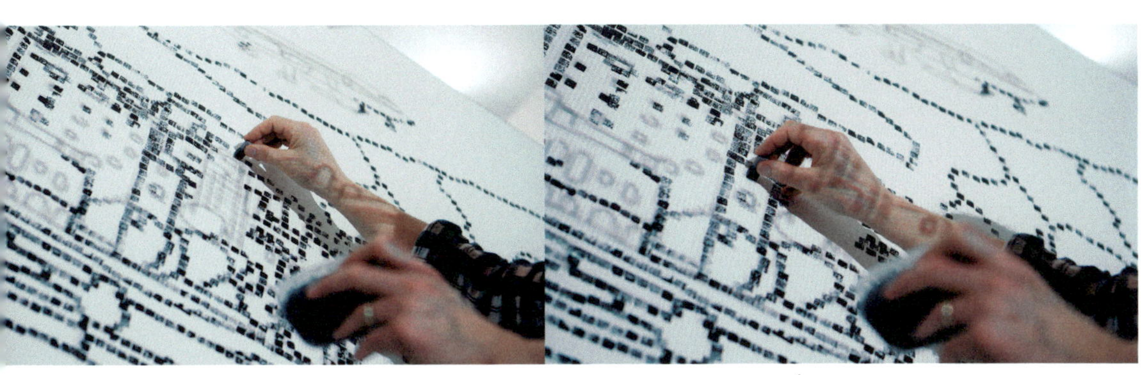

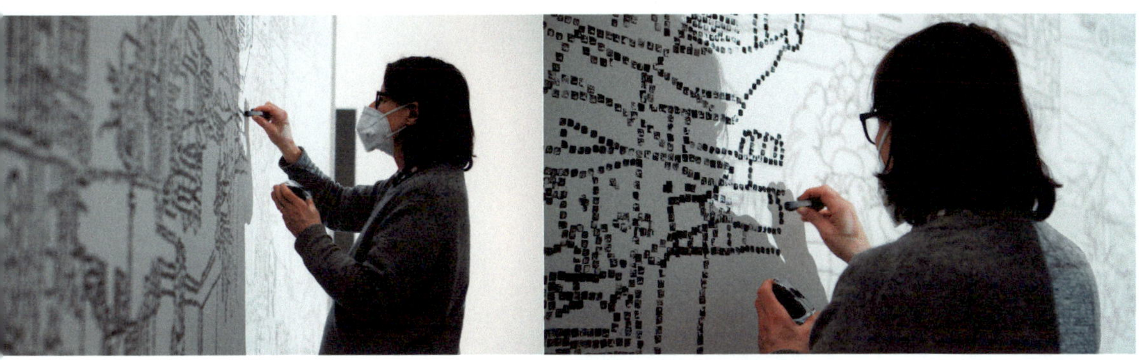

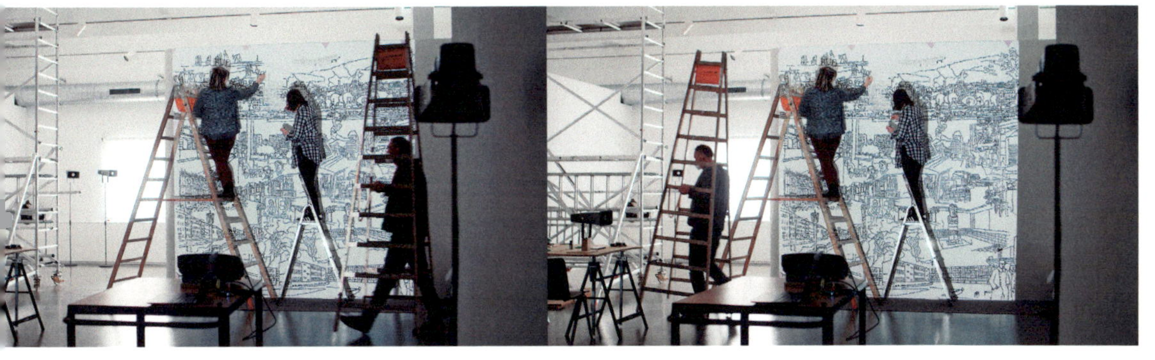

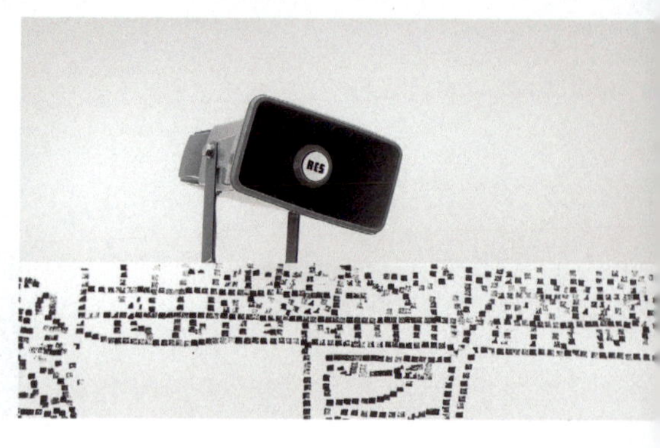

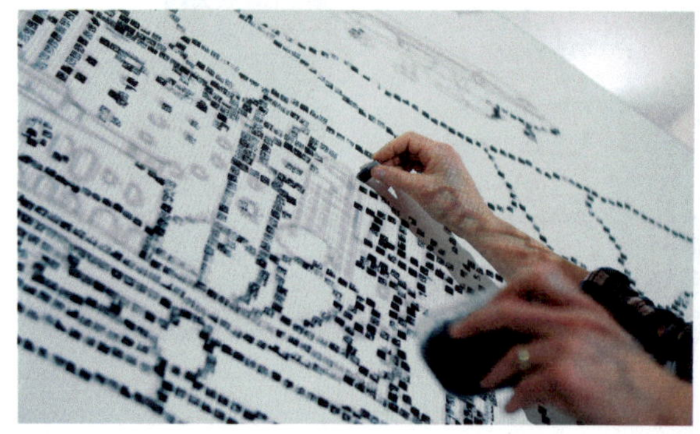

122   *Tania* (Mural, Sound installation)

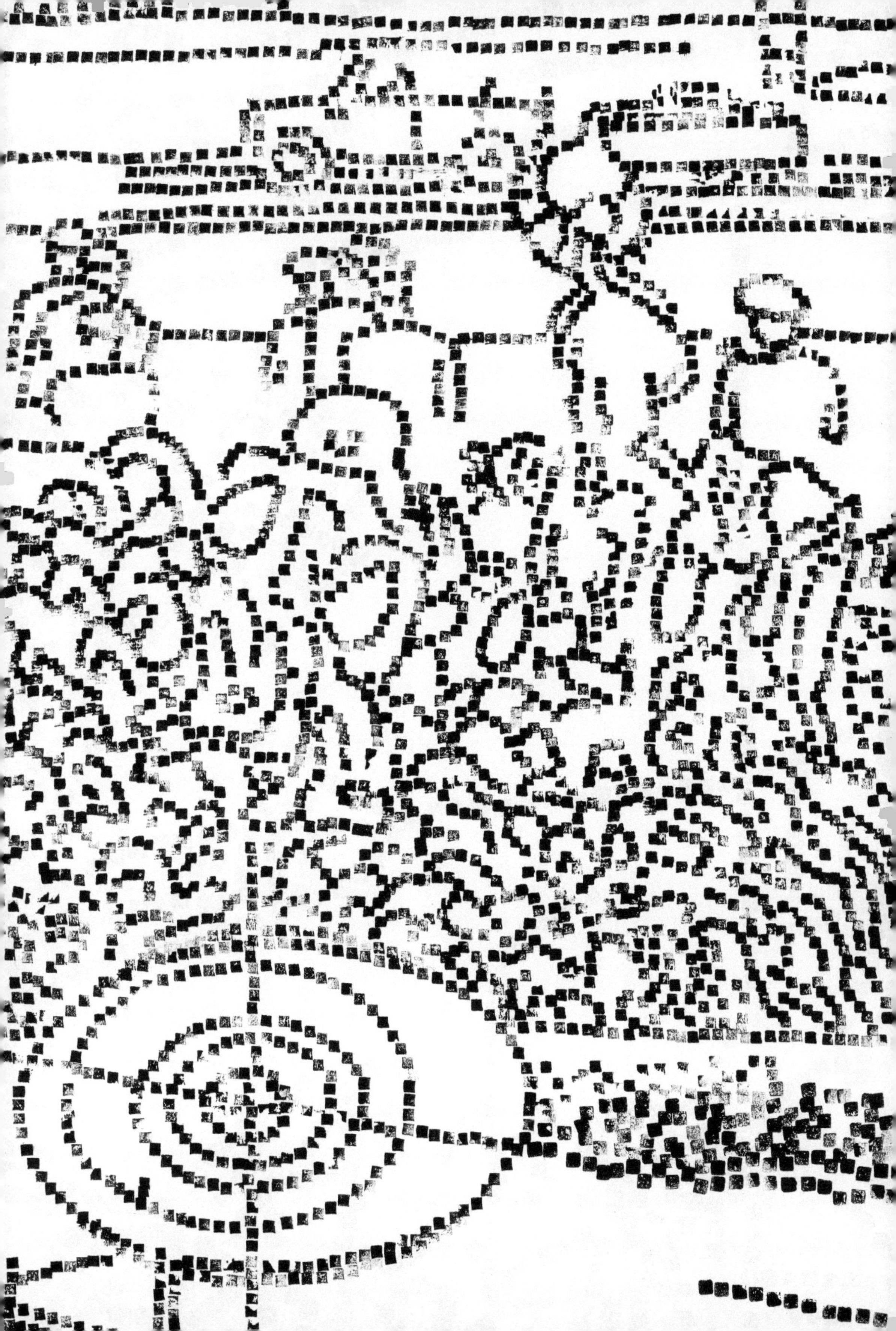

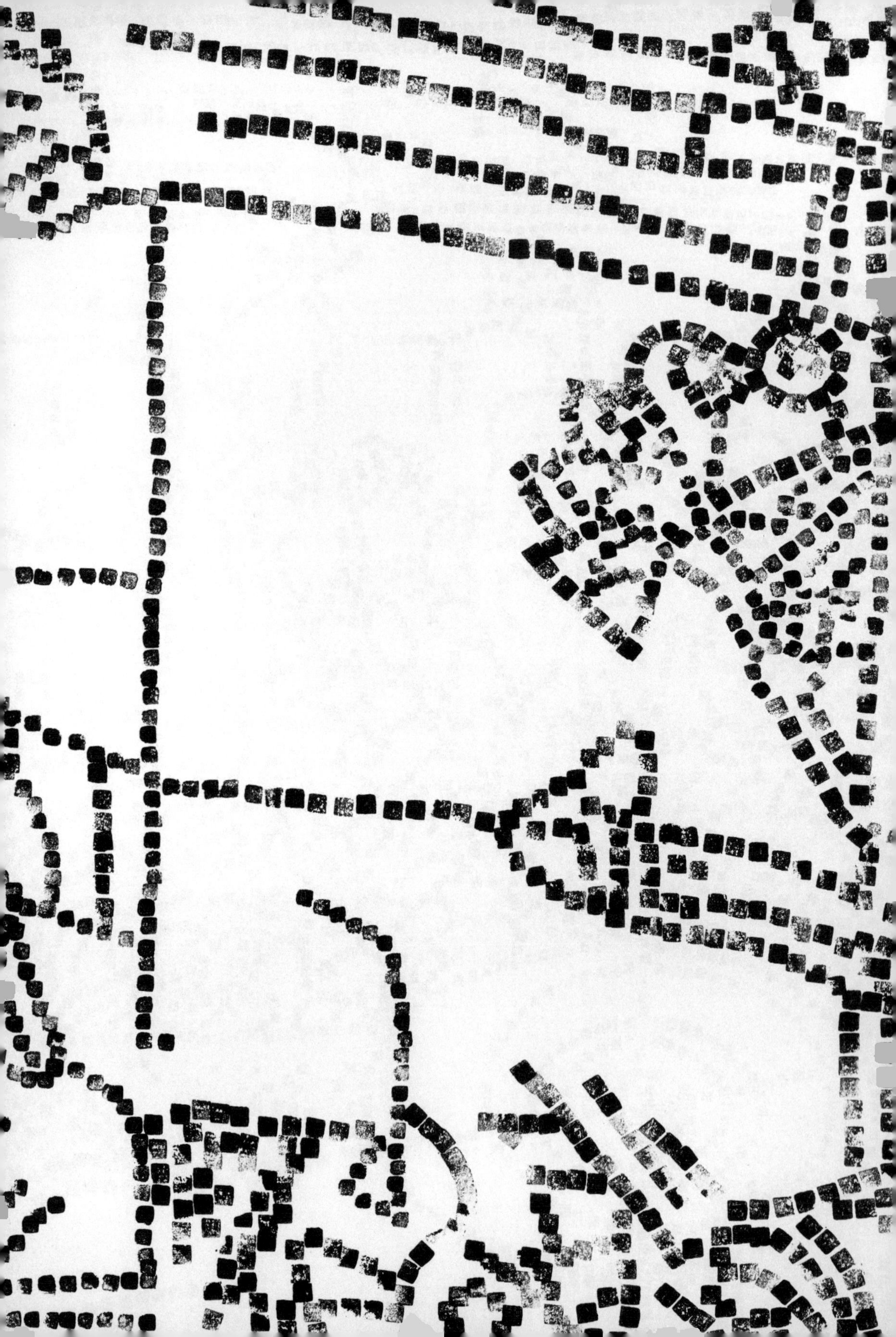

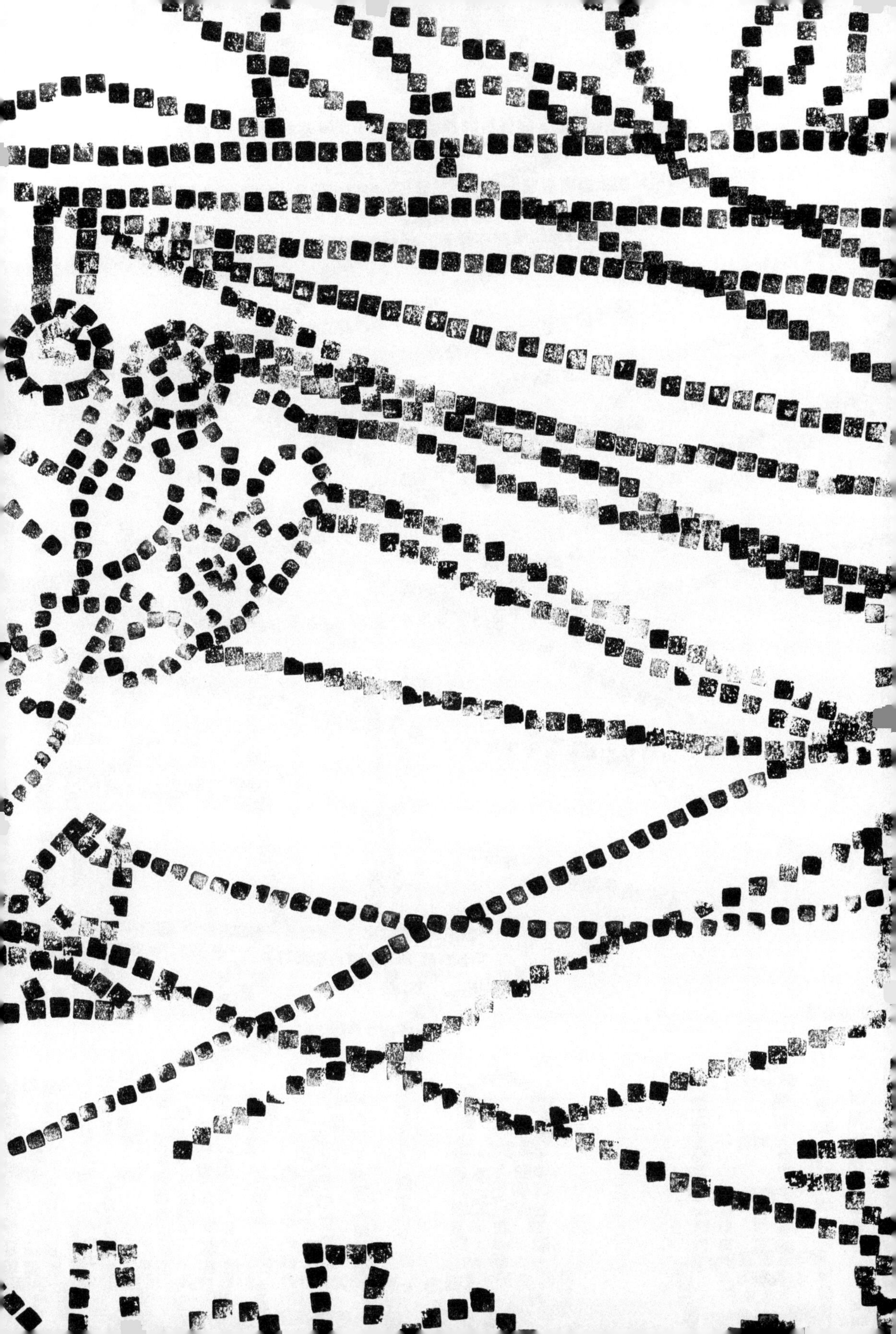

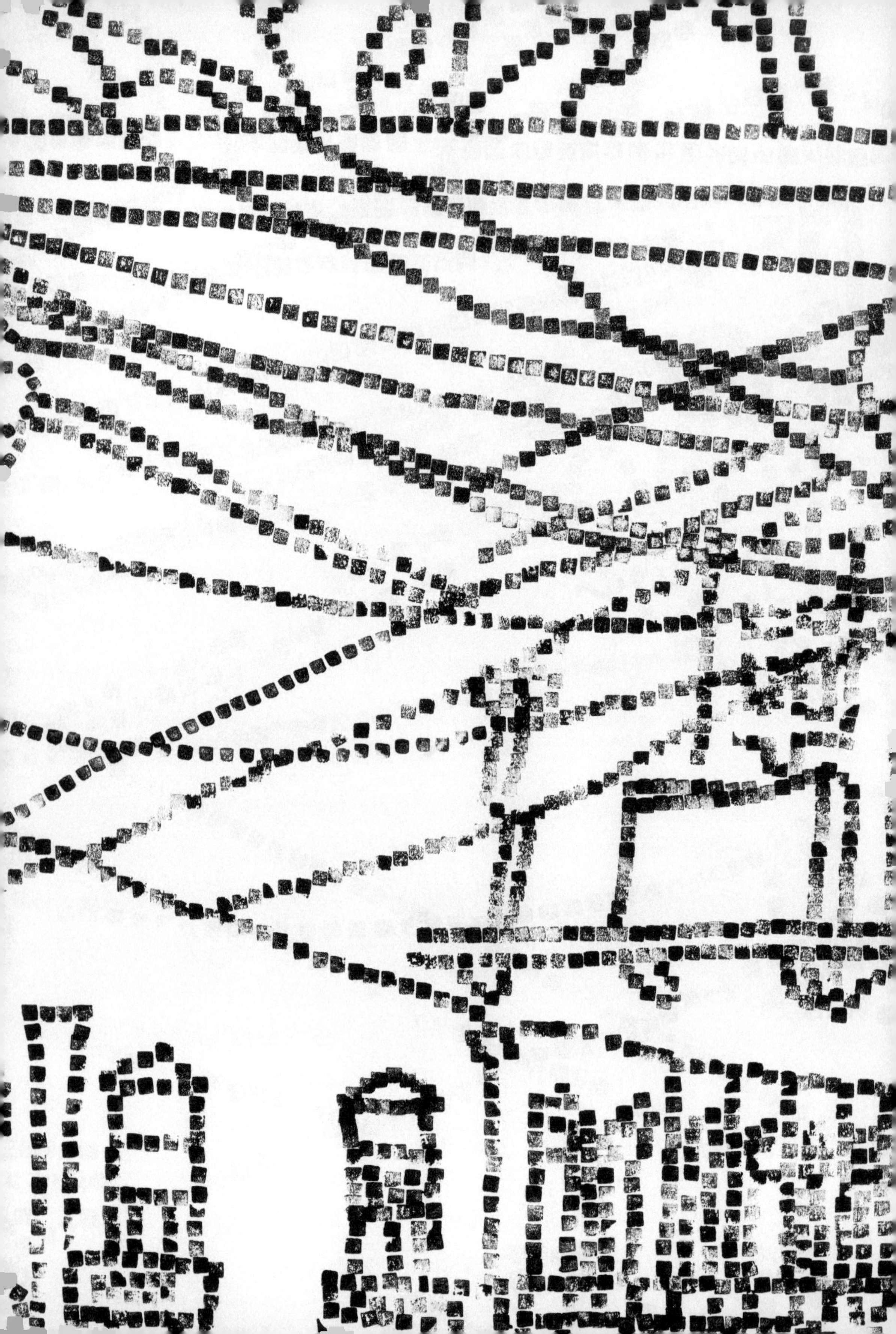

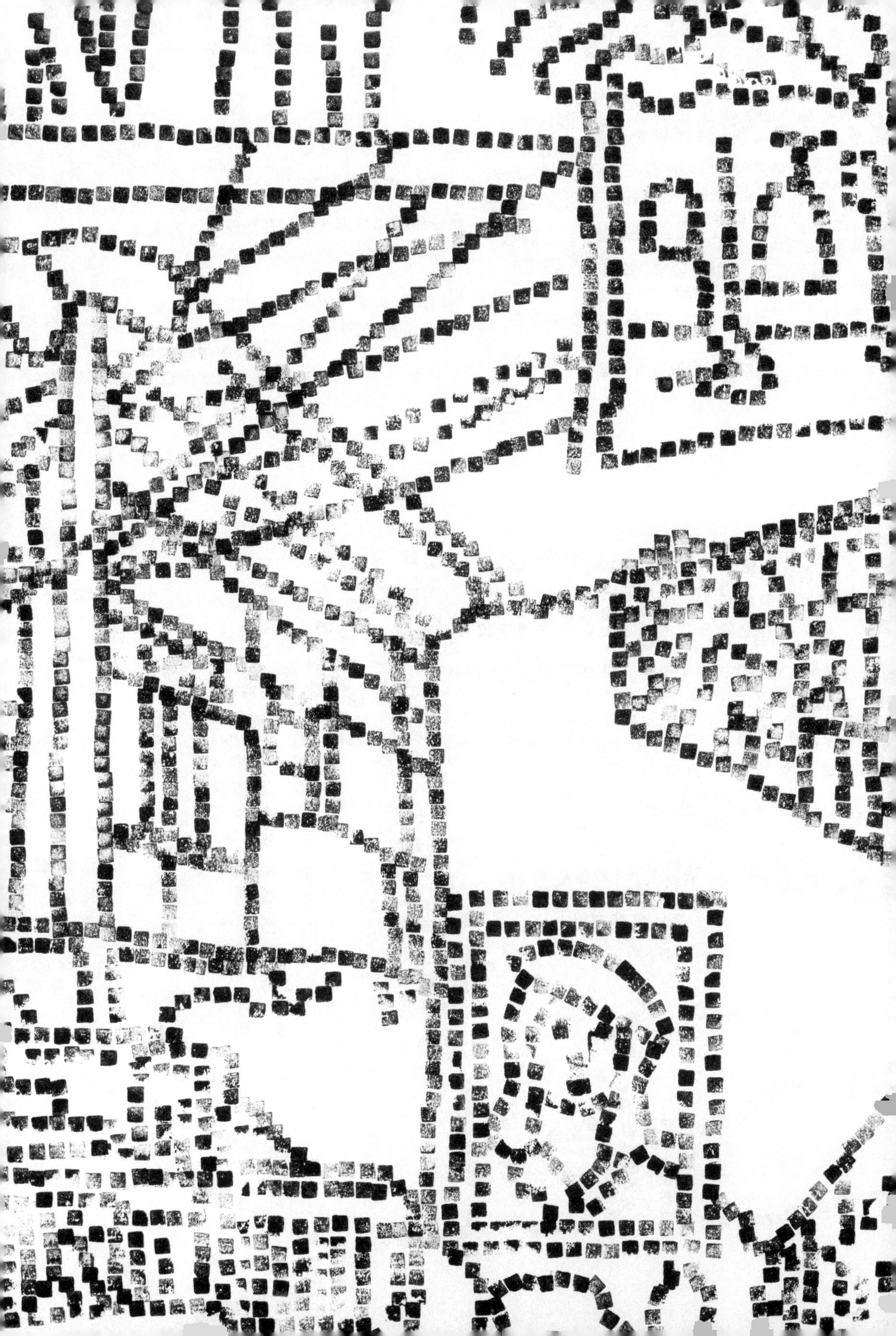

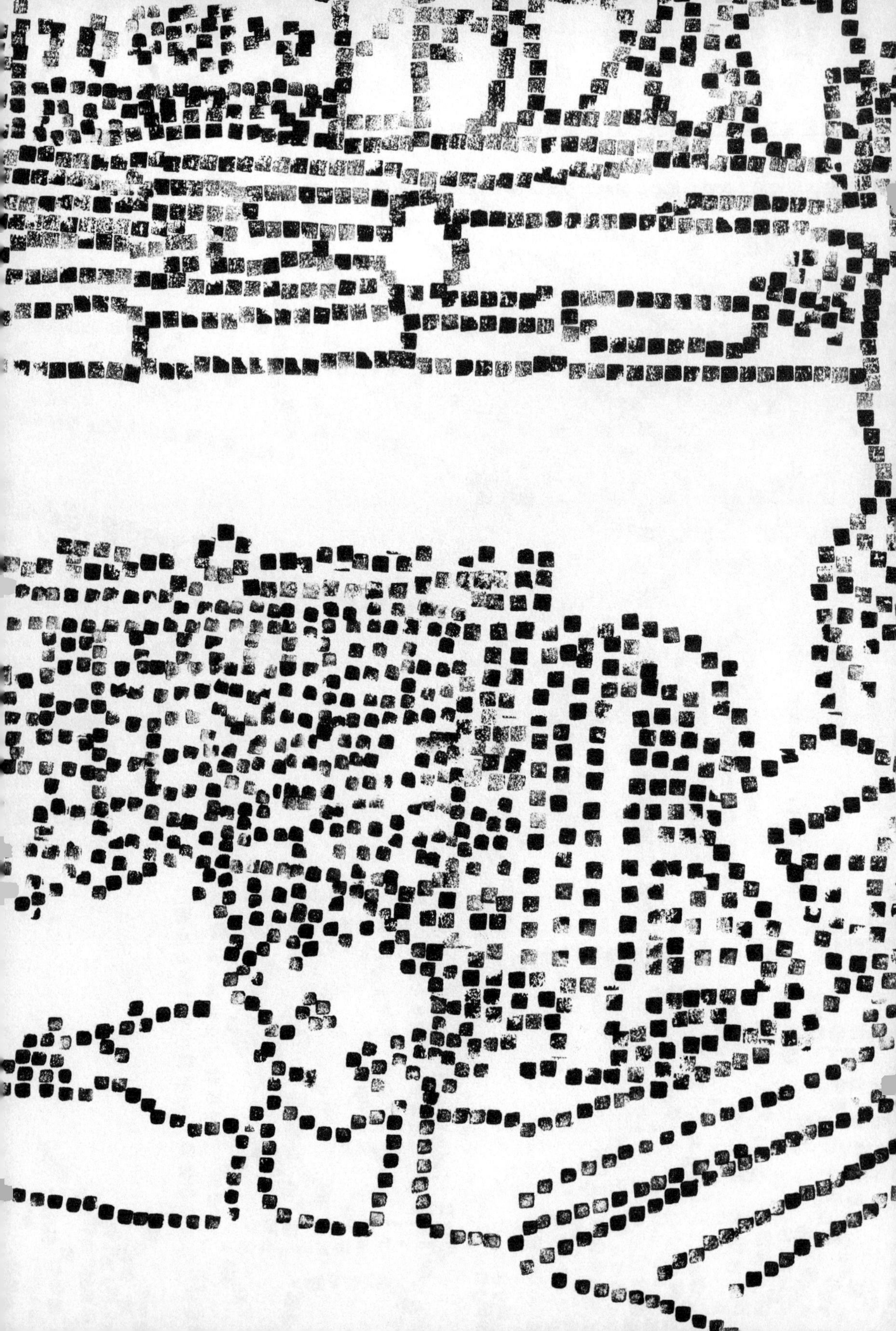

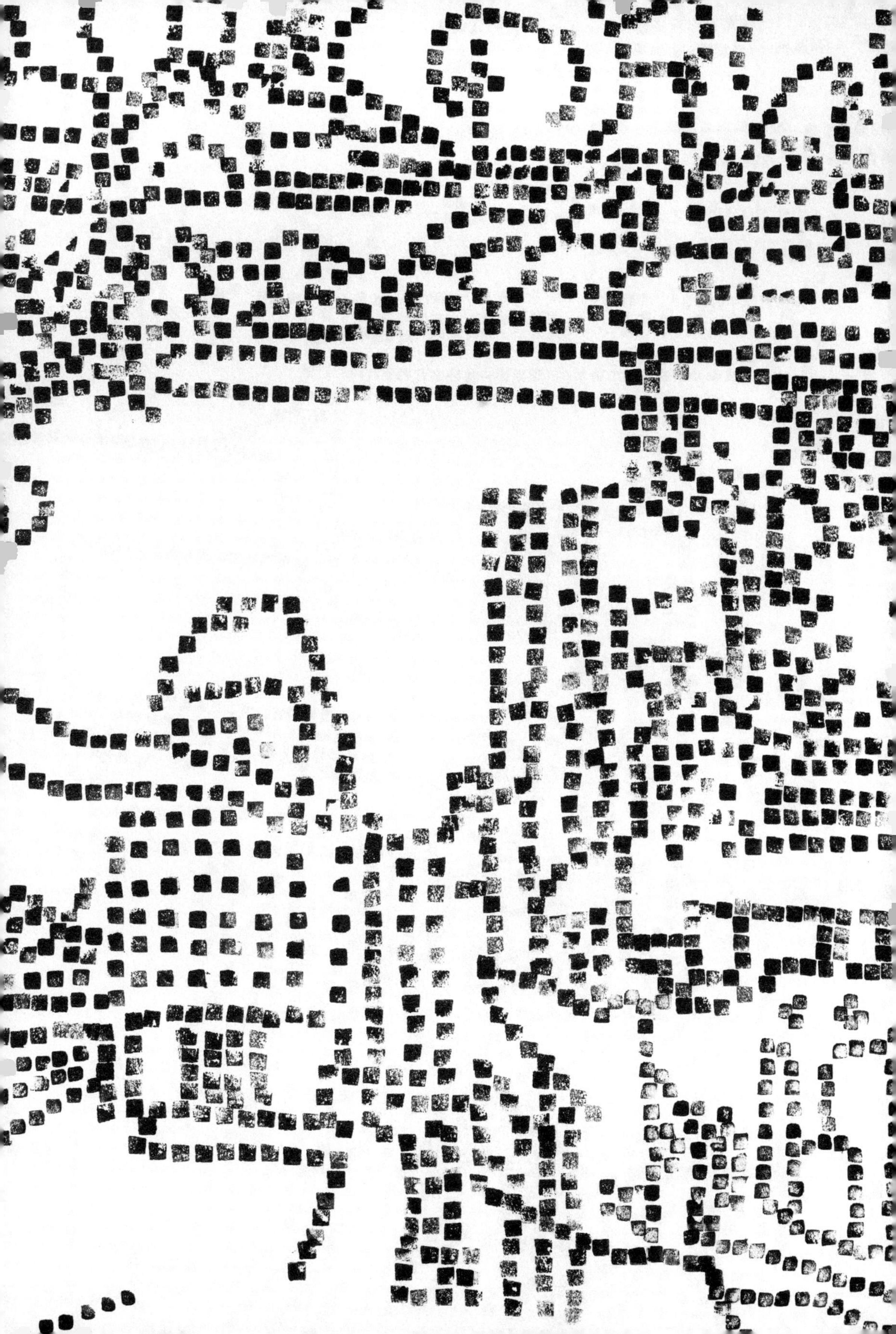

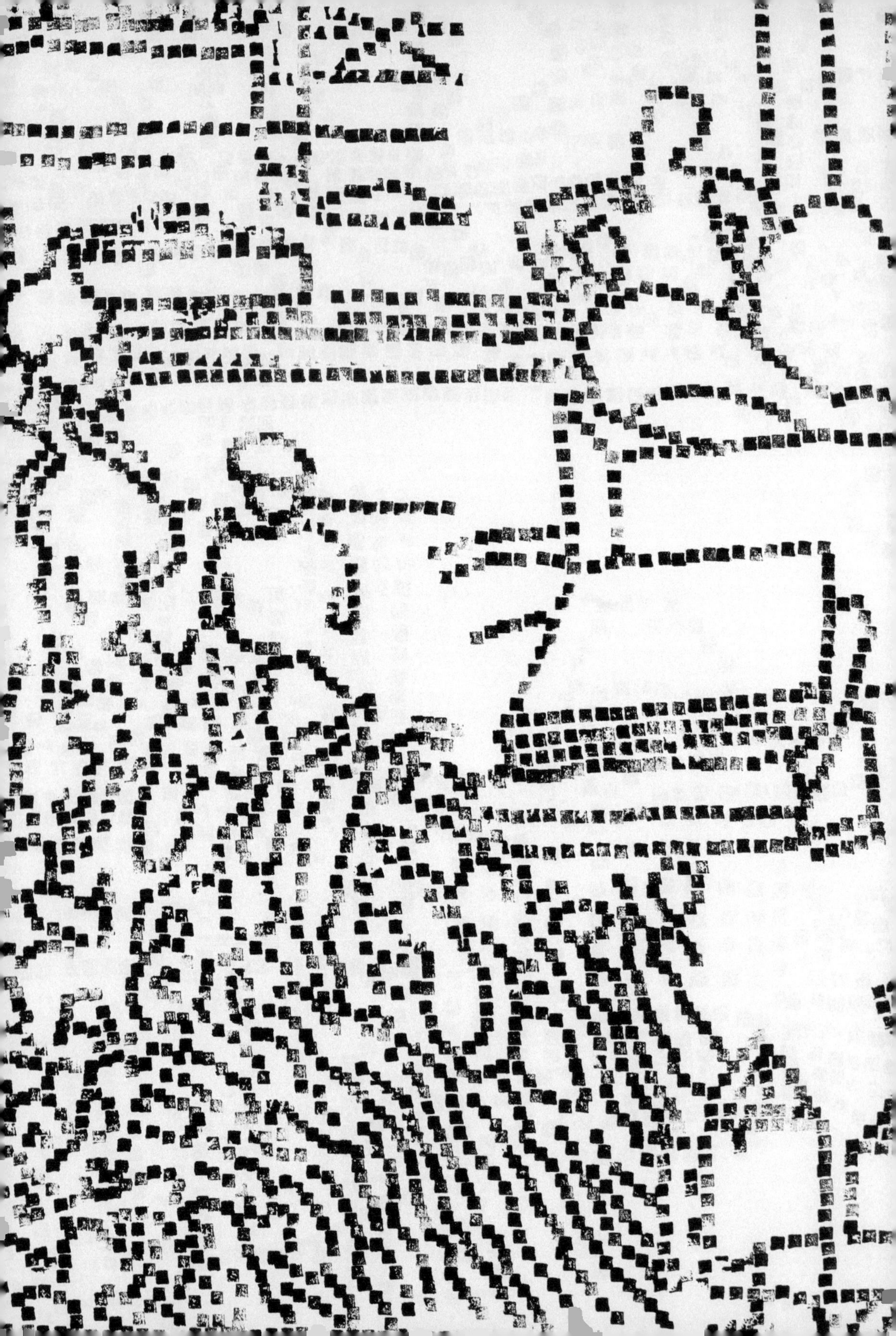

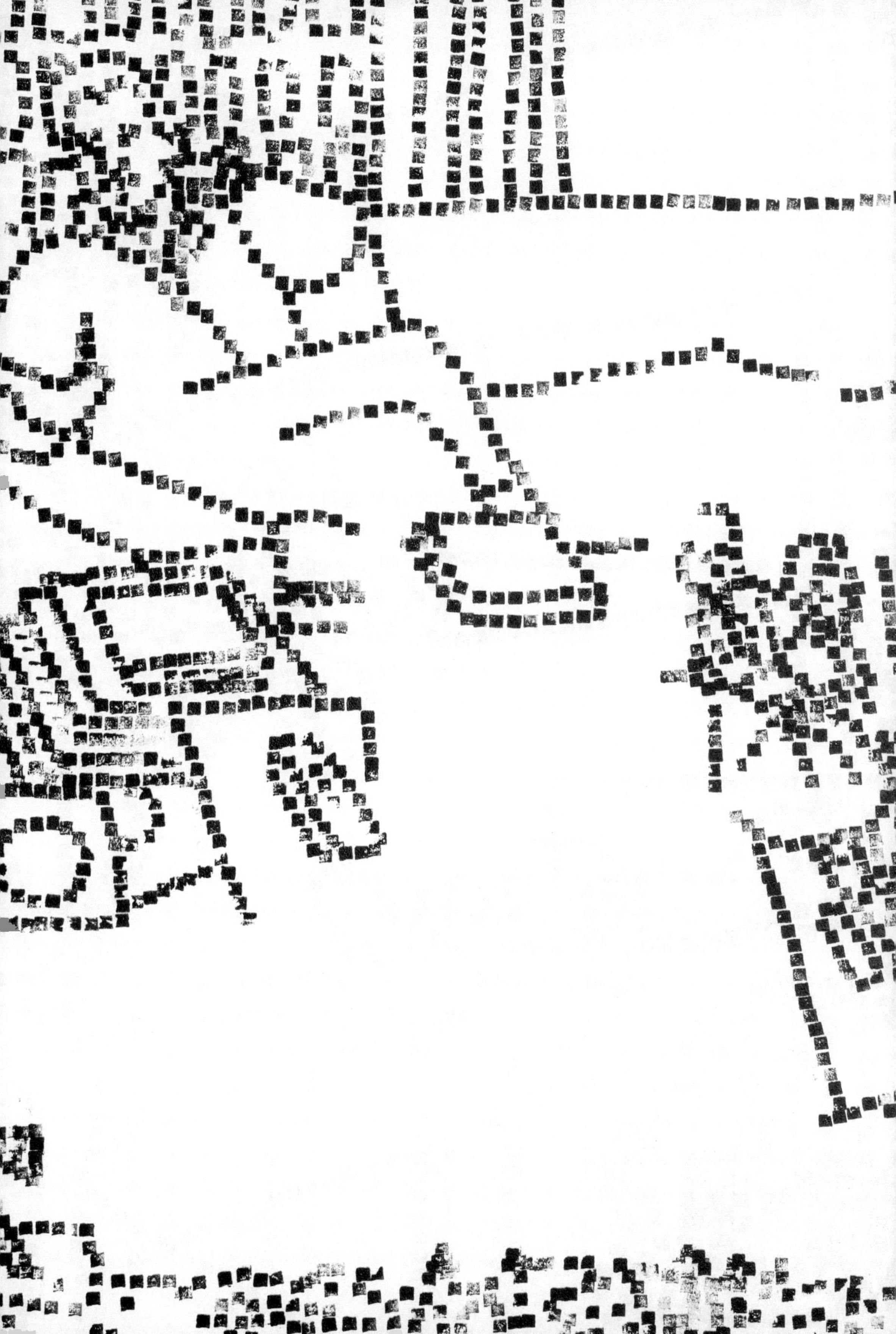

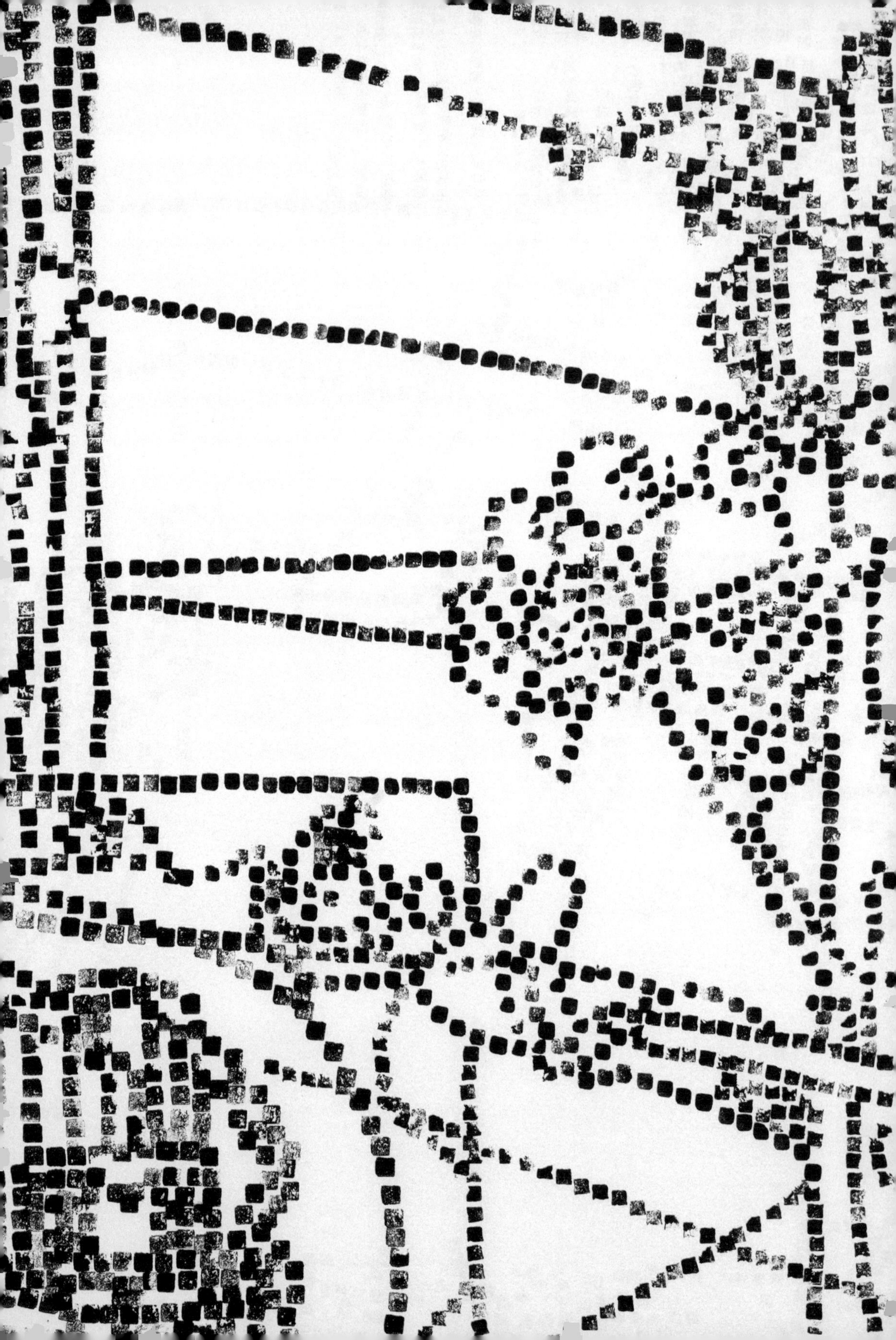

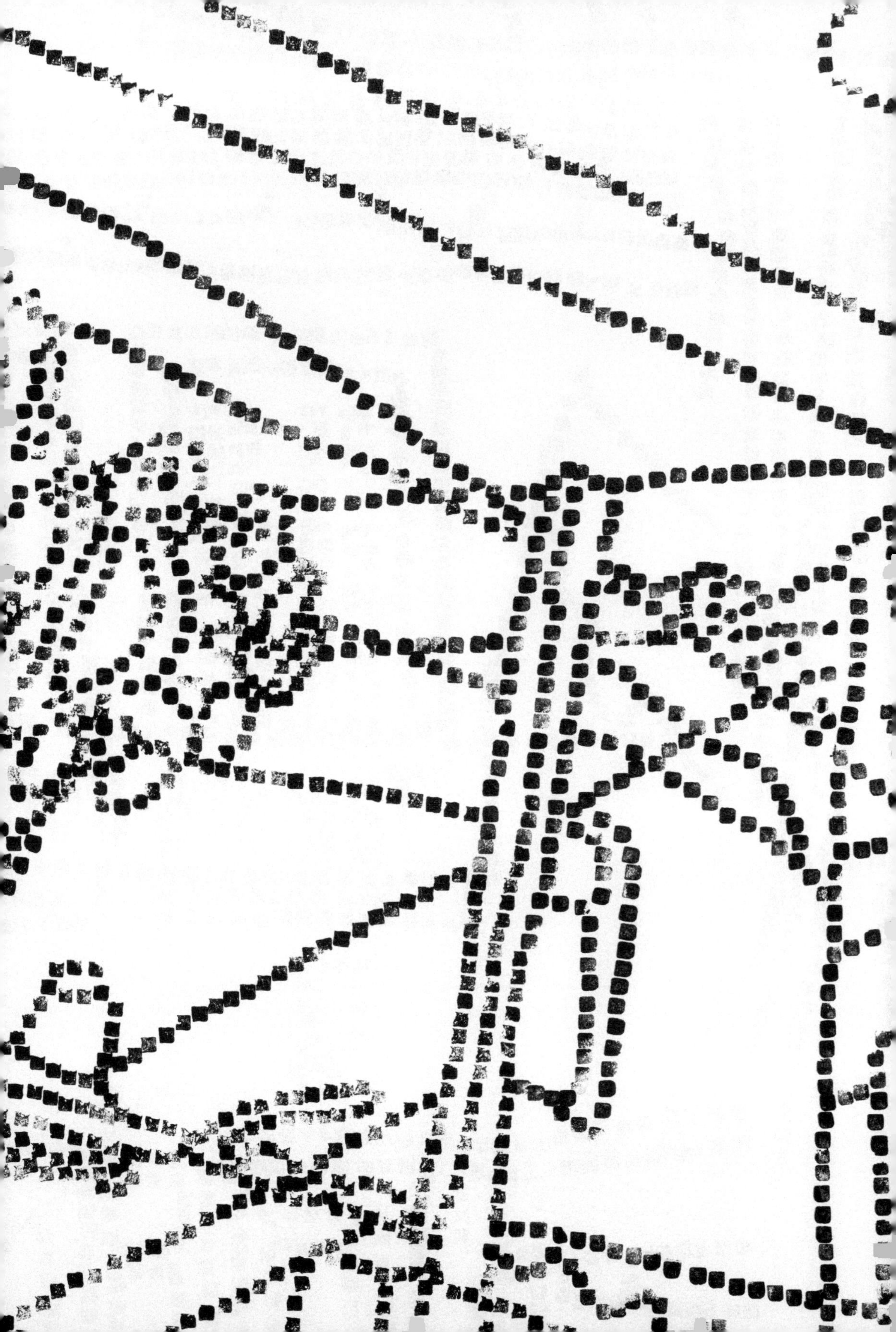

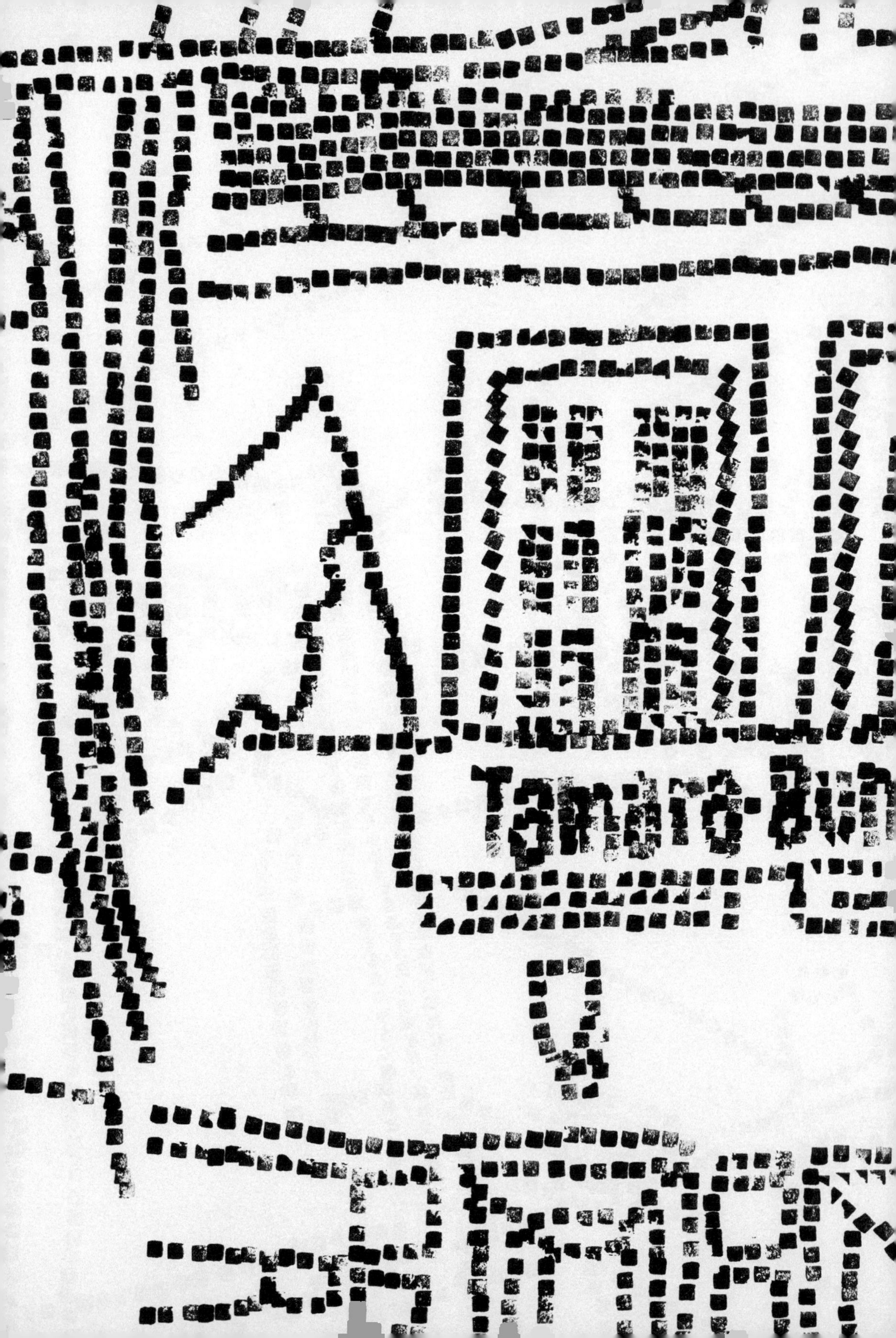
Tamara-Bun

Unterschied

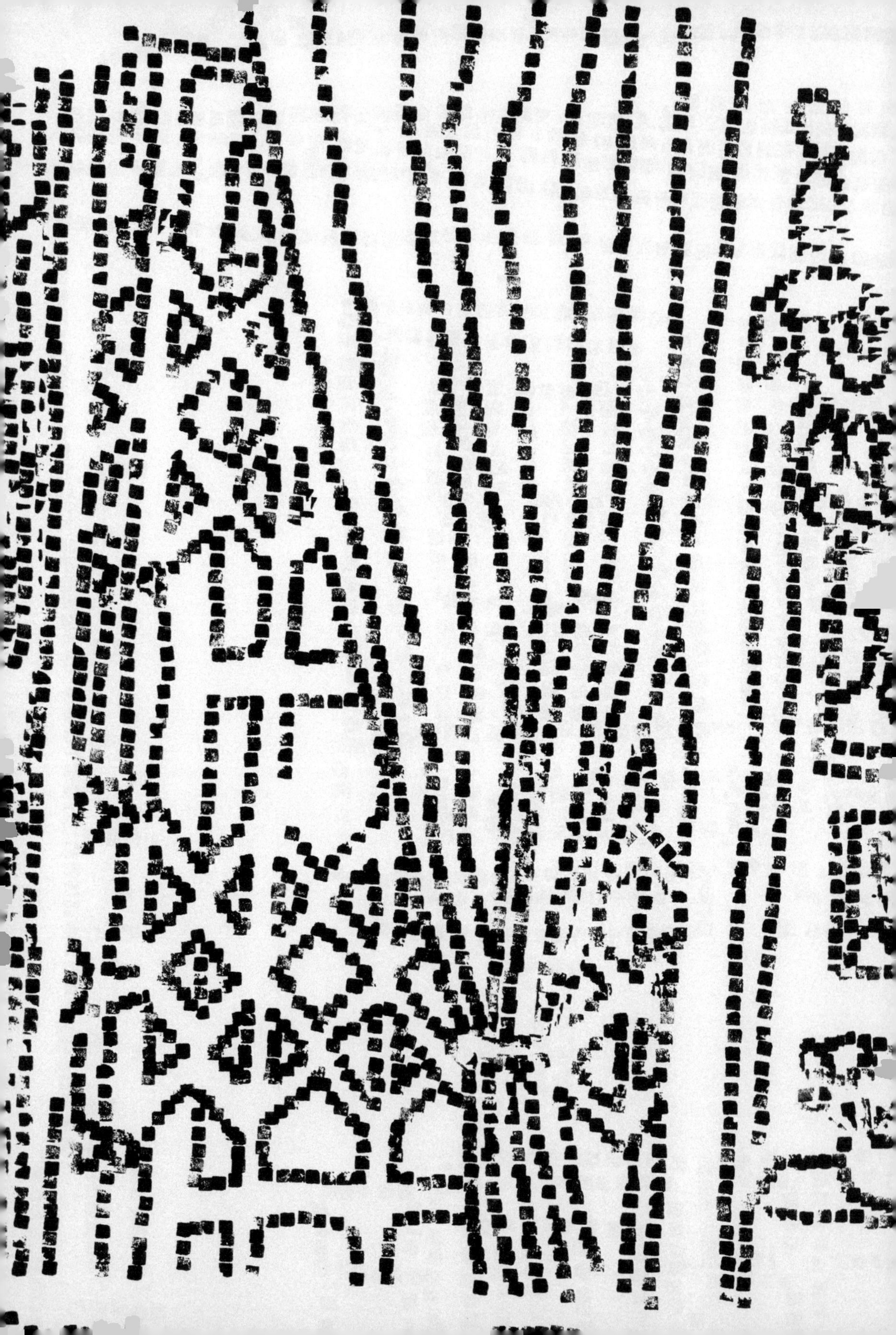

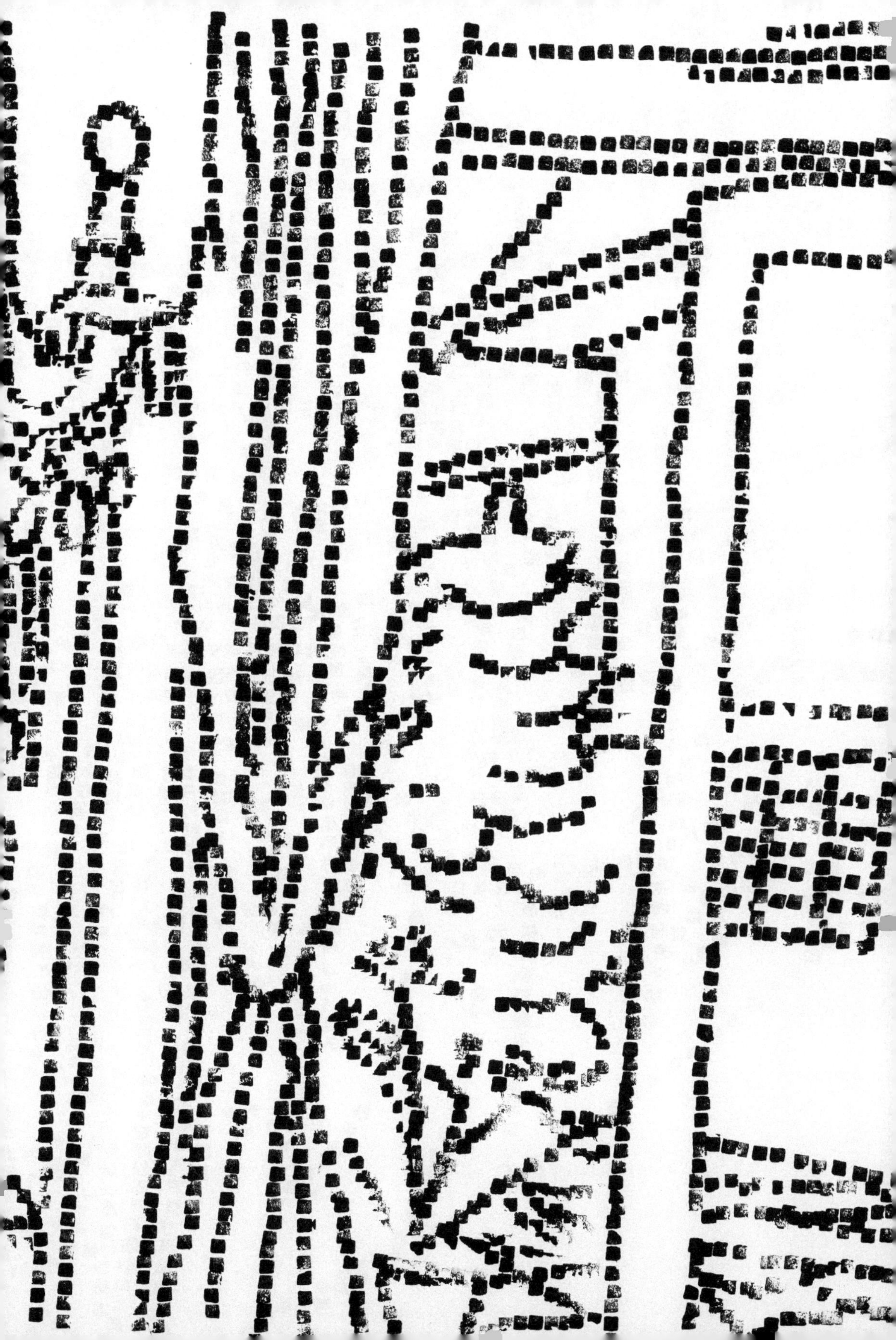

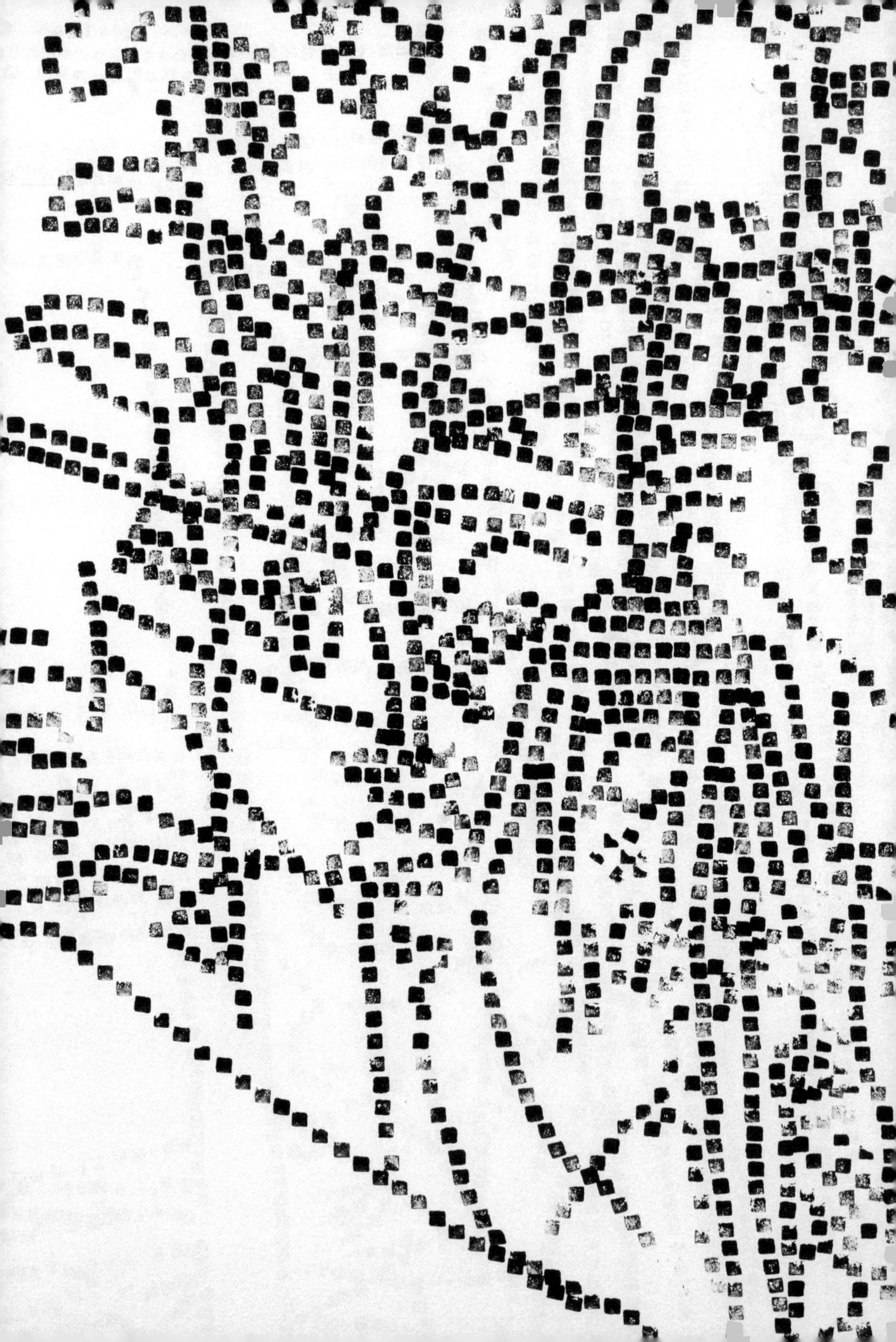

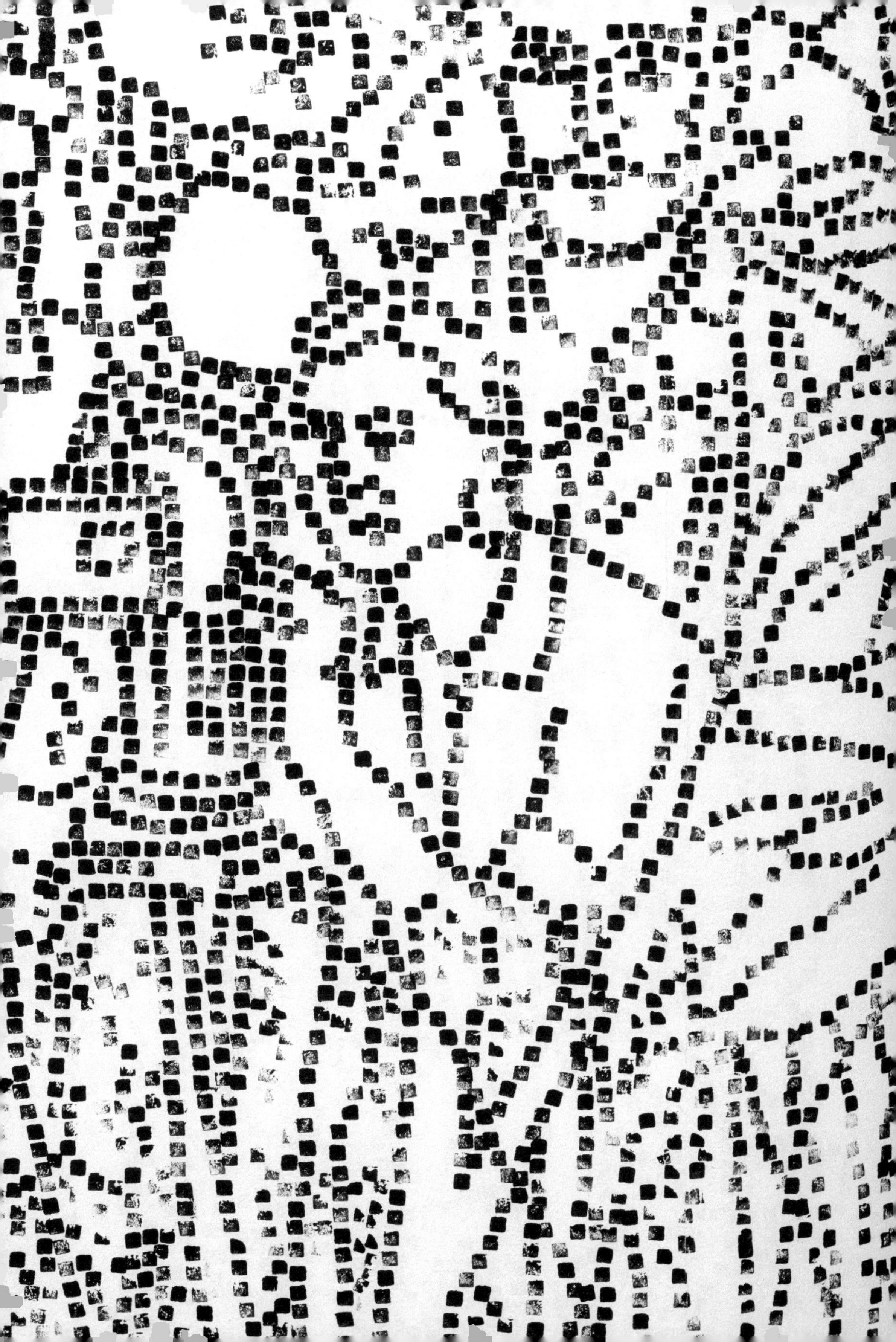

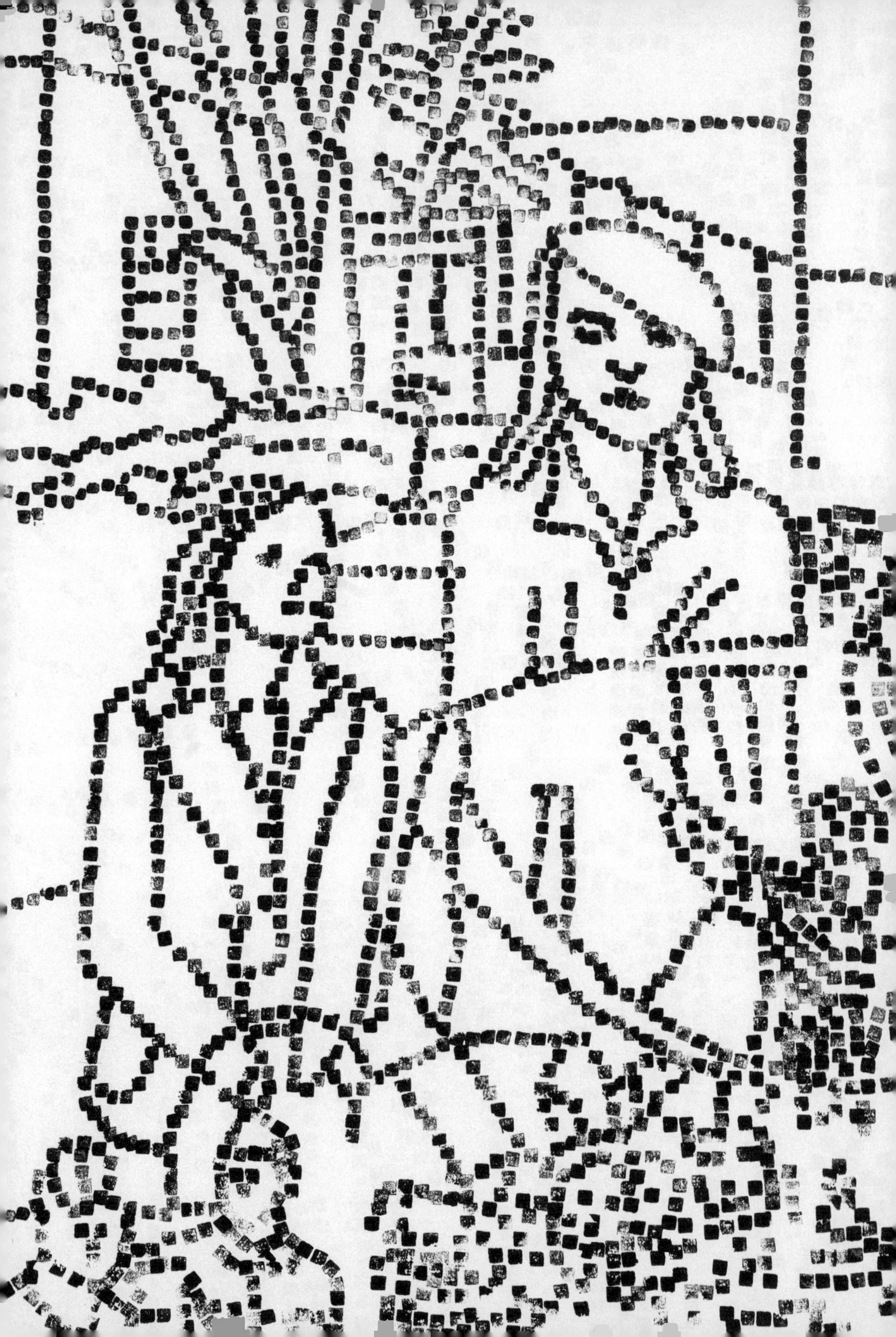

Michaela Melián

(* 1956 in Munich) is an interdisciplinary artist and musician as well as Professor of Mixed Media / Acoustics at the Hochschule für bildende Künste in Hamburg. She lives in Munich and Hamburg. Melián initially studied music at the Richard Strauss Conservatory in Munich before switching to fine arts at the Munich Akademie der Bildenden Künste and the Royal College of Art in London. In 1980, she formed the band F.S.K. together with Justin Hoffmann, Thomas Meinecke and Wilfried Petzi, where she continues to play and sing to this day. From 1980 to 1986 she was the editor of the literary magazine *Mode und Verzweiflung* (Fashion and Despair). Michaela Melián's artistic works are complex, transmedial layerings of images, sounds, objects and texts that are created by means of artistic research, montage and reproduction techniques. They are the result of intensive research. When Melián draws, stamps, superimposes, sews, composes and assembles, she puts politically and socially explosive topics, historical facts as well as private, unscripted stories into unexpected contexts and new perspectives.
Melián's work has received numerous awards, including the Edwin Scharff Prize (2018), the Roland Prize for Art in Public Space (2018), the Grimme Online Award (2011), the Kunstpreis of the town of Nordhorn (2011) and the Kunstpreis der Landeshauptstadt München (2010). Her work has been shown internationally in numerous solo and group exhibitions.

Solo exhibitions (selection):

2022
Red Threads,
KINDL – Centre for Contemporary Art, Berlin
Tout ce qui sonne,
Chambre Directe, St. Gallen
TeckTrack,
Kulturfestival KulturRegion Stuttgart, Kirchheim unter Teck
Past Statement,
Public Art München
2021
aufheben,
Burg Hülshoff, Center for Literature, Havixbeck bei Münster
Memory Loops,
permanent installation, NS-Dokumentationszentrum München
2020
Chant du Nix,
Kunstverein Harburger Bahnhof, Hamburg
2019
reiheM – Konzertreihe für Gegenwartsmusik, Elektronik und neue Medien,
Kölnischer Kunstverein, Cologne
Chant du Nix,
live radio performace, Deutschlandfunk Köln
2018
Dishammonia,
Schulterblatt 73, Hamburg
Music from a Frontier Town,
Public Art München
2017
Herminengasse,
Kunst im öffentlichen Raum Wien
2016
Electric Ladyland,
Städtische Galerie im Lenbachhaus, Munich
Barkarole,
Brückenmusik, Deutzer Brücke, Cologne
2015
Mannheim Chair,
Kunsthalle Mannheim
Wassermusik,
Stadtkuratorin – Kunst im öffentlichen Raum Hamburg
2014
Heimweh,
STORE und Kunsthaus, Dresden

In a Mist,
Badischer Kunstverein, Karlsruhe
2013
Hausmusik,
K' Galerie, Bremen
Else Lasker-Schüler,
Franz Marc Museum, Kochel
2011
House of Jacquard,
Städtische Galerie Nordhorn
2010
Memory Loops,
Public Art München
Rückspiegel,
Kunstverein Moers
2009
Speicher,
Lentos Kunstmuseum Linz / Ludlow 38, New York / Glasmoog, Cologne
2008
Speicher,
Ulmer Museum / Cubitt Gallery, London
2006
Föhrenwald,
Kunst-Werke, Berlin
2005
Föhrenwald,
Kunstraum München
2004
Locke Pistole Kreuz,
Kunstverein Langenhagen
2003
Panorama,
Galerie im Taxispalais, Innsbruck
2002
Triangel,
Kunstverein Springhornhof Neuenkirchen
Ignaz Guenther House,
Artothek München
2001
Moda y desesperación,
Goethe-Institut Madrid, Spain
1999
HysterikerIn,
Städtische Ausstellungshalle Hawerkamp, Münster
convention, The Better Days Project, Hamburg
1997
Bikini,
Kunstverein Ulm
1995
Tomboy,
Staatliche Kunsthalle Baden-Baden

**Group exhibitions
(selection):**

2022
Home and Abroad,
Museum of Modern Art Olomouc,
Czech Republic
Zusammen zeichnen. 201
Cadavres Exquis,
Museum im Bellpark, Kriens,
Switzerland
2021
To Reach a Star,
Gwangju Museum of Art,
Gwangju, South Korea
Auf ins Kaff רפכ,
Vorwerk Syke
Intimacy,
Schwules Museum, Berlin
2020
Black Album / White Cube,
Kunsthalle Rotterdam
Was wir sind und was wir tun,
Das Mitte Museum, Berlin
**Die Sonne um Mitternacht
schauen,**
Lenbachhaus, Munich
2019
**Tell me about ~~yesterday~~
tomorrow,** NS-Dokumentations-
zentrum München
Art sonor?,
Fundació Joan Miró, Barcelona
2018
Bouncing in the Corner,
Hamburger Kunsthalle
Radiophonic Cultures,
Museum Tinguely, Basel and
Haus der Kulturen der Welt, Berlin
WCW9 / WCWnine,
Ipanema Inn, Rio de Janeiro,
Brasil
2017
Truck Tracks Ruhr,
Urbane Künste Ruhr
2016
Geniale Dilletanten,
Museum für Kunst und
Gewerbe Hamburg
Land ohne Land,
Heidelberger Kunstverein
2015
Vot ken you mach?,
Muzeum Współczesne,
Wrocław, Poland

Geniale Dilletanten,
Haus der Kunst, Munich
Stadt der Frauen,
Münchner Opernfestspiele
2014
In a Mist,
Münchner Kammerspiele
A House of Passive Noise,
Ursula Blickle Stiftung, Kraichtal
Krankheit als Metapher,
Kunsthaus Hamburg
2013
Auf Zeit,
Staatliche Kunsthalle Baden-Baden
Sound Passagen,
Lentos Kunstmuseum Linz
2012
30 Künstler / 30 Räume,
Neues Museum Nürnberg
**Ulrike Müller – Herstory
Inventory,** Brooklyn Museum,
New York, USA
2011
Anfang gut, Alles gut,
Basso Berlin / Kunsthaus Bregenz
Pro & Contra,
MediaArtLab, Moscow
Kaunas Biennial, Lithuania
2010
Home Less Home,
Contemporary Art Museum
on the Seam, Jerusalem, Israel
2009
The Dwelling,
ACCA Melbourne, Australia
See the Sound,
Lentos Kunstmuseum Linz
2008
**ReCollecting. Raub
und Restitution,**
MAK, Vienna
Vertrautes Terrain,
ZKM | Zentrum für Kunst und
Medientechnologie, Karlsruhe
2007
Talkshow,
Tranzit Bratislava, Slowakia
Multispeak,
Witte Zaal, Gent, Belgium
2006
Das achte Feld,
Museum Ludwig, Cologne
**Von der Abwesenheit
des Lagers,**
Kunsthaus Dresden

2005
**Zur Vorstellung des
Terrors: Die RAF,**
Kunst-Werke Berlin and
Neue Galerie Graz
Slow Food. Bilder vom Stein,
Pinakothek der Moderne, Munich
**Boltanski, Ganahl, Melián,
Börnegalerie,**
Jüdisches Museum, Frankfurt
am Main
2004
**Common Property.
6. Werkleitz Biennale,**
Halle an der Saale
Gegen den Strich,
Staatliche Kunsthalle Baden-Baden
Atelier Europa,
Kunstverein München
2003
**Chironix fleckeri oder
Momente in der Schwebe,**
nGbK, Berlin
Ladyfest,
Westwerk, Hamburg
2002
Cardinales,
MARCO – Museo de Arte
Contemporánea, Vigo, Spain
Intermedium,
ZKM | Zentrum für Kunst und
Medientechnologie, Karlsruhe
Die zweite Haut,
Museum Bellerive, Zurich
2001
**CTRL [Space] – Rhetorics
of Surveillance from Bentham
to Big Brother,**
ZKM | Zentrum für Kunst und
Medientechnologie, Karlsruhe

**Monographies /
Exhibition Catalogues
(selection)**

Chant du Nix,
Salon Verlag, Cologne 2020.
Michaela Melián. Dishammonia,
Spector Books, Leipzig 2019
(With a text by Niklas Maak).
**Michaela Melián. Electric
Ladyland,** Munich 2016 (With texts
by Laurence A. Rickels, Jan Kedves
and Eva Huttenlauch; on the occa-
sion of the exhibtion of the same
name at Lenbachhaus München,
8.3.–19.6.2016).
**IEMANJÁ. Bembé do Mercado,
Santo Amaro, Bahia,**
Spector Books, Leipzig 2013
(with Thomas Meinecke).
House of Jacquard,
Nordhorn 2012 (With texts by
Veronika Olbrich and Kerstin
Stakemeier; on the occasion of the
exhibtion of the same name at
Städtische Galerie Nordhorn,
2.12.2011–12.2.2012).
**Rückspiegel. Michaela Melián
sprach mit Alexander Kluge,
Edgar Reitz, Josef Anton Riedl,
Hans-Jörg Wicha sowie
Kurd Alsleben über die Multi-
media-Arbeit VariaVision –
Unendliche Fahrt, das Studio
für elektronische Musik
und die HfG Ulm,**
Spector Books, Leipzig 2010.
Michaela Melián. Speicher,
Koenig Books, London 2009
(With texts by Jan Verwoert, Bart
von der Heide, Stella Rollig and
Brigitte Reinhardt; on the occasion
of the exhibition of the same name
at Ulmer Museum, 19.4.–22.6.2008,
Cubitt Gallery, London,
14.11.–14.12.2008 and at the Lentos
Kunstmuseum, Linz, 6.3.–2.6.2009).
Michaela Melián. Föhrenwald,
Revolver, Frankfurt am Main 2005
(With texts by Heike Ander,
Nikolaus Hirsch, Michael Hirsch,
Ronald Hirte, Thomas Meinecke,
Michaela Melián and Jim G. Tobias;
on the occasion of the exhibtion
of the same name at Kunstraum
München, 24.9–30.10.2005).

Michaela Melián. Triangel,
Lukas und Sternberg, Berlin 2003
(With texts by Heike Ander,
Jochen Bonz, Silvia Eiblmayr,
Sabine Himmelsbach, Didi Neidhart,
Dirk Snauwaert and Frank Wagner;
on the occasion of the exhibtion
of the same name Kunstverein
Springhornhof, Neukirchen,
14.7.–1.9.2002 and at Galerie im
Taxispalais, Innsbruck,
1.2.–23.3.2003).
Michaela Melián. Tomboy,
Baden Baden 1995 (With texts by
Jörg Heiser, Thomas Meinecke,
Thomas Palzer, Susanne Prinz,
Barbara U. Schmidt and Dirk
Teuber; on the occasion of the
exhibtion of the same name Staat-
liche Kunsthalle Baden-Baden,
16.12.1995–4.2.1996).
Michaela Melián,
Monographienreihe Förderpreise,
Munich 1994 (With a text by
Friederike Kitschen).
**Michaela Melián. Combat
and Survival,**
Kunstverein München, Munich
1993 (With texts by Helmut
Draxler and Thomas Palzer).
**Michaela Melián.
44 Zeichnungen,**
Éditions Traverses, Neuchâtel 1992
(With texts by Berg Lauchstaedt,
Thomas Meinecke and Thomas
Palzer).
Michaela Melián,
Monographienreihe Förderpreise,
Munich 1987 (With a text
by Tom Holert).
Michaela Melián,
Munich 1986 (With texts
by Maureen Paley and Roger
Willemsen; on the occasion of
the exhibtion of the same name
at Galerie der Künstler,
10.7.–10.8.1986).
**Der Sprengreiter #4.
Gospelausgabe,**
Kern Verlag, Munich 1984
(With texts by Daniel Leonhard
Henschel und Marc Sargent; on
the occasion of the exhibtion
Gospel at Künstleratelier Lothringer
Straße, 6.6.–9.7.1984).

**Texts by and about
Michaela Melián
(selection)**

**Ander, Heike: Luftbetriebene
Objekte,** in: Dziembowski, Bettina
von; Eiblmayr, Silvia; Schafhausen,
Nicolaus (Eds.), *Michaela Melián.
Triangel,* Lukas und Sternberg,
Berlin 2003, pp. 89–95.
**Bischoff, Juliane: Michaela
Melián. Man Family House,**
in: NS-Dokumentationszentrum
München (Ed.): *Tell me about
~~yesterday~~ tomorrow,* Munich 2020,
pp. 112–113.
**Bonz, Jochen: Funktion des
Schleiers,** in: Dziembowski, Bettina
von; Eiblmayr, Silvia; Schafhausen,
Nicolaus (Eds.), *Michaela Melián.
Triangel,* Lukas und Sternberg,
Berlin 2003, pp. 43–51.
**Bonz, Jochen: Kreuzstich durch
die Geschichte,** in: *Texte zur Kunst,*
48 (2002), pp. 204–205.
**Ehardt, Christine; Wieser,
Renate: Tune in to Reality.
Stimme und Geschlecht,** in: Ead.,
Pillgrab, Daniela; Rauchenbacher,
Marina; Alge, Barbara (Eds.),
*Inszenierung von „Weiblichkeit".
Zur Konstruktion von Körperbildern
in der Kunst,* Löcker, Vienna 2011,
pp. 143–161.
Eiblmayr, Silvia: Panorama,
in: Dziembowski, Bettina von;
id. Schafhausen, Nicolaus (Eds.),
Michaela Melián. Triangel,
Lukas und Sternberg, Berlin 2003,
pp. 59–65.
**Engelmann, Jonas: Erinnerungs-
räume,** in: *testcard # 20 – Access
Denied – Ortsverschiebungen,*
Ventil Verlag, Mainz 2011, pp. 84–87.
**Gerstner, Jan: Das postkoloniale
Wissen und die Fotografie.
Leonore Mau, Hubert Fichte,
Thomas Meinecke und Michaela
Melián in Bahia,** in: Beck, Laura;
Osthues, Julian (Eds.), *Postkolonia-
lismus und (Inter-)Medialität. Per-
spektiven der Grenzüberschreitung
im Spannungsfeld von Literatur,
Musik, Fotografie, Theater und Film,*
Transcript, Bielefeld 2016,
pp. 165–190.

Heiser, Jörg: Michaela Melián. Yes to the Modern World, in: Heiser, Jörg: *Double Lives in Art and Pop Music*, Sternberg Press, London 2019, pp. 143–157.

Heiser, Jörg: Michaela Melián. Ja zur modernen Welt, transatlantische Feedbacks, Feminismus, in: Heiser, Jörg: *Doppelleben. Kunst und Popmusik*, Fundus Verlag, Hamburg 2014, pp. 291–325.

Heiser, Jörg: What Is Appropriate? The Role of Art in Responding to the Holocaust, in: *frieze*, 130 (2010), pp. 92–97.

Heiser, Jörg: Wilde Spiele im Freien, in: Kunsthalle Baden-Baden (Ed.), *Michaela Melián. Tomboy*, Baden-Baden 1995, pp. 47–64.

Himmelsbach, Sabine: Mobile, in: Dziembowski, Bettina von; Eiblmayr, Silvia; Schafhausen, Nicolaus (Eds.), *Michaela Melián. Triangel*, Lukas und Sternberg, Berlin 2003, pp. 99–104.

Holert, Tom: Die Kunst der Michaela Melián, in: Kulturreferat München (Ed.), *Michaela Melián, Monographienreihe Förderpreise*, Munich 1987, pp. 3–4.

Kedves, Jan: Schwingungen und Geschichte. Ein „close listening" der Musik von Michaela Melián in 5 Abschnitten, in: Lenbachhaus München (Ed.), *Michaela Melián. Electric Ladyland*, Munich 2016, pp. 10–11.

Kitschen, Friederike: Noms de guerre, in: Kulturreferat München (Ed.), *Michaela Melián, Monographienreihe Förderpreise*, Munich 1994, pp. 2–3.

Loreck, Hanne: Michaela Melián. Lenbachhaus München, in: *frieze d/e*, 24 (2016), pp. 122–124.

Maak, Niklas: Die gezeichnete Moderne, in: *Michaela Melián. Dishammonia*, Spector Books, Leipzig 2019, pp. 5–12.

Melián, Michaela: Muttersprachen. Michaela Melián über Hélène Cixous' „Meine Homère ist tot …", in: *Texte zur Kunst*, 13.3.2020, online: https://www.textezurkunst.de/en/articles/melian-muttersprachen/.

Melián, Michaela: Arbeiten für das Radio / Arbeiten mit dem Radio, in: Neue Rundschau, 130 (3/2019), pp. 118–121.

Melián, Michaela: Assoziieren. Rückkoppeln, in: Sabisch, Andrea; Zahn, Manuel (Eds.), *Visuelle Assoziationen. Bildkonstellationen und Denkbewegungen in Kunst, Philosophie und Wissenschaft*, Textem, Hamburg 2018, pp. 204–214.

Melián, Michaela: Electric Ladyland. Ausstellung als Medium, in: Busch, Kathrin, Dörfling, Christina; Peters, Kathrin; Szántó, Ildikó (Eds.), *Wessen Wissen? Materialität und Situiertheit in den Künsten*, Brill / Fink, Paderborn 2018, pp. 151–165.

Melián, Michaela: Electric Ladyland, in: *Texte zur Kunst*, 112 (2018), pp. 92–101.

Melián, Michaela: Memory Loops, in: Hartel, Gaby; Goerke, Marie-Luise; Skoruppa, Ekkehard; Sarkowicz, Hans (Eds.), *Choreographie des Klangs – Zwischen Abstraktion und Erzählung | Choreography of Sound – Between Abstraction and Narration*, V&R, Göttingen 2015, pp. 181–182.

Melián, Michaela: Schleifen und Hallräume zwischen hier und dort und gestern und morgen, in: Lichtenstein Swantje; Metzger, Anneka (Eds.), *Ausfindig machen. Sprachkunst und textuelle Verfahren in den Künsten*, Verlag der Kunsthochschule für Medien, Cologne 2015, pp. 125–135.

Metzger, Stephanie: Zwischen Speicher und Ereignis – „Memory Loops" von Michaela Melián. Perfomativität und Ereignis im Rundfunk, in: Ernst, Wolf-Dieter; Niethammer, Nora; Szymanski-Düll, Berenika; Mungen, Anno (Eds.), *Sound und Performance. Positionen · Methoden · Analysen. Thurnauer Schriften zum Musiktheater*, 27 (2015), pp. 497–509.

Möntmann, Nina: Die treibende Kraft der mobilen Anpassung (unberechenbare Pässe!), in: *Lieber zu viel als zu wenig*, Vice Versa, Berlin 2003, pp. 98–105.

Mühleis, Volkmar: Michaela Melián, in: id.: *Ein Kind lässt einen Stein übers Wasser springen. Zu Entstehungsweisen von Kunst*, Brill / Fink, Paderborn 2011, pp. 147–158.

Nedo, Kito: Guerillera aus Stalinstadt, *art – Das Kunstmagazin*, (4/2022), p. 132.

Neidhart, Didi: Ignaz Guenther House, in: Dziembowski, Bettina von; Eiblmayr, Silvia; Schafhausen, Nicolaus (Eds.), *Michaela Melián. Triangel*, Lukas und Sternberg, Berlin 2003, pp. 109–120.

Nollert, Angelika: Michaela Melián, in: Rothenberger, Manfred; Schlecht, Anke (Eds.), *30 Künstler / 30 Räume*, Verlag für moderne Kunst, Nuremberg 2012, pp. 232–233.

Oswald, Nina: She Acts as a Woman Should, in: *Kunst-Bulletin*, (9/1999), pp. 14–19.

Plath, Nils: The Trace of Stones and Memory Work. Michaela Melián on the Historicity of Re-representations, in: Lasalle College of the Arts (Eds.), *Issue 08. ERASE*, Singapore 2019, pp. 81–83.

Plesch, Tine: Faden aufnehmen. Die Künstlerin Michaela Melián zeigt mit ihren Werken, was wie womit zusammenhängt, in: Herzing, Evi; Plesch, Hanns; Engelmann, Jonas (Eds.), *Tine Plesch. Rebel Girl. Popkultur und Feminismus*, Ventil-Verlag, Mainz 2013, pp. 215–217.

Prinz, Susanne: Subjekt – Prädikat – Objekt, in: Kunsthalle Baden-Baden (Eds.), Michaela Melián. Tomboy, Baden-Baden 1995, pp. 9–26.

Reichelt. Matthias: Michaela Melián. Red Threads. Ein Bericht vom Aufbau der Ausstellung im KINDL – Zentrum für zeitgenössische Kunst 27.3. – 24.7.2022, in: *Kunstforum international*, 281 (2022), pp. 244–245.

Rickels, Laurence A.: Speichern,
in: Lenbachhaus München (Ed.*),
Michaela Melián. Electric Ladyland*,
Munich 2016, pp. 6–7.
Sander, Christian: Michaela
**Melián. Neues Bauen und
Girl-Kultur**, in: *Weissenhof City*,
Staatsgalerie Stuttgart, 2019,
pp. 30–37.
**Schmidt, Barbara U.:
Täterin nicht auszuschließen,**
in: Kunsthalle Baden-Baden (Ed.),
Michaela Melián. Tomboy,
Baden-Baden 1995, pp. 35–43.
Schütz, Heinz: Michaela Melian.
Föhrenwald, in: *Kunstforum
international*, 178 (2005),
pp. 354–355.
**Shahan, Cyrus: Getting Lost.
Motion, Sound, and Image
in Michaela Melián's Rendering
of VariaVision. Unendliche Fahrt –
aber begrenzt**, in: Langston,
Richard; Adelson, Leslie A.; Jones,
N.D., Wilms, Leonie (Eds.),
The Poetic Power of Theory,
V&R unipress, Göttingen 2019,
pp. 291–310.
Smith, Roberta: Michaela
Melian. Ludlow 38, in: *New York
Times*, 13.2.2009, online:
https://archive.nytimes.com/query.
nytimes.com/gst/fullpage-
9E07E0DD1F3CF933A15751C
0A96F9C8B63.html.
Snauwaert, Dirk: Unter der
Haut …, in: Dziembowski, Bettina
von; Eiblmayr, Silvia; Schafhausen,
Nicolaus (Eds.), *Michaela Melián.
Triangel*, Lukas und Sternberg,
Berlin 2003, pp. 79–83.
**Stakemeier, Kerstin: Arbeiten
in der Kunst. Produktivistische
Avantgarde und repräsentative
Negativität**, in: Lenbachhaus
München (Ed.), *Playtime*, Munich
2014, pp. 37–38.
**Streitberger, Alexander:
Provokation, Dialog, Information.
Die Denkmalinschrift in der
zeitgenössischen Kunst,**
in: Rehm, Ulrich; Simonis, Linda
(Eds.), *Poetik der Inschrift*,
Winter Verlag, Heidelberg 2019,
pp. 209–231.

**Verwoert, Jan: Zurück zur
Zukunft**, in: Lentos Kunstmuseum;
Ulmer Museum; Cubitt Gallery
(Eds.), *Michaela Melián. Speicher*,
Koenig Books, London 2009,
pp. 57–77.
**Verwoert, Jan: Past, Present
and Future**, in: *frieze*, 105 (2007),
pp. 168–173.
**Vinken, Barbara: Have You
Ever Been to Electric Ladyland?
Barbara Vinken über Michaela
Melián im Lenbachhaus
München**, in: *Texte zur Kunst*,
102 (2016), pp. 162–165.
**Wagner, Frank: Low Tech –
High Concept**, in: Dziembowski,
Bettina von; Eiblmayr, Silvia;
Schafhausen, Nicolaus (Eds.),
Michaela Melián. Triangel, Lukas
und Sternberg, Berlin 2003,
pp. 7–25.
**Warsza, Joanna: Michaela
Melián. Music from a Frontier
Town**, in: Warsza, Joanna; Reed,
Patricia (Eds.), *City Curating
Reader*, Motto, Geneva / Berlin
2018, pp. 235–242.

**Interviews
(selection)**

**A Recurring State of Mist.
Interview mit Michaela Melián
von Lisa Bergmann,**
in: Feministisches Arbeits-Kollektiv
(Eds.), *Body of Work*, Motto,
Geneva / Berlin 2015, pp. 136–141.
**Ein letztes Mal in seiner
ganzen Göttlichkeit.
Michaela Melián im Gespräch
mit Max Dax**, in: Dax, Max;
Luckow, Dirk (Ed.), *Hyper!
A Journey into Art and Music*,
Snoeck, Cologne and Deichtor-
hallen Hamburg, 2019, pp. 214–223.
**Electric Ladyland. Gespräch
zwischen Michaela Melián
und Eva Huttenlauch,**
in: Lenbachhaus München (Ed.),
*Michaela Melián. Electric
Ladyland*, Munich 2016,
pp. 12–13.

"Ich bin argwöhnisch gegenüber
jeder staatstragenden Meta-
phorik." Michaela Melián im
Gespräch mit Kerstin Stakemeier
über Memory Loops, ihr virtu-
elles Denkmal für die Opfer des
Nationalsozialismus im Stadt-
raum München, in: *Texte zur Kunst*,
4.1.2011, online: https://www.
textezurkunst.de/en/articles/ich-
bin-argwohnisch-gegenuber-jeder-
staatstragende/.
**Kulturelle Diplomatie.
Michaela Melián im Gespräch
mit Sven Beckstette,**
in: Warsza, Joanna; Reed, Patricia
(Hg.), *City Curating Reader*, Motto,
Geneva / Berlin 2018, pp. 244–268.
**Künstlerinnen International.
Michaela Melián im Gespräch
mit Jörg Heiser**, in: *frieze*,
157 (2013), pp. 92–101.
**Michaela Melián. Deutschland
kommt in vielen Themen um
die Ecke. Interview mit Michaela
Melián von Maria Anna Tappeiner,**
in: *Kunstforum international*,
236 (2015), pp. 148–155.
**Really Dirty History.
Michaela Melián in Conversation
with Angus Cook and
Stefan Kalmár**, in: Maier, Tobi;
Lotz, Antonia (Eds.), *The first 3
Years @ Ludlow 38*, Spector Books,
Leipzig 2011, pp. 172–182.
**The Trace of Stones and Memory
Work. Michaela Melián on the
Historicity of Re-representations.
By Nils Plath**, in: Lasalle College
of the Arts (Eds.), *Issue 08:
ERASE*, Singapur 2019, pp. 84–105.
**Tonspuren. Freundliche
Übernahme. Ein Interview
mit Michaela Melián
von Aram Lintzel**, in: *Texte zur
Kunst*, 60 (2005), pp. 126–132.

Authors

Nadja Abt (née Vladimirovich) is an artist and author. She lives in Berlin and Lisbon. Abt studied literature and the history of art at Freie Universität Berlin as well as visual arts at Universität der Künste Berlin and Universidad Torcuato di Tella in Buenos Aires. From 2018 to 2020, she was editor of the journal *Texte zur Kunst*. In her artistic practice, she constructs feminist narratives that reference the worlds of literature and film. Abt is a member of the artist collective *Michelle Volta*. She has exhibited and performed internationally at institutions including Kunsthalle Freeport, Porto (2021), HUA International, Beijing (2021), KW-Institute for Contemporary Art, Berlin (2021), HKW, Berlin (2019) and Casa Triângulo, São Paulo (2018).

Kathrin Becker is a curator and as of 2020 artistic director of the KINDL – Centre for Contemporary Art in Berlin. From 2001 to 2019, she directed the Video-Forum of the Neuer Berliner Kunstverein (n.b.k.). In her curatorial work, Becker engages in feminist and postcolonial approaches. She also explores intercultural issues, such as the redefinition of the concept of culture in Western Europe and the post-communist countries through national, regional and, above all, particular cultural policy settings. Becker has been responsible for several exhibitions, most recently *Mona Hatoum, Rémy Markowitsch* and *Landscapes of Belonging* (all 2022, KINDL). She is the author of numerous publications, including *Time Pieces. Videokunst 1963 bis heute (Time Pieces. Video Art 1963 until today)* (2012, co-edited with M. Babias and S. Goltz).

Katja Kynast is a cultural scientist and head of communication at the KINDL – Centre for Contemporary Art. She works with the tools as a cultural historian and curator, with a focus on text, discourse and events, and she enjoys collaborative work. In 2022 she was awarded her PhD with a thesis on images in environmental theory. Kynast is a member of the editorial board of *ilinx – Berliner Beiträge zur Kulturwissenschaft*. Together with Hauke Ziessler, she curated *Unfinished Histories Vol. VI: The Better Alchemists*, Klosterruine Berlin (2019); with Isabel Jäger, Malte Pieper and Maja Smoszna, *Birds and Buoys,* Bärenzwinger Berlin (2021); with Magdalena Mai, KINDL *signs | soundtracks* (2022). Most recent publication: *Bilder der Umwelttheorie. Fotografien, Zeichnungen und Schemata bei Jakob von Uexküll (Images of Environmental Theory. Photographs, Drawings and Patterns by Jakob von Uexküll)* (2022).

Hanne Loreck is an art theorist and Professor of Art and Cultural Studies / Gender Studies at the University of Fine Arts Hamburg, where she was Vice President from 2006 to 2019. She is co-initiator of the university's artistic-scientific doctoral programme. Loreck writes about current art positions, the history of art, media and the subject in the 20th century, fashion phenomena and cultural theory, with a focus on questions of visibility, pictoriality and surfaces. Among other things, she is the author of the monographs *"Sissy stuff – mainly needlepoint." Anni Albers an der Staatlichen Kunstgewerbeschule zu Hamburg (Anni Albers at the State School of Applied Arts in Hamburg)* (2022) and *Geschlechterfiguren und Körpermodelle: Cindy Sherman (Gender Figures and Body Patterns: Cindy Sherman)* (2002).

Magdalena Mai is an art historian, curator and head of project at the KINDL – Centre for Contemporary Art in Berlin. She was a curatorial assistant from 2017 to 2020, working on various exhibition and publication projects. Most recently, she curated the exhibition *Ende Neu* (KINDL, 2021), together with Manuel Kirsch, and *KINDL signs | soundtracks* (KINDL, 2022), a site-specific sound work for the area of the former Kindl brewery in Berlin-Neukölln, together with Katja Kynast. Publications: Wenn ein Hase Bier trinkt. Andreas Fiedler und Magdalena Mai im Gespräch mit Jonathan Monk (When a Hare Drinks Beer. Andreas Fiedler and Magdalena Mai in conversation with Jonathan Monk), in: *Monk, Jonathan: Exhibit Model Four – plus invited guests* (2020); *Wolkenatlas. Michael Sailstorfers Wolkenskulpturen und die Materialisierung des Flüchtigen (Cloud Atlas. Michael Sailstorfer's Cloud Sculptures and the Materialisation of the Ephemeral)* (2022).

Ingrid Wagner holds a doctorate in art history and works as a freelance curator and publicist. From 2002 to 2020, she was Deputy Head of Department and Officer for Visual Arts, Dance and Literature at the Berlin Senate Department for Culture and Europe. She previously taught at numerous art colleges, including in Berlin, Braunschweig, Munich and New Brunswick. Wagner's curatorial and journalistic focus is on the presentation of contemporary artists and questions of identity politics in a social context. She was part of the nGbK working groups *Unbeachtete Produktionsformen (Overlooked Forms of Production)* (1981) and *Das Verborgene Museum (The Hidden Museum)* (1987) and author of numerous exhibitions such as *Im Unterschied (In Contrast)* (1991), *VALIE EXPORT* (2003) and *The New Normal?* (2020).

Joanna Warsza is a freelance curator, editor and writer. She lives in Berlin. She is interested in the workings of art beyond the protective shield of the white cube. Warsza was co-curator of the Polish Pavilion at the *59th Biennale di Venezia* (2022), the *3rd* and *4th Autostrada Biennale* in Kosovo (2021/ 2022), the *12th Survival Kit* in Riga (2021) as well as the exhibition *Die Balkone (The Balconies)* in Berlin (2020 and 2021). Since 2014, she has been the Programme Director of the CuratorLab at Konstfack University of Arts in Stockholm. Her recent publications include *Red Love. A Reader on Alexandra Kollontai* (2020, co-edited with Maria Lind and Michele Masucci) and *And Warren Niesłuchowski Was There. Guest, Host, Ghost* (2020, co-edited with Sina Najafi).

This Publication Is Published on the Occasion of the Exhibition

Michaela Melián
Read Threads
27.3. – 24.7.2022

KINDL – Centre for
Contemporary Art
Maschinenhaus M2
Am Sudhaus 3
12053 Berlin

Exhibition
Curators:
Kathrin Becker, Ingrid Wagner
Head of Project:
Magdalena Mai
Exhibition Technology:
Jürgen Galli, Karlsruhe
Head of Installation:
Marcus Trägner
Team:
Jakob Argauer,
David Möller,
Frederic Spreckelmeyer
Artist Assistant:
Luisa Koch
Courtesy Exhibits:
The Artist, except *Girl-Kultur*:
Collection Staatsgalerie Stuttgart

Published by:
Spector Books
Markus Dreßen, Anne König,
Jan Wenzel
Harkortstraße 10
04107 Leipzig
www.spectorbooks.com

Publication
Editor: Kathrin Becker
Texts:
Kathrin Becker, Ingrid Wagner
(pp. 5–6);
Magdalena Mai, Katja Kynast
(pp. 17–55);
Nadja Abt (pp. 67–75);
Hanne Loreck (pp. 97–105);
Joanna Warsza, Michaela Melián
(pp. 109–118)
Translations: Jan Caspers
Editing: Kat Lawinia Gorska
Copyediting: Jan-Frederik Bandel
Proof Reading: Jan Wenzel
Design:
Anna Lena von Helldorff
Photography: Jens Ziehe, Berlin,
except
pp. 8–16, p. 47, pp. 82–83,
p. 119: Michaela Melián;
pp. 22–25, pp. 62–65, pp. 77–81,
p. 108: Wilfried Petzi;
p. 106: Stephan Baumann;
p. 107: Staatsgalerie Stuttgart;
pp. 120 / 121, p. 122 below:
Oliver Puck
Image Processing:
ScanColor Leipzig
Printing and Processing:
Gutenberg Beuys Feindruckerei
GmbH Langenhagen

© 2022 Michaela Melián,
KINDL – Centre for Contemporary
Art, the authors, Jens Ziehe,
Wilfried Petzi, Spector Books

The Deutsche Nationalbibliothek lists
this publication in the Deutsche National-
bibliografie; detailed bibliographic data are
available on the internet at http://dnb.dnb.de

Team KINDL
Artistic Director:
Kathrin Becker
Head of Administration:
Georg Lehmann
Head of Project, Curator:
Magdalena Mai
Head of Communication:
Katja Kynast
Head of Project: Anke Grossmann
Event Management:
Filistin Younes
Office Management:
Bärbel Kirchhoff
Press: Denhart von Harling /
segeband.pr
**Coordination Visitor Service
and Ticketing:**
Forster Herchenbach
**Coodination of Museum
Attendants and Reception:**
Peter Hübert
Art Education:
Christian Brünner, Daniela Dahlke,
Janna Heiß
Outreach: Sadaf Vasaei
**Museum Attendants
and Mediation:**
Alejandra Borea, Ketevan
Gorgiladze, Peter Hess, Clara
Messerschmidt, Eda Nakiboglu,
Catarina Palma, Olga Solodova
Head of Installation:
Marcus Trägner
Technicians:
Edgar Goldstein, Marcus Goldstein
Café Babette:
Maik Schierloh, Thomas Welzel,
Hannah Chaker-Agha

Supported by
Hauptstadtkulturfonds

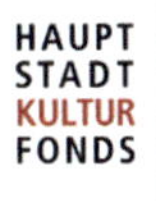

Distribution:
Germany, Austria: GVA, Gemeinsame Verlagsauslieferung
Göttingen GmbH&Co. KG, www.gva-verlage.de
Switzerland: AVA Verlagsauslieferung AG, www.ava.ch
France, Belgium: Interart Paris, www.interart.fr
Great Britan: Central Books Ltd, www.centralbooks.com
North, Central and South America, Africa:
ARTBOOK/ D.A.P., www.artbook.com
South Korea: The Book Society, www.thebooksociety.org
Japan: twelvebooks, https://twelve-books.com
Australia, New Zealand: Perimeter Distribution,
www.perimeterdistribution.com

Printed in Germany
First edition

ISBN 978-3-95905-640-3

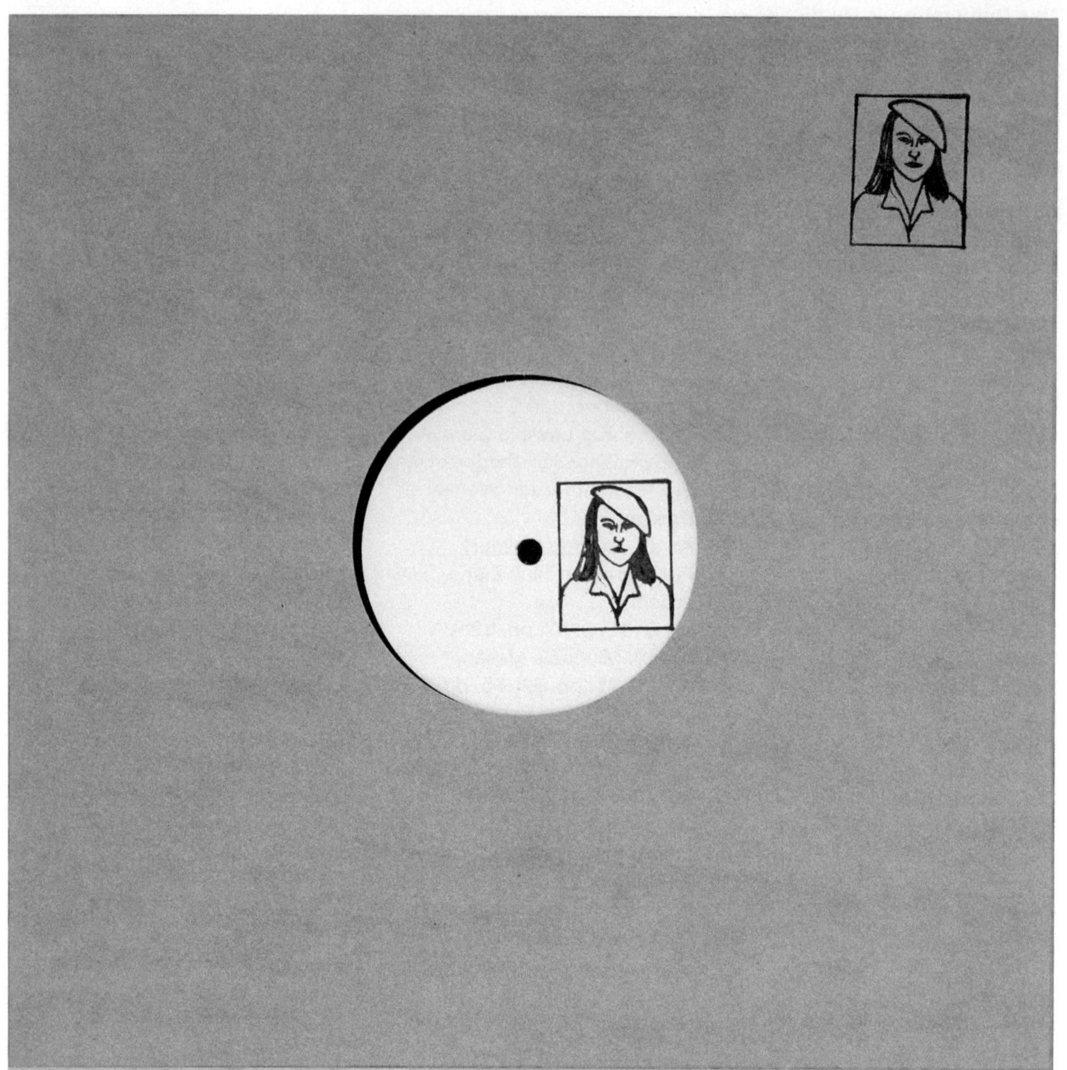

TANIA
45 rpm, 9:33 min., Edition 100, 2022
(12" EP, handstamped, signed and numbered)